Logion Press Books

Stanley M. Horton, Th.D.

General Editor

MINISTERIAL ETHICS: A GUIDE FOR SPIRIT-FILLED LEADERS

MINISTERIAL ETHICS

A Guide for Spirit-Filled Leaders

T. Burton Pierce

General Editor: Stanley M. Horton

LOGION
P R E S S
Springfield, Missouri
02-0320

Logion Press books are published by Gospel Publishing House.

Library of Congress Cataloging-in-Publication Data

Pierce, T. Burton, 1926–
    Ministerial ethics : a guide for Spirit-filled leaders / T. Burton Pierce ; Stanley M. Horton, general editor.
        p.   cm.
    Includes bibliographical references and indexes
    ISBN 0-88243-320-2
    1. Clergy—Professional ethics. 2. Pentecostal churches—Clergy—Professional ethics. 3. Assemblies of God—Clergy—Professional ethics. 4. Pastoral theology—Pentecostal churches. 5. Christian ethics—Assemblies of God authors. 6. Assemblies of God—Doctrines. 7. Pentecostal churches—Doctrines.   I. Horton, Stanley M.
    II. Title.
    BV4011.5.P54   1996
    241' .641—dc20   96-3636

Printed in the United States of America

Contents

Prologue

As ministers of the gospel we have a responsibility both to declare the truth and to live the truth. This involves both our relationship to God and to others. It means living in a way that upholds the ethical standards for conduct that the Bible teaches. In a day when relativism is rampant, the Bible still points us to God's own character as the standard we must, with the help of the Holy Spirit, strive to follow. It is not enough to follow the norms that the world around us accepts as ethical (Matt. 5:46-48). We also have the example of Jesus, and we can learn from the apostles as they followed Him (1 Cor. 4:16-17; 11:1).

To act ethically in a way that pleases God, we must seek to be like the Father, which also means to be like Jesus who reveals the Father (Matt. 11:27). Consider, then, the character of God revealed in the Bible. Holiness and love stand out. God is love by His very nature (1 John 4:8). When Moses repeated the Ten Commandments in Deuteronomy 5:6-21, he went on to say, "Love the LORD your God with all your heart and with all your soul and with all your strength" (Deut. 6:5). Then he added, "These commandments that I give you today are to be upon your hearts" (v. 6). In other words, the Israelites could not even begin to keep the Ten Commandments in a way that pleased God unless their whole being was going out to God in love.

The love God wanted was really a response to His love, for He loved them first (Deut. 7:7-8) and showed His love by delivering them out of Egypt by grace through faith. They had shown that faith by obedience as they sacrificed the Passover lamb, sprinkled its blood, and ate it with everyone dressed, packed up, and ready to go. The Book of Hosea demonstrated further that the kind of love God wanted included a loyalty that Israel throughout its history so often lacked.

Our response to His love must also make us a channel of His love to others. In the midst of the Law God said, "'Love your neighbor as yourself'" (Lev. 19:18). Then He added, in Leviticus 19:34, "'The alien living with you must be treated as one of your native-born. Love him as yourself, for you were aliens in Egypt. I am the LORD your God.'" Our God is the kind of God who loves foreigners. The Law also called for acts of love, even to an enemy. However, not many accepted the full meaning of love for the neighbor until Jesus made it real through the Parable of the Good Samaritan (Luke 10:25-37). Jesus also demonstrated divine love many times, for example, in Matthew 9:36: "When he saw the crowds, he had compassion on them, because they were harassed and helpless, like sheep without a shepherd." But no one really understood the fullness of God's love or the kind of love He expects us to show until Jesus died on the cross (John 3:16; Rom. 5:8). That same love—shown "while we were still sinners"—makes a full provision available to us that can not only save us but also see us all the way through to glory as we follow Jesus (Rom. 5:10). Just how necessary it is for believers to show this kind of love is one of the great themes of 1 John.

The Bible, however, does not make God's love central to His character. In Isaiah's inaugural vision, the seraphim ("burning ones") so reflected God's glory they seemed to be on fire. But they did not call out, "Love, love, love." They kept calling to one another: "'Holy, holy, holy is the LORD Almighty; the whole earth is full of his glory'" (Isa. 6:3). Holiness is central to God's nature. Even His love works in line with His holiness—as the Cross demonstrated. God could not be true to himself and simply excuse our sin because of His love. His holiness demanded that the penalty be paid, "for the wages of sin is death" (Rom. 6:23). So Jesus, the sinless Lamb of God, fulfilled the entire sacrificial system as well as Isaiah 53. He became our substitute and satisfied the holiness of God.

God's holiness must be the standard of our holiness. Isaiah repeatedly calls Him the Holy One of Israel. God commanded Israel to consecrate themselves and be holy because He is holy (Lev. 11:44-45; cf. 20:26). This involves our cooperation with God, who makes us holy (Lev. 20:7-8).

God's holiness has two aspects. The basic meaning of the Hebrew word for holiness is "separation." On one hand, God is totally separate from all sin and evil—quite unlike the false gods the pagans believed in, gods they thought could swap wives, kill each other, glorify drunken orgies, and do other evil deeds.

The other aspect of God's holiness is related to His faithfulness. He has separated himself to the carrying out of His great plan of redemption and to the completing of His purpose to bless all the families of the earth (Gen. 12:3). He will bring people from every nation, tribe, people, and language to share His glory and to be with Him forever (1 Thess. 4:16-17; Rev. 7:9).

Jesus demonstrated these two aspects of holiness. He rejected Satan's temptations, using something that is available to us: God's Word (Matt. 4:1-10). He also demonstrated the positive aspect by identifying himself with us and taking the place of a humble servant of His Father and of God's people. He told His disciples, "'You know that the rulers of the Gentiles lord it over them, and their high officials exercise authority over them. [That is, they love to play the tyrant and show their authority.] Not so with you. Instead, whoever wants to become great among you must be your servant, and whoever wants to be first must be your slave—just as the Son of Man did not come to be served, but to serve, and to give his life as a ransom for many'" (Matt. 20:25-28). Then, in His prayer in the Garden of Gethsemane, He declared His total submission to His Father's will (Matt. 26:39,42).

So, too, our holiness must have two aspects. We must turn our backs on sin and evil. We must also take up our cross and follow Jesus (Matt. 10:38; 16:24). The latter is what really makes us holy. We can see this illustrated by the holy vessels of the Old Testament tabernacle and temple. They were separated from ordinary use; they could not be used in the homes of the Israelites. But that is not what made them holy. They became holy when they were taken into the temple and used in the worship and service of the Lord. In a similar way, our holiness involves consecration and dedication of ourselves to the worship and service of the Lord.

However, neither our holiness nor our love is a matter of mere human effort. Nor is it merely our human response to God's holy love. Jesus was the divine Helper for His disciples while He was on earth. He restrained them when they wanted to bring fire down from heaven (Luke 9:54-55). He directed them to feed the multitude (Matt. 14:15-21). He gave them authority and power to heal the sick and drive out demons (Matt. 10:1). Then He promised them "another Counselor" (John 14:16). The basic meaning of "Counselor" is simply "Helper," and "another" means "another of the same kind." Thus the Holy Spirit is our Helper; God pours out His "love into our hearts by [His] Holy Spirit" (Rom. 5:5). He does this not simply for us to enjoy, but to make us channels of that Calvary love, that self-giving love that is to extend even to our enemies.

The Holy Spirit also helps us along the highway of holiness. On the one hand, this means He helps us to reject sin and evil and guides us along "the paths of righteousness" (which in Psalm 23:3 could be translated "ruts of righteousness," well used by godly people who have gone before us and well marked in Scripture).

On the other hand, the Holy Spirit helps us dedicate ourselves to the worship and service of the Lord. He has gifts and ministry for every believer. But the Holy Spirit distributes His gifts not according to our desires but "just as he determines" (1 Cor. 12:11).

Our part is to be open to the Spirit's guidance and responsive to His promptings. Believers are not to decide on their own what ministry they want to become involved in. Neither do we put one kind of ministry on a higher level, or consider it more important, than others. First Corinthians 12:14–26 emphasizes the importance of each member of the Body and the necessity and value of every ministry, including those that are unseen or in the background.

The Spirit will guide us in many ways. In the Book of Acts the Holy Spirit used several means. Sometimes He used circumstances, as when the persecution after the stoning of Stephen caused the believers, except the apostles, to scatter in all directions, preaching the Word wherever they went (Acts 8:4). Sometimes He sent an angel, as when God wanted Philip to leave the revival in Samaria and go south to the old, deserted Gaza road that practically no one used anymore (Acts 8:26). But when Philip obeyed, he didn't need another angel to tell him to run alongside the chariot of the Ethiopian eunuch: By his initial obedience he had become more sensitive to the voice of the Holy Spirit, and that was all he needed (vv. 29–30).

Sometimes the Lord does use unusual means to turn people around. He did with Saul the persecutor on the Damascus Road (Acts 9:1–6), and even after Saul became the apostle Paul, at Troas, God used an unusual dream to give him the Macedonian call (Acts 16:9–10).

Acts has no formal ending. The acts of the Holy Spirit, along with His guidance and power, are meant to continue today. I found that out in a real way when God used various means to give direction to my life. When I was a student majoring in science at the University of California in Berkeley, some friends wanted me to quit the university, for they considered it a godless place. I prayed and could get no peace until I said, "Lord, if You want me to finish and get my degree in science, I will." Then a warm feeling went from the top of my head to my toes. God knew a science background would be helpful in my future teaching.

After graduation I worked for the Bureau of Chemistry of the California Department of Agriculture in Sacramento. One Sunday afternoon I was alone in the prayer room of Bethel Temple, and the Lord spoke to me in an audible voice and told me to go back to school and prepare to teach in Bible school. I was vice president of the young peoples' group, teaching a junior boys' class in Sunday school, going to street meetings and convalescent homes—I thought I was doing everything the Lord wanted me to do. I had no thought of further ministry, and neither did anyone else suggest any such thing to me. That is probably why God had to speak audibly to me.

Then the Lord used pastor W. T. Gaston and Harold Needham, president of Southern California Bible College, to encourage me. I wrote to various schools, and a seminary in Texas seemed best. So I filled out an application and was about to sign it when I felt a definite check from the Holy Spirit. I prayed again and again felt restrained. So I put the application in my desk drawer without signing it and worked another year in the chemistry laboratory. God often tests our faith and obedience by delay. During that year God used an evangelist to tell me about the school that I would finally attend in Boston. God had another reason for sending me there, for there I found my wife, Evelyn, who has been a wonderful help to me for over fifty years.

Turning to Paul's epistles, we find that each begins with teaching and then goes to a practical section, where Paul deals with questions and problems that arose in the Early Church. For some of them he had a word from the Lord. That is, he had a saying or teaching of Jesus to answer their questions or their need. In Galatians he lets us know that he learned from Jesus himself the things He did and taught, probably during Paul's three years in Arabia (1:11–12,15–18). But where Paul did not have a word of Jesus to give the recipients of his letters, he had the inspired word of the Holy Spirit.

Peter's epistles also are full of guidance for every aspect of Christian living. In our day, perhaps 1 Peter 4:19 is appropriate: "Those who suffer according to God's will should commit themselves to their faithful Creator and continue to do good." "Suffer" means to endure. It is the same word used of the sufferings of Jesus. The faithful Creator is the one who made us and who sent His Son to die on the cross. Committing ourselves to Him means taking up our cross daily and following Him. Doing good then means doing the kind of good He did, telling the good news of the gospel, healing the sick, casting out demons, and encouraging people to turn to Jesus. We are to live for Him. This includes acting ethically in all our relationships and in all we do. For example, we must not put our religion in a watertight compartment so that it does not affect our business dealings, as some do. It will help us to act ethically also if we remember that as believers we are waiting for Jesus to come again from heaven, for He has promised to rescue us from the coming wrath that will fall on the unbelief, violence, and immorality of a Christ-rejecting world (1 Thess. 1:10).

STANLEY M. HORTON, TH.D.
*Distinguished Professor Emeritus
of Bible and Theology
at the Assemblies of God
Theological Seminary*

Preface

In line with the usage of both the KJV and the NIV, "LORD" is used in capitals and small capitals where the Hebrew of the Old Testament has the personal, divine name of God, Yahweh (which was probably pronounced *'ya-wā*).[1]

In quoted Scripture, words I wish to emphasize are in italics.

For easier reading, Hebrew, Aramaic, and Greek words are all transliterated with English letters.

These abbreviations have been used:

KJV: King James Version
NCV: New Century Version
NKJV: New King James Version
NRS: New Revised Standard
Phillips: *The New Testament in Modern English, Translated by J. B. Phillips*
RSV: Revised Standard Version
TEV: Today's English Version
TLB: *The Living Bible*

---

[1]The Hebrew wrote only the consonants YHWH. Later traditions followed the New Latin JHVH and added vowels from the Hebrew for "Lord" to remind them to read *Lord* instead of the divine name. This was never intended to be read "Jehovah."

Introduction

Christian ethics is not easily defined, though most discerning Christians can usually determine when an action is ethical or unethical. Former Supreme Court Justice Potter Stewart, when asked to define graphic art that would be unacceptable to the court in meeting community standards, responded, "I can't define it, but I know it when I see it."[1] Most of us have a similar instinct about the absence or presence of Christian ethics in a given situation.

A definition must of necessity make a distinction between "secular ethics" and "Christian ethics." It must also distinguish between ethics and morality. In the broader secular sense, ethics combines fair play with a healthy respect for the laws of the land, modified by a mild appreciation for the Ten Commandments. By contrast Christian ethics rises to a higher level on the basis of Scripture, including the law of Moses, the Sermon on the Mount, and the Pauline epistles. Despite its loftiness the Christian ethic can be achieved and maintained through the grace and love of God, the redeeming work of Calvary, and the faithfulness of the Holy Spirit, who lives within the believer.

How does ethics differ from morality? The terms are similar in derivation. The word "ethics" comes from the Greek word *ethos*, which means "custom."

---

[1]See Robert Bendiner, "The Law and Potter Stewart: An Interview," *American Heritage* 35 (December 1983): 99–104.

The Latin equivalent, *mormos,* has the same meaning as the Greek word and is the root of our English word "morals." This is not to say that ethics is a study of what is customary in a given situation; rather it is what *ought* to be customary. While ethics is primarily deciding what our action shall be, morality is the action itself. Ethics can be viewed as an intellectual and spiritual exercise. Morality is the carrying out of the ethical premise. Ethics has to do with our aspirations, our goals, our judgments of one another, but morality is the putting of them into practice or not putting them into practice, as the case may be.

That is to say, one may have high ethical standards and yet fail to act morally on some occasion, and, conversely, an individual who might not have lofty ethical principles could act morally in certain circumstances.

The challenge of developing a definition of Christian ethics has produced some interesting observations by ethicists. Norman Geisler, for example, contends that norms or rules are both "inescapable and essential for a meaningful ethic." They are inescapable because they are needed to help evaluate what is meant by "good" or "better." They are essential because there must be a noncontradictory way of expressing the ethical idea.[2] Henlee H. Barnette sees the task of ethics as defining the "Highest Good" and determining the nature and purpose of God's ideal for human action (blended with insights of philosophy, history, and social sciences).[3] "Ethics is prescriptive, not simply descriptive," observes Philip E. Hughes. "Its domain is that of duty and obligation, and it seeks to define the distinction between right and wrong, between justice and injustice, and between responsibility and irresponsibility."[4] On the

---

[2]Norman L. Geisler, *Ethics: Alternatives and Issues* (Grand Rapids: Zondervan Publishing House, 1971), 27.

[3]Henlee H. Barnette, *Introducing Christian Ethics* (Nashville: Broadman Press, 1961), 3–4.

[4]Philip Edgcumbe Hughes, *Christian Ethics in Secular Society* (Grand Rapids: Baker Book House, 1983), 11.

other hand, many believe and practice situation ethics, grounding ethics in the situation rather than in universals; then ethics means different things to different people.

Why should we study the subject of Christian ethics? I suggest these reasons:

1. Every Christian needs a solid foundation for living a consistent Christian lifestyle. Jesus made it clear that the person who heard and did the things He taught was like the wise man who built his house on a rock, enabling it to weather any storm. By heeding the Lord, we shall be able to withstand any pressure (Matt. 7:24–25).

2. It is the responsibility of the servant of God to proclaim the Christian ethic, whether to a Sunday morning congregation or a neighborhood Bible study. We are all called to witness (Acts 1:8), and witnessing is simply proclaiming what we have seen and what we know.

3. To study ethics is to study Scripture. To probe the basis of moral and civil law is to probe the Word of God. In so doing, we follow the example of the Bereans who "received the message with great eagerness and examined the Scriptures every day" (Acts 17:11).

4. Self-examination is healthy. Auditing one's ethics is more critical than watching for the signs of cancer. It keeps us alive morally.

5. No Christian is more powerful than the example he or she sets. Our children, our friends, our neighbors—all are affected by how well we have grasped and put into practice sound ethical principles. I am "my brother's keeper" whether I choose that role or not (Gen. 4:9).

In treating the subject of Christian ethics we will move from the foundation of the Ten Commandments, the Mosaic codification of the Law, and Old Testament teaching to the rarefied air of the Sermon on the Mount, the parables and teachings of Christ, and the challenging concepts of the Pauline epistles.

This upward theological mobility, enabled by the Spirit, can be described as being led from Law to grace, from judgment to mercy, from divine disfavor to God's holy love.

My major premise is that godly love is essential for attaining godly ethics. This godly love must emanate from God himself, who "first loved us" (1 John 4:19); it then must possess the heart of the Christian, who in turn so loves God that he cannot bear to grieve Him with unbecoming desires. Next comes love for others, which naturally follows love for God. In fact, the Bible clearly teaches that it is impossible to love God and at the same time not love one's brothers (1 John 4:20). Finally comes love for self in the sense of self-respect or a humble recognition of self-worth because of the price paid for us at Calvary (1 Cor. 6:20).

Jeremiah 9:24 (NRS) beautifully expresses the basis for ethical conduct as coming from God himself: "Let those who boast boast in this, that they understand and know me, that I am the LORD; I act with steadfast love, justice, and righteousness in the earth; for in these things I delight." Here are given the three great attributes of God to be reflected in all ethical conduct: His love, which exceeds human understanding; His justice, which is exacting and meticulously fair; and His righteousness, which simply means doing the right thing in the right way at the right time. What a beautiful balance! The justice of God demands a penalty for every person's wrong actions; His love provides the means of taking care of that penalty at Calvary; His righteousness is made available to humankind by the sanctifying power of the Spirit. We know that "the Judge of all the earth" will always do right (Gen. 18:25). Of and by His Spirit He enables His children to do right as well. We have been placed on solid ethical ground.

Part 1

The Basis for Christian Ethics— Scripture

Part 1: The Basis for Christian Ethics— Scripture

Chapter 1

The New Morality of Christ: Ethics Defined

Chapter 2

The Basis of Morality: The Ten Commandments

Chapter 3

Transition from Law to Grace: The Sermon on the Mount

Chapter 1

The New Morality of Christ: Ethics Defined

FLESH, SPIRIT, AND POPULAR THEOLOGY

Though taught by the apostle Paul, the concept of flesh (the sinful nature) versus Spirit—and the Spirit's ultimate triumph—has not been espoused in either the seminaries or the pulpits of most evangelical churches. Neither is the concept of an internal spiritual struggle found any longer among Holiness groups. In most charismatic churches the tendency is to believe a personal devil or demon is the cause of the foibles and failures of the child of God. Apparently the Church needs only to point in any direction other than inward to identify the source of spiritual shortcomings.

It is time for Christians, especially ministers, to accept and promote personal responsibility for high ethical standards rather than making human failure into a spiritual whipping boy. Being an overcomer is not a matter of gritting one's teeth in the face of temptation and holding on to integrity by sheer willpower. As we walk in faith in this sin-darkened world, God provides for victorious living; appropriating His resources becomes a fulfilling experience, affording peace of mind and heart.

NEW BIRTH, NEW NATURE

Before experiencing salvation, everyone is both dead and alive: spiritually dead in sin but physically alive to sin. Without being fully aware of the jeopardy

27

Part 1

Chapter 1
The New
Morality of
Christ:
Ethics
Defined

they face, people are potentially doomed, threatened daily by the possibility of eternal damnation. They may have little or no interest in matters of the Spirit or in enjoying the transformed life of a child of God.

Despite being without God, they may hold to a high code of conduct and personal integrity, rivaling that of some professing Christians. Philip E. Hughes reflects on this paradox:

> That ethical standards are seriously regarded by the secular authorities as well as by the Christian church is not questioned. The presence of police forces and courts of law throughout the world testifies to concern for what is socially fair and equitable. . . .
>
> It would, however, be a mistake to conclude that Christian and secular ethics must be virtually identical simply because both have a concern for decency and order and profess antipathy to injustice.[1]

At their virtuous best, secular ethics are the product of each individual's upbringing, what we may refer to as "generation ethics." Thus evolves a form of morality that springs from the unregenerate conscience. Each individual holds to a personal set of values profoundly affected by the contemporary moral climate. As a result, the ethical standards of our society spiral downward.

What is the solution? The greatest love story of all time, drawn from the Scriptures. The more persistently people have rejected God, the more persistently His love has pursued them. God "so loved" that He sent His holy, spotless Son; "Salvation is found in no one else" (Acts 4:12).

Christ took the occasion of welcoming a despised tax collector into the Kingdom to clearly state His mission: "The Son of Man came to seek and to save what was lost" (Luke 19:10). At Calvary He paid to

---

[1]Philip Edgcumbe Hughes, *Christian Ethics in Secular Society* (Grand Rapids: Baker Book House, 1983), 11–12.

provide the divine energy for the plan of redemption, which had been in place since "the creation of the world" (Rev. 13:8; cf. 1 Pet. 1:20).

In an interview with a righteous religious leader and teacher of Israel, Nicodemus, Jesus described the dynamic change necessary for even him, the most ethical of men: the new birth. This radical moral transformation begins with humble repentance, a permanent turning away from the old life to the new. The Holy Spirit monitors the process whereby the Father forgives and Christ redeems, rescuing the soul from the evil one. Thus a Christian stands, a completely justified son or daughter, before a God who maintains the highest standard of ethical excellence. Second Corinthians 5:17 neatly sums up the new status: "If anyone is in Christ, he is a new creation; the old has gone, the new has come!"

With this newness of life comes a newfound ability to live with integrity and morality—befitting a child of God. The new birth not only brings new life but also renders one dead to sin, without any conscious act on one's part. Romans 6:11–12 explains it particularly well: "Count yourselves dead to sin but alive to God in Christ Jesus. Therefore do not let sin reign in your mortal body so that you obey its evil desires."

Although redeemed believers are dead to sin, their wills are never violated. Therefore, they can and must choose to remain "dead," unresponsive to the natural urges to revert to their old ways, old habits, old patterns of ethics. On the other hand, they must respond to motivation to pursue the new and higher lifestyle. "Since, then, you have been raised with Christ, set your hearts on things above, where Christ is seated at the right hand of God. Set your minds on things above, not on earthly things" (Col. 3:1–2).

Consistently taking the high road, honoring God, is not a simple matter; the negative influences in one's upbringing and the corrupt thought patterns of the old life must continually be dealt with. As David Read notes: "[T]he 'old man' is always waiting in the

Part 1

Chapter 1
The New
Morality of
Christ:
Ethics
Defined

Part 1

Chapter 1
The New
Morality of
Christ:
Ethics
Defined

wings."[2] But the greatest incentive for ethical wholeness in the life of new converts is their newfound
love for the Lord.

Furthermore, the Spirit-quickened conscience gives
guidance over uncertain paths. Ephesians 2:1 (NKJV)
points out that we are no longer "dead in trespasses
and sins"; by God's grace we have been *"made
alive."* And more than that, restoration work has begun in us—restoration of the image of God. "The conscience is a line connecting man to his Creator: it is
one aspect of the image of God in which man was
created. It demarcates man from the rest of the animal creation as essentially a moral being who is answerable for his actions—answerable primarily and
ultimately to God—and whose behavior should reflect the holiness and lovingkindness of his Creator."[3]

Since receiving a quickened conscience, the child
of God is ready for a new set of values, which grow
out of the moral climate of the local church as well
as that of the Church universal. Hopefully the ethical
norms of the Church will reflect the work of the Spirit and not the debilitating influence of the world. So
getting the new Christian into a study of the Scriptures is imperative for establishing sound ethical
norms. Key passages are the Ten Commandments, the
Sermon on the Mount, and the Pauline epistles, the
latter particularly for their practical flavor.

RESTITUTION

Turning from the theoretical to the practical aspects of the new birth experience, the blessing of
restitution should never be overlooked. While restitution is not a scriptural requirement for salvation, it
becomes an important building block in the character
and ethical strength of the Christian who responds to

---

[2]David Haxton Carswell Read, *Christian Ethics* (Philadelphia:
J. B. Lippincott Co., 1968), 19.

[3]Hughes, *Christian Ethics in Secular Society*, 27.

Part 1

Chapter 1
The New
Morality of
Christ:
Ethics
Defined

the urging of the Holy Spirit. For example, the Law required that damaged or lost goods or livestock be restored: "If a man steals an ox or a sheep and slaughters it or sells it, he must pay back five head of cattle for the ox and four sheep for the sheep" (Exod. 22:1). If a man committed a violation related to holy things, "he must make restitution for what he . . . failed to do in regard to the holy things, add a fifth of the value to that and give it all to the priest, . . . and he will be forgiven" (Lev. 5:16).

The concept of restitution, doing more than expected, is certainly implied in the "second mile" teaching in the Sermon on the Mount: "'If someone wants to sue you and take your tunic, let him have your cloak as well. If someone forces you to go one mile, go with him two miles. Give to the one who asks you, and do not turn away from the one who wants to borrow from you'" (Matt. 5:40–42). Here the basic principles of steadfast love, justice, and righteousness far exceed the requirements of the Law.

By accepting the hospitality of a notorious tax collector, Zaccheus, Jesus inspired him to make things right with the people. Upon seeing Zaccheus's generous response, Jesus saw proof that he had accepted salvation and so announced it (Luke 19:9). The act of restitution reinforces one's ethical posture still today.

In the late 1920s my father, who in a few years would be called into ministry, was converted. He had just completed four years in the Navy and was living the usual carefree, sinful life of a young man with little thought of character development. However, when he found the Lord, he was transformed. The Holy Spirit whispered and brought his conscience to life. He responded by returning a set of tools he had stolen from an unsuspecting elderly friend, confessing his misdeed. His friend, who was not a Christian, wept with him as they reveled in the grace of God. The return of the tools was evidence that the power of the Spirit had taken my dad to a new ethical plane.

Part 1

Chapter 1
The New
Morality of
Christ:
Ethics
Defined

The same precepts apply from generation to generation. After a number of false starts, I was genuinely converted as a teenager. Since early childhood I had been trained to be truthful, but I couldn't be consistently straightforward until the Lord saved me. Even as a new Christian I had my moments of weakness in this area. Working at a summer job at an Army depot, I had a minor accident that damaged a piece of equipment on the truck I was driving. Afraid of losing my job, I did not report the accident and for years afterward rationalized that had I done so I would have been cleared of any liability. My rationalization satisfied my heart that I had not committed an immoral act, but the Holy Spirit continued to remind me that I had acted unethically and needed to make restitution for His sake as well as my own. I found a sweet release the day I finally sent off a sizable check to the Army Engineers' conscience fund.

THE PLEASURE PRINCIPLE

Unfortunately, the person who remains responsive to the promptings of the Spirit in ethical matters is usually thought of as frustrated, unhappy, and guilt-ridden. This assumption is reinforced by a social climate that emphasizes a pleasure-packed life in the fast lane. But not all pleasure produces joy; neither does joy always lead to lasting happiness. However, for the Christian, wholesome pleasure brings joy, and the joyful life produces happiness and fulfillment. The question then becomes, Are there both good pleasures and bad pleasures, and if so, how does one determine the nature of each?

Sidney Zink in *The Concepts of Ethics* approaches the question based on his determination that pleasure is a feeling or an experience that includes good, "the good of feeling or experience. The most obvious evidence that we do think pleasure a good thing is that we reward persons by giving them pleasure (and punish them by giving them pain). . . . But there is also

Part 1

Chapter 1
The New
Morality of
Christ:
Ethics
Defined

contrary evidence in that we think some pleasures are bad—for example, revenge, rage, lust."[4]

Zink further explains a distinction between the sources of the two kinds of pleasures: "There are other sorts of cases which show that what we admire in the so-called good pleasures, and what we deplore in the bad ones, are not these as states of feeling but as the expression of states of character."[5] It becomes necessary, then, in a study of the ethics of flesh versus spirit to determine when pleasure is bad, especially since pleasure is a goal of so many of our activities. The following typically engender bad pleasures:

1. When self-love dominates the pleasure-seeker's heart

A degree of self-love is only natural and proper. Scripture supports this premise, both Old and New Testaments. For example, Leviticus 19:18 states: "'Love your neighbor as yourself.'" Jesus sums up the Law and the Prophets in terms of loving God and your neighbor as yourself (Matt. 22:37–40). And Paul does the same in his epistle to the Romans: "'Love your neighbor as yourself'" (Rom. 13:9).

Furthermore, the ethicist can argue that we even have a responsibility to God to care for ourselves: "Agape-love requires that one properly care for himself . . . for the sake of service to God and man. Such concern and care of self turns out to be more of a duty to God than to self."[6]

The problem that may arise then in enjoying pleasure is doing so selfishly at the expense of others. Milton Rudnick views this self-centered approach to pleasure as a reflection of the times. He observes: "The 'new morality' that we have been experiencing is, . . . in fact, an ethical revolution in which the prin-

---

[4]Sidney Zink, The *Concepts of Ethics* (London: Macmillan & Co., 1962), 97.
[5]Ibid., 99.
[6]Ibid., 106.

Part 1

Chapter 1
The New
Morality of
Christ:
Ethics
Defined

ciples of Christian ethics have been assaulted and re-
pudiated by many. . . . 'If you enjoy it, it is good,'
many would say. Others with more social sensitivity
might put it this way: 'If most people in a given situation enjoy it or benefit from it, it is good.'"[7]

Rudnick summarizes the accepted evangelical posture on the subject by concluding that "few Christian
ethicists, even those who question the concept of di-
vinely revealed ethical norms, come out in favor of
this kind of pleasure-centered and self-centered approach."[8]

*2. When pleasure is harmful to oneself or to oth-
ers*

Most Christians would agree that masochistic activity seriously violates acceptable norms. To enjoy abusing oneself or being abused hardly seems compatible
with the changed life that flows from being born-
again. However, it is not uncommon for otherwise
conscientious believers to develop harmful eating
habits; to drive with abandon and unfastened seat
belts; or to be involved in vigorous recreational activity without adequate preparation, proper equipment,
or reasonable safeguards. We have all known apparently levelheaded persons who deliberately refused to
care for a serious injury or who, apart from faith for
divine healing, discontinued prescribed medication,
evidently getting a masochistic charge from the experience. Such willfulness approaches impropriety if
one believes the body is indeed the temple of the
Holy Spirit.

If pleasure from self-abuse is undesirable, pleasure
in harming or demeaning others is absolutely repre-
hensible. Tragically, in a world jaded by poverty, rac-
ism, and radical nationalism, the practice of inflicting
harm on another has almost become a pastime for

---

[7]Milton L. Rudnick, *Christian Ethics for Today: An Evangelical Approach* (Grand Rapids: Baker Book House, 1979), 18–19.
[8]Ibid., 19.

Part 1

Chapter 1
The New
Morality of
Christ:
Ethics
Defined

pockets of society, both in our nation and throughout our world. Especially when the pleasure is elicited from an act of revenge, it cannot be justified as acceptable. In this connection Sidney Zink makes the point that "taking any pleasure in a thing is generally a sign that one does like and desire the thing; and if a person does, even on a single occasion, feel pleasure in an act of revenge, this is some evidence that he is a vengeful person. It is this inference to a desire which leads us to call the revenge bad. It is a confusion of the pleasure in the act with the act as the expression of a personal desire which causes us to call the pleasure itself bad."[9]

3. When pleasure seeking becomes obsessive

God created human beings to appreciate and enjoy pleasure to His glory, but not to the satisfying of every whim and self-interest. Even as Christ in bearing up the weak did not please himself, so His followers should give themselves to others and love their neighbors as themselves. Of course, not all ethicists concur. Ayn Rand epitomizes a worldly viewpoint on this matter in rather shocking terms: "[B]y the grace of reality and the nature of life, man—every man—is an end in himself, he exists for his own sake, and the achievement of his own happiness is his highest moral purpose. The purpose of morality is not to teach one to suffer for others and die, but to enjoy himself and to live."[10]

In contrast, Augustine confessed to the Lord his struggle to overcome just such a lifestyle: "I was an unhappy young man, wretched as at the beginning of my adolescence when I prayed you for chastity and said: 'Grant me chastity and continence, but not yet.' I was afraid you might hear my prayer quickly, and that you might too rapidly heal me of the disease of

---

[9]Zink, The *Concepts of Ethics*, 98.

[10]Ayn Rand, *For the New Intellectual* (New York: New American Library, division of Penguin, USA, 1961), 123.

Part 1

Chapter 1
The New
Morality of
Christ:
Ethics
Defined

lust which I preferred to satisfy rather than suppress."[11]

In anguish he opened a New Testament and read: "Let us behave decently . . . not in orgies and drunkenness, not in sexual immorality and debauchery, not in dissension and jealousy. Rather, clothe yourselves with the Lord Jesus Christ, and do not think about how to gratify the desires of the sinful nature" (Rom. 13:13–14). At that moment, Augustine writes, "It was as if a light of relief from all anxiety flooded into my heart. All the shadows of doubt were dispelled. I [was delivered] out of the bonds of sinful desire with which I was so firmly fettered."[12] One cannot but marvel at the liberating power of the gospel. The very same power remains today for living on a joyful plane of Christian ethics and morality.

4. When pleasure seeking is with the wrong crowd

Bad pleasures often proceed out of unwholesome associations. Although we are able to live in the world without being of the world, if we become more comfortable with worldlings than with believers, soon we will be indulging in diversions foreign to the Christian ethic. What may appear a harmless association can destroy both ministry and minister. I recall a fellow minister I befriended shortly after he joined my district fellowship. An affable man, he had an infectious grin and an upbeat personality—an outstanding pastor. His parishioners loved him, but he reserved his warmest friendships and moments of recreation for his non-Christian neighbors. Like the Lord himself, he was a friend of sinners, but unlike the Lord, he lacked the desire to live an exemplary life among them. Had he been able to keep his friendships in the community and hold a Christ-honoring standard, he might have won them over. However,

---

[11]Augustine, *Confessions* (trans. Henry Chadwick) VIII. 7.
[12]Ibid., VIII. 12.

Part 1

Chapter 1
The New
Morality of
Christ:
Ethics
Defined

today he is out of the ministry, struggling to hold a job in a small retail store.

5. When the pleasure seeker is engaged in pleasure and the Lord's presence is not enjoyed

How blessed we would be if we were as sensitive to the Spirit as Joseph when responding to the seductions of Potiphar's wife: "'How . . . could I do such a wicked thing and sin against God?'" (Gen. 39:9).

For avoiding unethical pleasures, particularly in a sophisticated society like ours, a major step is seeing the act for what it is. Milton L. Rudnick in *Christian Ethics for Today: An Evangelical Approach* notes: "The problem is not simply that people are sinning more and obeying less. The problem is, rather, that a growing number of people in the world, as well as in Christian circles, refuse to consider many types of behavior as sin. These people insist on approving certain activities and attitudes though they are clearly identified as sin in the Scripture. Homosexuality, self-assertion, and revolution are some examples."[13] Regardless of how we label our pleasures, if we can't enjoy them and at the same time enjoy the presence of God, we risk being unprepared to enter the fullness of joy when we depart for the next world.

But now after having considered circumstances that result in bad pleasures, we must certainly give equal time to proper attitudes toward pleasure. As Christians, we need not keep a list of no-no's in order to enjoy a life of joy and fulfillment. We can find pleasure at every turn, in places and situations we would never have supposed before we found Christ. The freedom and delight that accompany the Christian experience come from within and tend to heighten the moments of pleasure we share. So although wholesome, pleasureful acts are important and legitimate, they are not essential to our enjoyment of life in Christ.

---

[13]Rudnick, *Christian Ethics for Today*, 19.

Part 1

Chapter 1
The New
Morality of
Christ:
Ethics
Defined

Like most experiences in life, we will find that pleasures are more fulfilling and memorable when they are shared, as well as when they are wholesome. It is the steadfast love of God's ethic that does away with our selfish motives, allowing us to engage in shared pleasure. To the world, there is mystery about this unselfish love manifested by God's people. As Henlee Barnette observes:

> Psychiatrists and psychologists . . . deny selfless love because they tend to approach the problem from the human side. From the divine perspective the theologian sees a distinct type of love, a love not wholly unrelated to duties to self. This unique type of love is epitomized by our Lord in John 13:34: "A new commandment I give to you, that you love one another; even as I have loved you." The differentia of the Christian ethic is that of love to one another, *not as we loved ourselves* but *as Christ loves us.*[14]

Because of the high motivation that divine love produces in us, we will be naturally Christ-honoring in our activities, regardless of the pleasure.

But we must find a balance between the pleasurable aspects and the sober responsibilities of the Christian walk. Indeed, the experience of living for Christ in a sinful world has been described in Scripture as a marathon, a warfare, not a stroll through the park. The more serious side of our commitment to God and His kingdom will prevent our joys from becoming frivolity; rather our "good" pleasures will lift our spirits in the heat of battle.

THE POWER OF THE CROSS

The new birth brings a positive change. The believer becomes a new creation, spiritually alive and perceptive. Yet the saint remains human: The struggle to be a consistently ethical person becomes a daily experience. The problem we face as children of God is

---

[14]Barnette, *Introducing Christian Ethics*, 103-4.

Part 1

Chapter 1
The New
Morality of
Christ:
Ethics
Defined

that, essentially, we are not by nature good. In fact, such passages as that of Paul's in Romans 7:18-19 profile a hopeless character study: "I know that nothing good lives in me, that is, in my sinful nature. For I have the desire to do what is good, but I cannot carry it out. For what I do is not the good I want to do; no, the evil I do not want to do—this I keep on doing." It appears that we are compulsive sinners, doomed to fail.

But, thank God, in our new lives in Christ there is bright hope. We can rise by faith from guilt and frustration into a consistently victorious position in Christ. "Therefore, there is now no condemnation for those who are in Christ Jesus" (Rom. 8:1), and "I can do all things through Christ who strengthens me" (Phil. 4:13, NKJV). I can and will reach a level of ethical living beyond human comprehension. My secret? I have realized that while it is true I am not capable of being virtuous and victorious in my own capabilities, I have the source of genuine spiritual power— the cross of the Lord Jesus Christ.

Consider the powerful message of Romans 6:6: "We know that our old self was crucified with him so that the body of sin might be done away with, that we should no longer be slaves to sin." The process whereby the "old self," the sinful self-life, is nailed to the cross *has already* taken place. It need not be repeated. At the same time, it is not a process I can carry out alone; I cannot crucify myself. Only in the power of the Spirit am I able to submit to the cross as Christ did.

Galatians 2:20 concurs: The action is in the past tense. And it is made clear that we have the honor of sharing the crucifixion and the power of resurrected life with Christ. "I *have been* crucified with Christ and I no longer live, but Christ lives in me. The life I live in the body, I live by faith in the Son of God, who loved me and gave himself for me." Christ lives in me as the crucified but risen Christ, and I share

Part 1

Chapter 1
The New
Morality of
Christ:
Ethics
Defined

the life and power of His resurrection by faith in His finished work, done on my behalf.

I will not consider myself worthy of my position in Christ or boast of ethical or spiritual attainment. I will echo Paul: "May I never boast except in the cross of our Lord Jesus Christ, through which the world has been crucified to me, and I to the world" (Gal. 6:14).

As a further act of faith in dealing with the ethical problems presented by the fleshly nature, one should heed this admonition: "Put off your old [corrupt, KJV] self, which is being corrupted by its deceitful desires; . . . be made new in the attitude of your minds; and . . . put on the new self, created to be like God in true righteousness and holiness" (Eph. 4:22–24). To aid me in putting off the old self-life, we are told specifically what we are to put out of our lives by faith: "sexual immorality, impurity, lust, evil desires and greed, which is idolatry . . . anger, rage, malice, slander, and filthy language" (Col. 3:5,8). Once having done that, we are able to "put on the new self, which is being renewed in knowledge in the image of its Creator. . . . [And as one of] God's chosen people, holy and dearly loved, [I can clothe myself] . . . with compassion, kindness, humility, gentleness and patience" (Col. 3:10,12).

In taking on these godly qualities we begin almost effortlessly to act in a wholesome manner among those about us. Verse thirteen of this passage indicates we will be able to be patient with others of like precious faith and forgive their offenses even as Christ has forgiven us. Then, best of all, we will reach the epitome of ethicality as we take the ultimate step of faith: "Over all these virtues put on love, which binds them all together in perfect unity" (Col. 3:14). Once again we are pointed to the lofty pattern of ethical practice, predicated on divine love, recorded in Jeremiah 9:24, "'I am the LORD; I act with steadfast love, justice, and righteousness in the earth, for in these things I delight'" (NRS).

THE SECRET OF VICTORY: SPIRIT OVER FLESH

Part 1

**Chapter 1
The New
Morality of
Christ:
Ethics
Defined**

The Holy Spirit is depicted in the Old Testament as having a somewhat impersonal ministry, filling only a few and often coming upon individuals temporarily to empower them for specific actions to the glory of God. Even Samson and Elijah, who were richly endowed of the Spirit, needed a special anointing for a given act of service to God.

In the New Testament the Holy Spirit came upon and dwelled within the persons who were to be uniquely used of God. For example, the Holy Spirit came upon Mary at the conception of Christ. There is reason to believe that He remained within her in a remarkable way, at least until the birth of Christ, as evidenced by the witness of the Spirit to the embryonic John the Baptist, himself filled with the Spirit in Elizabeth's womb (Luke 1:15).

Jesus, filled with the Spirit when He was baptized by John the Baptist, was also led by the Spirit directly from the Jordan into the wilderness temptations (Luke 4:1). Returning triumphant from His confrontation with the devil, Jesus came into the synagogue at Nazareth, stood, and proclaimed that the Spirit was inaugurating His ministry: "'The Spirit of the Lord is on me, because he has anointed me to preach good news to the poor'" (Luke 4:18). By a divine anointing He would heal the brokenhearted, deliver the captives, heal the blind, free the oppressed, and generally "proclaim the year of the Lord's favor" (Luke 4:19). Attesting that Jesus' ministry relied on the Holy Spirit, the Gospel writers, in recording His miracles, often refer to the Spirit (Luke 4:14; 5:17).

At Pentecost the Spirit was poured out for the first time on the young Church to uniquely equip every member with anointing and power for witnessing and preaching the gospel. As the Holy Spirit came upon them, all spoke in languages they had never learned. Apparently each person spoke in a different tongue; the Spirit was doing an intensely personal work in

Part 1

Chapter 1
The New
Morality of
Christ:
Ethics
Defined

each life. In the same way, the Spirit has come to hungering, thirsting believers over the centuries to prepare them uniquely and personally for service to God.

Besides bringing empowerment for service, the Spirit, as predicted by Christ, comes as the Comforter (Helper, Counselor), the Guide into truth, the Teacher who reiterates and reinforces the ethical teaching of the Master himself. The Spirit is able to search out the "deep things of God" and reveal them to the simplest among us (1 Cor. 2:10). Taking our individual needs on His own heart, "the Spirit himself intercedes for us with groans that words cannot express" (Rom. 8:26). Each of these functions of the Spirit helps us retain victory over the sinful nature.

Where do we find the assurance that each day we can enjoy the Spirit's dominion over the sinful nature? In the teaching of Galatians 5:19–21 Paul lists the sins of the flesh, ranging from adultery, licentiousness, and idolatry to heresies, murders, and drunkenness. Then in the next two verses he identifies the ninefold fruit of the Spirit: "love, joy, peace, patience, kindness, goodness, faithfulness, gentleness and self-control." It is noteworthy that this grouping of attributes is headed by the single most important quality—godly love.

The secret, then, of a life that enjoys the mastery of the spirit over the flesh is simply to choose consistently the high road: "Live by the Spirit, and you will not gratify the desires of the sinful nature" (Gal. 5:16). The battle is already won.

STUDY QUESTIONS

1. What is the secret of becoming a spiritual overcomer?

2. How are our wills involved in the life of the Spirit?

3. What should a person do when restitution is not possible?

4. On what basis should a Christian determine which pleasures are acceptable and which are not?

5. What help do we have to deal with the old sinful (fleshly) nature, and what steps do we need to take to live in continuous victory?

Part 1

Chapter 1
The New
Morality of
Christ:
Ethics
Defined

Chapter 2

The Basis of Morality: The Ten Commandments

BACKGROUND OF THE LAW

JACOB AND HIS SONS

The ethical principles undergirding the law of Moses can be traced back to the life of Jacob. The name "Jacob" itself is significant: From birth he was a heel grabber, a deceiver (Gen. 25:26). As a young man he defrauded his brother, Esau, of his birthright (25:31–34) and later deceived his nearly blind, elderly father to obtain his blessing (27:19). After escaping his uncle Laban, who defrauded him, Jacob faced the truth about his past as he anticipated meeting Esau. At Peniel he wrestled with an angel, clinging to him despite the excruciating pain of a hip out of joint. Having forced a confession of his identity as Jacob the deceiver, the divine wrestler renamed him "Israel," the man who struggled with God and overcame (Gen. 32:28). He limped away from his lesson in ethics, realizing that God places a higher premium on good character than on good health. Israel would remain a cripple for the rest of his days.

Character is not transmitted from generation to generation, however. Most of Jacob's sons seemed bent on evil. Settled in Canaan where their clan seemed to have been received, their sister was raped by a Canaanite. When her brothers heard of this, they pretended to accept the Canaanite's offer of marriage. Instead—going far beyond the eye-for-eye, punishment-fitting-the-crime justice of God—they wiped out an

Part 1

Chapter 2
The Basis of
Morality:
The Ten
Commandments

entire Canaanite community; this forced Jacob and the rest of his clan to move (Gen. 34:1-31).

Jacob did have at least one outstanding son, Joseph. Although a youth of integrity, he was perhaps a little egotistical and far too frank and naive for his own good. He foolishly revealed his dreams to his family, making it clear that he would someday take precedence over not only his jealous brothers but his father and mother as well (Gen. 37:5-11). God arranged for the grudging brothers to sell him into Egyptian slavery (45:5-8), but Joseph carried his high standards along. Severely tested in the home of his master, Potiphar, he clung to his godly principles, only to wind up in prison (39:9,20). The keeper of the prison recognized strong character and put Joseph in charge of the prison (39:22). Ultimately, he emerged from jail second to Pharaoh himself (41:39-43). By his beautifully consistent ethical practice he was enabled by God to feed his family along with all of Egypt. As an intriguing final touch to his career, he made sure to get a pledge from his family that they—or their descendants—would carry his bones out of Egypt (Gen. 50:25). This was an expression of faith in the promises God had given to Abraham (Gen. 12:3; 15:13-16,18-21).

MOSES AND THE CHILDREN OF ISRAEL

Nearly four centuries later the groaning of the Hebrew slave nation touched the heart of God, and He prepared them a deliverer. The preparation had begun with the birth of Moses. Because of the Hebrew midwives who feared God and ignored Pharaoh's policy of infanticide for the male Hebrew babies, he was spared (Exod. 1:17). Even though the midwives lied to Pharaoh to protect the baby boys (1:19), God was gracious, forgiving and blessing the midwives because they feared Him (1:20-21).

Also in the providence of God, Moses was grounded in the Hebrew ethic at his mother's knee before being educated in Egypt's royal palace (Exod. 2:8-

10). One day he walked into the fields and witnessed mistreatment of a Hebrew. Moses felt such abuse was unjust although the Egyptian's action was hardly a serious violation of the ethical code of his culture, that is, what was considered customary under the circumstances. Yet Moses reacted to it by committing a brazen, immoral act in killing the Egyptian and burying his body in the sand. When his crime was found out, he fled to Midian (Exod. 2:11-15).

This series of events, however, was a matter of God's causing "the wrath of man" to praise Him (Ps. 76:10, KJV), leading Moses to stumble onto the household of his future father-in-law, Jethro. Again Moses' sense of fair treatment caused him to interpose himself, this time between some bullying shepherds and the daughters of Jethro; thus he earned the right to marry one of the daughters—only to become a sheepherder himself for the next forty years (Exod. 2:17,21).

God, in His own good time, visited Moses to announce His plan to deliver the Israelites (Exod. 3:2,10). One aspect of the plan seemed to involve questionable ethics. The Israelites were to ask for jewels, silver, and gold for the journey to the Promised Land. God wanted them to leave not as slaves sneaking away but as His triumphant army, having plundered the enemy—fulfilling a promise He had made to Abraham (Gen. 15:14). To make this possible, God gave the Israelites such favor with the Egyptians that they freely surrendered their treasures by the time of Israel's departure (Exod. 3:21-22; 11:2-3; 12:35-36).

In the meantime, the plagues became a test of the ethical consistency of Israel as well as of Pharaoh. The Israelites had to remain in their homes and in their assigned territory to avoid the calamities that were befalling Egypt. The final, decisive plague presented the most exacting test of obedience for the Israelites. They were to follow God's instructions—without variance—for what would become the first Passover: The lamb was to be carefully selected,

Part 1

Chapter 2
The Basis of
Morality:
The Ten
Commandment

Part 1

Chapter 2
The Basis of
Morality:
The Ten
Commandments

roasted, and the whole of it eaten or its leftovers burned. God's people were to be ready to travel even as they ate. But the most crucial directive called for the lamb's blood to be applied to the sides and tops of the door frames of every home (Exod. 12:7). Also, at the inception of the greatest of the Jewish feasts, the Passover, God gave careful instructions for observing it in the future (12:14).

The Israelites' final response to the test of their integrity is richly appropriate. Moses, man of principle and leader of the Exodus, rose to the centuries-old challenge of Joseph, man of sterling character who helped save the nation of Israel in his own day. Exodus 13:19 provides the record of this historic moment: "Moses took the bones of Joseph with him because Joseph had made the sons of Israel swear an oath. He had said, 'God will surely come to your aid, and then you must carry my bones up with you.'"

The lessons Moses learned through obedience during the Exodus experience put iron into his soul, the iron needed by a leader whose integrity and ethics must be respected by his followers, especially in times of crisis. As they approached the Red Sea, pursuit by Pharaoh's army was the Israelites' first emergency. Moses was able to offer the word for the hour: "'Do not be afraid. Stand firm and you will see the deliverance the LORD will bring you today. The Egyptians you see today you will never see again. The LORD will fight for you; you need only to be still'" (Exod. 14:13–14). Taking confidence in their godly leader, the multitude stepped into the dry seabed and walked across on dry ground. On the other bank, with the bodies of dead Egyptians washing ashore, Israel in one hour came to fear the Lord and believe His word, as well as that of His servant Moses. A great seaside praise rally followed (Exod. 15:1–21).

Shortly, faced with a different kind of water problem—none to drink—Israel complained against both Moses and God. God gave Moses precise instructions for quenching their thirst. Moses was to strike a rock with his rod. He obeyed and water gushed out (Exod. 17:6).

Part 1

Chapter 2
The Basis of
Morality:
The Ten
Commandment

Some years later, as the journey continued, the sequel to this miracle resulted in a lesson in ethics. Again Israel was in need of drinking water, but God's command to His servant was to *speak* to the rock to get the water. But Moses, in anger this time and taking credit for himself and Aaron as suppliers of the water instead of God, struck the rock. Although the water poured out, Moses, now the disobedient leader, was deprived of the Promised Land (Num. 20:8–12). The lesson is simple, basic: the how of ministry is more important than the results of ministry.

As the time for receiving God's commandments approached, it was essential that Moses and his people learn more lessons in the ethics of obedience. Jethro, Moses' father-in-law, joined the march and noticed that Moses so involved himself in the minutiae of administration that he was neglecting other responsibilities. Recognizing this counsel as from God, Moses appointed capable judges to share leadership roles in the camp (Exod. 18:13–26). Later, Israel's elders were allowed to attend an awesome meeting with the Lord (24:9–11). But boundaries were set to safeguard the people during the actual giving of the Law. To trespass was to face sudden death (19:12–13).

Moses was called by God to join Him on the mount for forty glorious days of communion and the giving of the Law (Exod. 24:18). Yet even as the commandments and statutes were being given, the Hebrews began violating the very code of ethics they had adopted at the Red Sea when they committed themselves to respect and obey their leader. They doubted Moses would ever return, and they looked to Aaron to lead them onward in their wilderness journey.

No spiritual leader ever acted more unethically than Aaron: He collected gold from the people and fashioned a calf to receive the worship due the God who was at that very moment acting in their behalf a

Part 1

Chapter 2
The Basis of
Morality:
The Ten
Commandments

short distance away. Completely forsaking their scruples, the people "sat down to eat and drink and got up to indulge in revelry" (Exod. 32:6). Verse 25 says, "The people were running wild . . . out of control," and sexual immorality may be implied.

Moses' response to the news of this debauchery and shame was powerful. Interceding with an angry God, Moses asked that the rebels be spared—not because of their merits but for God's glory. And God, true to His description of himself to Jeremiah centuries later, showed that He would always "act with steadfast love, justice, and righteousness in the earth" (Jer. 9:24, NRS). Only token judgment followed.

When Moses finally returned to the camp, he was so overwhelmed with righteous wrath that he smashed the tablets of the Law, ground the golden calf to powder, spread it on the drinking water, and forced the people to drink the concoction (Exod. 32:19–20). God's justice demanded that the Levites take sword in hand and destroy three thousand of the rebellious Israelites (32:27–28). Again Moses stood between God and the people, having the integrity to offer the classic plea of the intercessor: "'Please forgive their sin—but if not, then blot me out of the book you have written'" (32:32).

God's love prevailed; fresh mercy was granted. Needing his faith renewed, Moses requested and was granted another audience with the Lord. Heeding God's directions, he hewed out two more tablets of stone, and God again wrote down the commandments by His own finger (Exod. 34:1). Then God gave him a new directive: His people were to eliminate pagan worship and shun intermarriage in the Promised Land (34:10–16).

With the Law also came instruction in ethical worship, calling for a proper attitude. Acceptable offerings for the building of the tabernacle would come only from "everyone who [was] willing" (Exod. 35:5). Artisans for the intricate work on the tabernacle had to be called of God, their hearts having been stirred by Him and filled with His Spirit to perform the appointed tasks and to apprentice others (Exod. 35:30 to 36:2).

Part 1

Chapter 2
The Basis of
Morality:
The Ten
Commandment

The priests had to be clothed in specially tailored garments. The priests were to be trained with care to offer the various sacrifices required of the Lord. They must order their lives to follow the regulations He laid out for them. When the sons of Aaron, perhaps reflecting their father's immoral example at Sinai, were destroyed for offering "unauthorized fire" to the Lord, he was not permitted to mourn (Lev. 10:1-3,6-7). He had to accept God's judgment. Yet the rest of the nation was allowed to lament this tragedy, a vivid object lesson demonstrating God's view of integrity in ministry. This tragedy also was the background for the instituting of the annual Day of Atonement (Lev. 16:1). It would provide forgiveness for all the sins of the Israelites (16:34).

As the long journey continued, Miriam, along with her brother, Aaron, became the unhappy subject of another of God's lessons in proper conduct in ministry. The two of them criticized Moses' leadership. Miriam was smitten by God with leprosy, of which she was healed in seven days but only through Moses' intercession (Num. 12:1-15).

At Kadesh Barnea, Israel learned a profound lesson in the ethics of faith versus fear. When the twelve spies returned from their trip into the Promised Land and gave a divided report, the people rejected the minority opinion of Caleb and Joshua that the Lord could keep His promise of a "land flowing with milk and honey" (Num. 13:30-31; 14:5-10). After God condemned that generation to stay and die in the desert, they decided to enter the land. Their disobedience and presumption caused their rout at the hands of the enemy (Num. 14:30-35,40-45; Deut. 1:44), followed by many more years of futile traveling around in the desert, though led by the cloud of God's presence.

Part 1

Chapter 2
The Basis of
Morality:
The Ten
Commandments

Shortly before they approached the land of promise for the last time, they were victimized by Balaam, the pagan prophet who wanted remuneration more than God's will. His counsel to trespass against God caused the deaths of twenty-four thousand Israelites (Num. 25:1-9; 31:16).[1]

As Israel approached the land of promise, Joshua and Caleb, the spies with faith, were the only persons of their generation allowed to enter (Num. 26:65). Joshua became the God-ordained, Spirit-filled leader of Israel (27:22-23). And the first instruction he received from God was to meditate on the Book of the Law day and night until its ethic became second nature (Josh. 1:8). His first challenge as leader was to demonstrate confidence in the integrity of God's Word. At God's command the priests bearing the ark stepped into the floodwaters of the Jordan; the waters piled up to the north; and Israel marched across, as their forebears had with Moses, on dry ground (Josh. 3:13-17).

Twelve large memorial stones from the east bank of the Jordan were deposited in the riverbed; twelve from the riverbed were placed on the west bank, all as a monument to God's faithfulness (Josh. 4:3-9). The stone tablets of the Law marked a covenant with God that would sustain Israel as it began its existence as a free nation; the memorial stones marked a fresh covenant with God that would provide strength and encouragement for occupying the Promised Land.

In conquering Jericho, the first city in Israel's path, an ethical dilemma challenged Joshua more critically

---

[1]A sidelight to the story of Balaam comes from his journey to do Balak's bidding, contrary to God's primary will. Anna B. Lock, an outstanding evangelist of the 1940s, would cite this incident (characteristically with tongue in cheek) to illustrate God's willingness to use a female to speak His word. For a careful reading of the episode brings out the gender of the donkey Balaam was riding: "Then the Lord opened the donkey's mouth, and *she* said to Balaam, 'What have I done to you to make you beat me these three times?'" (Num. 22:28).

The Ten Commandments   **53**

Part 1

Chapter 2
The Basis of
Morality:
The Ten
Commandment

than the massive walls of the city. When the city fell to Israel's army, would this man of God honor the agreement between his spies and a prostitute of the city, Rahab? To his eternal credit he spared her and her family, although the city and the rest of its inhabitants were destroyed, dedicated to God's judgment as the firstfruits of the conquest (Josh. 6:21,24-25). The amazing sequel to the story is the place given this woman of poor reputation but rich faith—in the direct line of none other than the Messiah himself (Matt. 1:5).

THE TEN COMMANDMENTS

The events and personalities related to the giving of the Law are intriguing, but for grandeur and importance, the giving of the Ten Commandments at Sinai is without equal.

The significance of the Ten Commandments cannot be overstated. Though given to Israel to help them keep their relationship with God, their application is universal: to the Jew, to the Christian, to all humanity. To capture some of the significance of this monumental moral code, we need to review the events and the setting of its presentation.

Moses returned to Horeb, where God had called him from a burning bush. With him was all Israel, two million strong, about to witness an even more awe-inspiring manifestation of the Lord's presence than Moses had seen. In preparation, boundaries for the people were set, and the people themselves were consecrated. Thunder crashed across the mount; lightning flashed; holy fire glowed as a cloud settled over the mountain peak. Smoke made its way heavenward; the earth quaked; a trumpet blew; and God called out an invitation for Moses to join Him on the mount for the oral giving of the Law (Exod. 19:16-20).

It is the next phase of this series of events that highlights the nature of God and His divine purpose

Part 1

Chapter 2
The Basis of
Morality:
The Ten
Commandments

in giving the commandments. The Lord, whose every
action reflects His basis for conduct—"steadfast love,
justice, and righteousness" (Jer. 9:24, NRS)—made it
clear that love is His primary motivation. He extended a personal invitation to Moses, Aaron, Nadab, Abi-
hu, and the seventy elders of Israel to join Him for a
fellowship meal on the mountainside, during which
"they saw God, and they ate and drank" (Exod. 24:9-
11). This warm gesture added emphasis to God's purpose for the commandments: not to intimidate and
terrorize His people but to guide them into happy
compliance with His will for their lives. His love
shines through even in the giving of the second commandment (Exod. 20:6): Idol worship would not go
unpunished, but love and obedience would be repaid
by divine love (Deut. 7:9).

Next came specific instructions for building and
furnishing the tabernacle, guidelines for the ministry
of the priesthood, and directions for the order of the
sacrifices to be offered for the sins of the people and
for occasions designated as feast days. Then Moses
went to the top of Mount Sinai for the stone tablets
prepared and inscribed by God. During this interval
the people of Israel, led so foolishly by Aaron, degen-
erated into carousing idol worshipers. Shocked by
this scene, Moses broke the tablets and dispensed
God's justice (Exod. 32:19-20).

God, true to His merciful nature, met once again
with Moses on the mount—this time to write on the
tablets that Moses prepared. The Lord descended in a
pillar of cloud and proclaimed His name and His passion for His people: "'The LORD, the LORD, the compassionate and gracious God, slow to anger,
abounding in love and faithfulness, maintaining love
to thousands, and forgiving wickedness, rebellion and
sin. Yet he does not leave the guilty unpunished; he
punishes the children and their children for the sin of
the fathers to the third and fourth generation'" (Exod.
34:6-7; see also Deut. 7:9-10).

A study of the Ten Commandments reveals qualities

not in any other code of ethics or guidelines for morality. Among these unique qualities are the following:

Part 1

Chapter 2
The Basis of
Morality:
The Ten
Commandment

1. The Ten Commandments, given by God, hold for the Jews a significance similar to that held by the Sermon on the Mount, given by God's Son, for Christians.

2. The Ten Commandments are concise but complete; they reflect divine authority, not mere human idealism. They possess an eternal quality, a grandeur as though they belong to the ages.

3. The Ten Commandments are closely interrelated. It is virtually impossible to break only one at a time. For example, it has been observed that to commit adultery may well involve violating five other commandments (see p. 57). The Holy Spirit takes it a step further, however, in James 2:10: "Whoever keeps the whole law and yet stumbles at just one point is guilty of breaking all of it."

4. The Ten Commandments have application to all people, to all cultures, to all time. The first five apply to the human race's duty to God (obedience to parents was considered part of their obedience to God), the remaining five to the human race's duty to itself.

5. The Ten Commandments go beyond the external and moral aspects of proper conduct. As Henlee Barnette points out in *Introducing Christian Ethics:* "Respect for parents, personality, marriage, property, and truth are the distinctively ethical obligations of the Commandments."[2]

A brief synopsis of the commandments (quoted in the King James, as they are in public places) will serve to point out their ethical as well as their practical aspects.

1. "Thou shalt have no other gods before me" (Exod. 20:3). There is one God and He must reign supreme and alone in the human heart. Total dedication to the Lord is basic to all true faith.

---

[2]Henlee H. Barnette, *Introducing Christian Ethics* (Nashville: Broadman Press, 1961), 25.

Part 1

Chapter 2
The Basis of
Morality:
The Ten
Commandments

2. "Thou shalt not make unto thee any graven image" (20:4). No material substitute for His spiritual presence is acceptable. No image of himself, much less of another deity, is to be formed (cf. Deut. 4:15–19). The Lord states in Exodus 20:5 that He is "'a jealous God, punishing the children for the sin of the fathers to the third and fourth generation of those who hate [Him and who continue in the sins of their fathers].'" Yet in verse 6 His love shines through in His promise of "'showing love to a thousand generations of those who love [Him] and keep [His] commandments.'" His love is far greater than His judgment!

3. "Thou shalt not take the name of the Lord thy God in vain" (20:7). Just as one cannot make a mockery of His divine form by fashioning an image, neither can one mock His nature by careless use of His holy name. To quote the Psalmist: "O Lord, our Lord, how majestic is your name in all the earth!" (Ps. 8:1). His name represents His nature and character and is worthy of reverence.

4. "Remember the Sabbath day, to keep it holy" (20:8). Here is the perfect example of the perfect work ethic. God worked six days and rested on one; His people were *commanded* to do the same, arranging their work schedule so nothing would be left hanging and they would be free to worship on the seventh day. It is unfortunate that no such enforced day of rest is listed in the average minister's calendar for the week. Even the minister's "day off" usually involves the frantic pursuit of one activity or another. Nonetheless, the law of the Sabbath is built into our world. Humans must have periodic rest and relaxation to function at their best. Work animals require a day of rest each week. Even the machines that are so important to our way of living cannot continue indefinitely without rest.[3]

---

[3]Harold Lindsell, "The Lord's Day and Natural Resources," in *The Lord's Day*, comp. James P. Wesberry (Nashville: Broadman Press, 1986), 143–44.

Part 1

Chapter 2
The Basis of
Morality:
The Ten
Commandment

5. "Honor thy father and thy mother" (20:12). God designed the family. He is the role model, the respected, beloved, revered Father. This commandment, so often ignored by those who appear to be highly ethical otherwise, is unique in that, when kept, it carries a promise of longevity.

6. "Thou shalt not kill [murder]" (20:13). God is the Giver of Life; sin is the producer of death. When God breathed into the nostrils of the inanimate Adam, He was breathing the breath of *lives,* according to the original Hebrew text for Genesis 2:7. The God-spark of life has been passed from generation to generation. Thus human beings remain in the image of God to this day. It is impossible to destroy this likeness without being accountable to God personally (Gen. 9:6); doing so gave grounds for capital punishment under the Law.

7. "Thou shalt not commit adultery" (20:14). Adultery, despite the wretched moral climate of our world, remains a terrible offense against the individual, against society, and against God. As noted earlier in this chapter, this particular sin may involve the violation of as many as six commandments: the first (no other gods), the fifth (dishonoring parents), the seventh (adultery), the eighth (stealing), the ninth (lying), and the tenth (coveting).

8. "Thou shalt not steal" (20:15). This prohibition is not only directed at the dishonest handling of money and tangible objects but carries other ethical implications also. "'You shall not steal'" another's honor, friends, reputation, affection, due credit, time, or anything that is not rightfully yours. In short, "'You shall not steal'" anything!

9. "Thou shalt not bear false witness" (20:16). This commandment specifically prohibits making false statements about the character and actions of one's neighbor. But the question arises, as it did in Jesus' day, "'Who is my neighbor?'" (Luke 10:29). Obviously, His answer cannot be improved upon: even the total stranger must be respected as a neighbor (Luke

Part 1

Chapter 2
The Basis of
Morality:
The Ten
Commandments

10:30–37). The commandment does not mention other types of lying, but it becomes a background for prohibiting lying in general (Lev. 6:2–7; Prov. 14:5; cf. Col. 3:9). To be known as a person of the truth in all situations is to be esteemed as a person of high principles.

10. "Thou shalt not covet" (20:17). Of all the commandments this one falls most clearly into the category of pure ethical instruction; it addresses not the fruit of sin but its root, the heart. And whether or not it leads to the act itself, it is prohibited. Covetousness gnaws from within, leaving people frustrated and unfulfilled, causing them to yearn for what they know they should not have. Nevertheless, as Jesus would indicate in the Sermon on the Mount, to lust or desire wrongfully is to actually commit the deed in one's heart (Matt. 5:27–28).

APPLICATION OF THE STATUTES TO ETHICAL CONDUCT

According to the calculations of Richard Higginson, the Mosaic law included 613 commands—248 prescriptions, 365 prohibitions—which fall into five categories: criminal, civil, familial, cultic, and charitable. (The cultic statutes are defined as having to do with laws of cleanliness.[4]) Often the statutes have ethical connotations rather than moral implications. That is, they may call for a high level of conduct, even under difficult circumstances, although to follow an inferior course of action would not be immoral. Three examples will suffice to illustrate:

1. In Exodus 21:2–6 is the regulation concerning the Hebrew servant or slave who was bought by one of his own nation and served faithfully for six years. At this point the qualities of God's standard of excellence—"steadfast love, justice, and righteousness" (Jer. 9:24, NRS)—came into play. Justice dictat-

---

[4]Richard Higginson, *Dilemmas, A Christian Approach to Moral Decision Making* (London: Hodder & Stoughton, 1988), 56.

Application of the Statutes to Ethical Conduct   **59**

Part 1

Chapter 2
The Basis of
Morality:
The Ten
Commandment

ed that the slave was to be free after the six-year tenure of service, but if he was given a wife while serving and loved her and his master, he could elect to remain a slave in his master's house with his family until death. He was then taken to the judges where his ear was bored, and he was then a love-slave for life.

2. In Exodus 21:35-36, if a man's bull hurt another man's bull so severely that the bull died, the live bull had to be sold and the proceeds divided between the two owners. The carcass of the dead bull was to be divided equally between the owners as well. This procedure helped make certain there was no violation of sound ethics: The settlement was equitable for both parties. However, if the owner of the live bull was aware that his animal was dangerous, he was to exchange his live bull for the dead one as penalty.

3. The following series of practical stipulations is recorded in Exodus 23:4-9:

"'If you come across your enemy's ox or donkey wandering off, be sure to take it back to him'" (v. 4). This was an act of love for the enemy.

"'If you see the donkey of someone who hates you fallen down under its load, do not leave it there; be sure you help him with it'" (v. 5). This also was an act of love.

"'Do not deny justice to your poor people in their lawsuits'" (v. 6). This called for loving concern for the poor.

"'Have nothing to do with a false charge and do not put an innocent or honest person to death, for I will not acquit the guilty'" (v. 7). Love and justice meet in this.

"'Do not accept a bribe, for a bribe blinds those who see and twists the words of the righteous'" (v. 8).

"'Do not oppress an alien; you yourselves know how it feels to be aliens, because you were aliens in Egypt'" (v. 9). God loved you while you were foreigners, and He expects you to love foreigners (see Lev. 19:33-34).

Part 1

Chapter 2
The Basis of
Morality:
The Ten
Commandments

RELATIONSHIP TO NEW TESTAMENT ETHICS

The body of the Old Testament law—the commandments, the statutes, the judgments—is holy, just,
good, spiritual. Its application, however, proves people to be unspiritual and sinful (Rom. 7:12-14). Thus
the Law, which is good, becomes a curse to people
(Gal. 3:10). To remove the curse requires the grace of
God, made manifest and available to humankind only
through God's gift of His Son. At Calvary, Christ took
upon himself the curse of the Law and redeemed us
(Gal. 3:13). Now on the strength of this new covenant, or testament, we are saved by grace through
faith (Eph. 2:8). Until the moment Jesus died on the
cross and put the new covenant into effect, Jews
who trusted God were kept in the protective custody
of the Law. Therefore, the Law can be aptly described as a tutor or guide to bring the Jews down
through the centuries to Christ, that they "might be
justified by faith" (Gal. 3:23-24). The ethical aspects
of the transition from Law to grace are best understood in light of the teachings of Christ's Sermon on
the Mount, which will be treated in a subsequent
chapter.

SIGNIFICANCE OF THE LAW IN TODAY'S WORLD

The Ten Commandments, even apart from the
teaching of the Church, are regarded as the basis of
morality and right living in most civilized areas of the
world to this day. They may be found on plaques in
courthouses and other public buildings; they are often referred to by the secular media in their reports
on issues dealing with morals or ethical values. They
have been accepted as basic to the Judeo-Christian
heritage of America and many other nations (though
some are trying to strip them away).

American civil law, as well as criminal law, has the
Ten Commandments as a major part of its basis. Yet
in order to apply the commandments to social behavior, it has been found necessary to expand them into

Part 1

Chapter 2
The Basis of
Morality:
The Ten
Commandment

thousands of sections of law to form the criminal and civil codes that govern the nation. The question arises, How shall the Church relate to civil law, which, although based on divine law, at times seems to be in conflict with godly principles? Leon O. Hynson offers guidance on the subject in his analysis of Romans 13:1-7.[5] In this passage he sees Paul's dealing with the Christian responsibility to the state as being reducible to five primary statements.

1. The state exists by divine purpose and permission—ultimately God is over all.

2. The state is ordered (appointed, assigned, arranged) under God, providing for orderly life through the state.

3. Christians are called to submit to the governing authorities. This submission means voluntary respect or adherence. However, this is not to elevate the state above the Church; the state is to function in coordination with the Church.

4. The state has a responsibility to execute justice, based on the assumption that the government itself is just.

5. When Paul appeals to conscience (Rom. 13:5), he may be referring to the possibility of obedience to the just state and disobedience to the unjust state. The Christian's relationship to the state is sharply qualified by his relation to Christ. Paul is neither giving the state a blank check for requiring Christian obedience nor releasing Christians from responsibility to the state.

Despite the ethical and moral import of the Ten Commandments and the laws, statutes, edicts, judgments, precepts, stipulations, codes, and legal opinions based on them, it is impossible to insure the good conduct of this country's people. The trend in

---

[5]Leon O. Hynson, Lane A. Scott, eds., "The Ordered State and Christian Responsibility," in *Christian Ethics: An Inquiry into Christian Ethics from a Biblical Theological Perspective* (Anderson, Ind.: Warner Press, 1983), 264-67.

Part 1

Chapter 2
The Basis of
Morality:
The Ten
Commandments

America is to minimize the influence of biblical law—and the resultant slide in national morality is all too apparent. Nothing can arrest this trend but a spiritual revival from the Author of the commandments themselves. Only the transforming power of the Cross and the dynamic of the Holy Spirit are able to make the Law genuinely effective. The Spirit of God will enable us to live as God intended when He gave the Law to Moses.

STUDY QUESTIONS

1. What lessons do you see as you compare the lives of Jacob and Joseph?

2. Moses saw how God made "the wrath of man" to praise Him (Ps. 76:10, KJV). How have you seen this in your own life and in your church?

3. What events or actions show that God delivered Israel out of Egypt by grace through faith?

4. How should you apply Jethro's advice to Moses and God's taking of the Spirit that was on Moses and putting it on the seventy elders?

5. What does the Bible show about the relationship of love and heart attitude to the Law?

6. In what ways did God show His faithfulness to Israel during their journeys in the wilderness and the entrance to the Promised Land?

7. The Christian is not under Law. How should we view and apply the Ten Commandments?

8. How should we respond to civil law and ordinances (including such things as the speed limit)?

Chapter 3

Transition from Law to Grace: The Sermon on the Mount

SIGNIFICANCE OF THE SERMON

The Sermon on the Mount is the greatest sermon ever preached. It has been characterized as a sermon addressed primarily to disciples but overheard by the crowd, spoken to the Church and overheard by the world. Given by Jesus at the height of His popularity, it stands as "a systematic statement of the main elements of the Christian ethic."[1]

In the sermon Jesus introduced much of what He would teach and preach during His earthly itinerary. The message, drawn from the major precepts of the Law, is reported by Matthew and Luke (though the latter's is less concentrated). In Luke, Jesus applauded the expert of the Law who recognized its core: "'Love the Lord your God with all your heart and with all your soul and with all your strength and with all your mind,' and, 'Love your neighbor as yourself'" (Luke 10:27). Jesus then illustrated His meaning of neighborly love by telling the story of the Jericho road casualty and the Samaritan who showed him compassion.

In Matthew (23:23) Jesus rebuked the teachers of the Law and the Pharisees for keeping the letter of the Law but violating the basis of divine ethics, recorded in Jeremiah 9:24 (NRS), where God insisted

---

[1]Henlee H. Barnette, *Introducing Christian Ethics* (Nashville: Broadman Press, 1961), 50–51.

Part 1

Chapter 3
Transition
from Law to
Grace: The
Sermon on
the Mount

that He practices and delights in "steadfast love, justice, and righteousness in the earth." Jesus charged that the Pharisees had "neglected the more important matters of the law—justice, mercy, and faithfulness" (Matt. 23:23). He concluded His rebuke of the Pharisees in verse 28 with a reference to one of the underlying themes of the sermon: On the outside you appear to people as righteous, but on the inside you are full of hypocrisy and wickedness. Throughout His sermon He denounced the sham of religiosity and advocated sincere, godly love.

BLESSINGS FROM ABOVE—DESERVED AND UNDESERVED (MATT. 5:1-16)

The first three Beatitudes focus on the lowly of heart. "'Blessed are the poor in spirit, for theirs is the kingdom of heaven'" (5:3). They can look forward to exaltation, in contrast to the fall awaiting the spiritually proud Pharisees and teachers of the Law, who boasted of their attainments in law keeping. To be poor in spirit means we are not self-sufficient. We need the help of the Holy Spirit to live righteous lives and inherit the Kingdom. Righteousness is an integral part of God's ethical standard, but it must proceed from a love for God, never from a love for self.

"'Blessed are those who mourn, for they will be comforted'" (v. 4). Christ here introduced the remarkable concept of mourning over the things that hurt or grieve God as well as the joy of suffering with Christ. He had not yet gone to the cross. At this point His followers did not understand suffering as a godly virtue but as God's punishment for disobeying the Law. (The Master further explores the concept of victorious suffering in verses 10-12 of this passage.)

"'Blessed are the meek, for they will inherit the earth'" (v. 5; see Ps. 37:11; Zeph. 3:12.) The students of the Law, scattered among the listeners on the hillside, never understood the full meaning of meekness. Moses, "a very humble man" (Num. 12:3), became the chief of Israel when Aaron and Hur held up his arms on the hilltop (Exod. 17:10–13). Saul and David, in reigning over Israel, were not noted for meekness. Not even Solomon, the least warlike of Israel's early kings, could be described as a meek man, in view of his ruthless dealing with Shimei, his marriage to many foreign wives, his alliances with heathen kings, and his dependence on a strong army. To Christ's audience, meekness, in the sense of a humble selflessness that neither exalts nor deflates itself but depends on God, was a novel concept ("the way down is the way up"; cf. 2 Cor. 10:1)[2]—it still is!

"'Blessed are they who hunger and thirst for righteousness, for they will be filled'" (Matt. 5:6). This appetite is fundamental to godly, ethical living. A healthy spiritual condition depends on it, as does our experiencing the presence of God and communion with Christ.

"'Blessed are the merciful, for they will be shown mercy'" (v. 7). Closely akin to meekness is showing mercy. At first mercy seems foreign to the Law, yet it is reflected in the Psalms, particularly in 103:8,11,17, where the Lord is described as "compassionate and gracious," having "great . . . love for those who fear him," and manifesting His love "from everlasting to everlasting [to] those who fear him." (See also Ps. 25:6; Isa. 55:7; 63:9; Hos. 6:6; Mic. 6:8; 7:18; Hab. 3:2.) Clearly, mercifulness is a basic element of God's nature. In the Sermon on the Mount this quality was reemphasized as an ethical requirement for humankind.

"'Blessed are the pure in heart, for they will see God'" (Matt. 5:8). The pure in heart are "happy" (TLB) because they have the bright hope of seeing God. Here again Christ points to the nature of His Father: In Him alone is the ideal expression of purity of the heart. Nor does He condone hypocrisy in the heart of His children. Just as He is transparently ethi-

Part 1

**Chapter 3
Transition
from Law to
Grace: The
Sermon on
the Mount**

---

[2]Robertson McQuilkin, *An Introduction to Biblical Ethics* (Wheaton, Ill.: Tyndale House Publishers, 1989), 135.

Part 1

Chapter 3
Transition
from Law to
Grace: The
Sermon on
the Mount

cal, purity of heart is a requirement of those who would enjoy the revelation of His presence, that is, "see God," both now and in eternity.

"'Blessed are the peacemakers, for they will be called sons of God. Blessed are those who are persecuted because of righteousness, for theirs is the kingdom of heaven'" (Matt. 5:9-10). These final two groups labeled "blessed" are the peacemakers and the persecuted: champions of both the aggressive and passive sides of peace (5:9-10). Christ, the Prince of Peace, commends those who initiate the peace process. The peace in view, however, is the peace that Christ gives (John 14:27), and peacemakers by their witness and life seek to bring others to that peace. *The Living Bible* provides a unique insight into Matthew 5:9: "Happy are those who strive for peace." It seems that securing peace is not always easy. But herein is true happiness for those who in the pursuit of peace take their place in the ranks of the "sons of God."

Yet, much like a referee who steps in to settle a dispute, the peacemaker easily becomes the persecuted, receiving the wrath of the very persons he or she is attempting to help. Then the same ethic that calls for intervening on behalf of peace demands a happy attitude when the peacemaker himself comes under attack (cf. 2 Tim. 3:12). The peacemaker may suffer a fate similar to that of the Old Testament prophets who faced persecution. But if giving a cup of water in a prophet's name qualifies one for receiving a prophet's reward, then to receive their treatment is to share their reward as well (Mark 9:41).

By observing the Beatitudes, the Church becomes salt and light (Matt. 5:13-16). What a wholesome influence the Church has on the earth! As salt, it adds flavor and preserves. Often, all that preserves a community or a nation is the "salty" saints whose prayers hold back the forces of evil. Their godly examples set a pattern of conduct for all who surround them. It is a sad day when they lose their witness. They are then surrounded by those who are ready to cast them out and trample them underfoot at the first opportunity.

The symbolism of light implies that godly deeds are not done in a corner but in full view. Only under the rarest circumstances can we glorify God as silent witnesses or hidden followers. Ethical conduct cannot be hidden. It is so exceptional that the ethical person becomes like a "city on a hill" (Matt. 5:14).

The remarkable transition from Law to grace occurs in verses 17 and 18. "'Do not think that I have come to abolish the Law or the Prophets; I have not come to abolish them but to fulfill them. . . . Until heaven and earth disappear, not the smallest letter, not the least stroke of a pen, will by any means disappear from the Law until everything is accomplished.'" What a powerful mission statement! Christ's purpose was not to do away with the Law or to enforce the death penalty inherent in its commands. He had come to carry out its mandates and to demonstrate by His life that the demands of the Law could be met and were met in Him. Henlee H. Barnette in his *Introducing Christian Ethics* reasons that "[h]e fulfilled the law in several ways. First, he simplified it by making love central, reducing the six-hundred and thirteen laws of the Jews to the law of love to God and neighbor. . . . [H]e alone kept the law and exemplified it in his own life, thus revealing its deeper significance. Hence, Jesus did not come to abrogate the law, but to complete it—not to suspend, but to supplement it."[3]

In Him was complete fulfillment of the Law's demands. Before the new birth, outlined for Nicodemus, it was impossible to keep the Law because of human weakness (Rom. 8:3). Now by the power of the Spirit the impossible becomes the norm. Just as "the wind blows wherever it pleases" (John 3:8), the Spirit can bring new birth to whomever He pleases.

---

[3]Barnette, *Introducing Christian Ethics*, 56.

Part 1

Chapter 3
Transition
from Law to
Grace: The
Sermon on
the Mount

Then, as we learn to depend on Him, He enables us to do the good things God desired when He gave the Law.

Just as the Ten Commandments came directly from God, so Christ—the Word (John 1:1)—came directly from God. Thus He is the fulfillment, the embodiment, of the Law in every way. Whereas the Law was written on tablets of stone, the Holy Spirit says, "'I will put my laws in their hearts, and I will write them on their minds'" (Heb. 10:15-16). The Law will never fade away—not because of its intrinsic eternal qualities, but because it must remain, fulfilled in Christ and His followers.

Christ is the fulfillment of the symbolism of the Old Testament: the bronze serpent in the wilderness, the bread of heaven (manna), the desert rock that issued water. He comes as the great High Priest who "went through the greater and more perfect tabernacle that is not man-made. . . . He did not enter by means of the blood of goats and calves; but he entered the Most Holy Place once for all by his own blood" (Heb. 9:11-12). Thus, the Old Testament takes on meaning, vitality, and eternal significance because Christ fulfills it. The ethics of the Old Testament were merely theoretical—because of their sinful nature, people could not fully meet the requirements of the Law (Rom. 8:2-4,7). But in Christ the theoretical becomes actual and practical. He is the fulfillment of the Law.

TRANSITION FROM MERE MORALITY TO PURE SPIRITUALITY (MATT. 5:20-22,28; 6:1-8,16-18)

Christ demanded a higher code of conduct than the external righteousness of the teachers of the Law and the Pharisees: "'Unless your righteousness surpasses that of the Pharisees and the teachers of the law, you will certainly not enter the kingdom of heaven'" (Matt. 5:20). The behavior of these religionists was based on the letter of the Law, mere outward forms of morality, whereas spiritual life in Christ is based on principles of the heart.

Part 1

Chapter 3
Transition
from Law to
Grace: The
Sermon on
the Mount

Accordingly, for the individual who hopes to enter heaven someday, "You shall not murder" (Ex. 20:13) becomes "You shall not hate" (Matt. 5:21-22). Christ here begins to deal with sins of the heart—sins just as contemptible in the sight of God as any sinful deed.

The Law is at this point being superseded by grace. The Law, despite its severe penalties, was given by God in an act of love toward His people. Now comes the message of grace that more clearly reflects divine love; the application of love takes ethics to a higher level than has ever been known before. Now instead of merely curbing your anger at a brother, you will in love seek out a brother who is angry with you. Such behavior speaks volumes to the unbeliever. As David H. C. Read puts it, "The pagan world knew that a new ethical power was abroad not when they read a copy of the Sermon on the Mount, but when they saw a Christian Church and said: 'See how these Christians love one another.'"[4]

Just as Jesus dealt with the commandment prohibiting murder, He, in Matthew 5:27-29, attacked the sin of adultery. To look lustfully at a woman is to commit adultery in one's heart. Until this hour, conviction for the sin of adultery demanded witnesses, evidence, the passing of judgment, and the death penalty. The process of rendering judgment was highly public and empirical. Now the Master Teacher says that what happens in the mind and heart is as serious as what happens in the world at large—a violation of God's laws can occur either place. He underscores the culpability of the mental adulterer by suggesting that it is better to go through life blind than to allow the eyes to destroy one's ethical wholeness.

Not satisfied just to shatter the concept of law keeping as righteousness, Jesus, in Matthew 6:1-6 and 16-18, moved into what the Pharisees and teach-

---

[4]David Haxton Carswell Read, *Christian Ethics* (Philadelphia: J. B. Lippincott Co., 1968), 35.

Part 1

Chapter 3
Transition
from Law to
Grace: The
Sermon on
the Mount

ers of the Law considered their province: religious practices for which they were admired and revered by the people on the street. He examines almsgiving, public prayer, and ritual fasting.

He labels those individuals hypocrites who must alert the public when they are about to contribute to the needy at the synagogue. They succeed only in eliciting the passing praise of the people; God ignores them. But He blesses the humble servant of the Lord who gives in secret. Thus it is possible to violate God's code of ethics even in such a noble act as benevolence. And, of course, the same is true of one's attitude in prayer. If the purpose of prayer is to impress an audience, it is wasted time: Only those within earshot heed the prayer; God is not interested.

But fasting appears to call for reverse ethics, for the practitioner to be somewhat hypocritical: Jesus told him to anoint his head and to wash his face so he would not appear to be fasting. We can apply this to all outward show of religious forms. As God said to Samuel when he was looking to anoint one of Jesse's sons: "'Man looks at the outward appearance, but the LORD looks at the heart'" (1 Samuel 16:7). From the day the tall, handsome Eliab was consecrated to join in the worship and stood for Samuel's inspection until this day, God's guidelines for judging a person remain unchanged.

THE DISCIPLES' PRAYER (MATT. 6:7–15)

We turn from the mode of prayer to the content of prayer. We are warned about offering repetitious phrases rather than heartfelt prayer. Such praying is variously described as "vain repetitions" (KJV), "babbling like pagans" (NIV), "heap[ing] up empty phrases" (RSV), "saying things that mean nothing" (NCV). In short, God is not as concerned with the amount of our prayers as with their sincerity: "'Your Father knows what you need before you ask him'" (Matt. 6:8).

Part 1

**Chapter 3
Transition
from Law to
Grace: The
Sermon on
the Mount**

Then follows the model prayer for the disciples of Christ through the centuries. In Jesus' introduction to the prayer and in the prayer itself one can see a reemphasis of God's standard of conduct—described in Jeremiah 9:24 ("steadfast love, justice, and righteousness" [NRS]) and reiterated in Matthew 23:23 and Luke 10:27—the essence of the Sermon on the Mount. The provision of steadfast love appears in Matthew 6:8, "Your Father knows what you need." Again in verse 9 God chooses to be addressed as "Our Father" when we approach His throne. The presence of justice in the prayer is found in the phrases "as we also have forgiven our debtors" (v. 12) and "deliver us from the evil one" (v. 13). God's concern for righteousness is apparent in the expressions "hallowed be your name" and "lead us not into temptation."

The prayer holds many implications. (1) We honor God when we hold His name sacred (v. 9). (2) God's will is to be respected by both people and angels (v. 10). (3) The debts of others must be forgiven to ensure God's forgiveness of our obligations to Him (v. 12). (4) The cry of the human heart must always be for guidance away from the snare of the evil one and deliverance from ethical and moral failure (v. 13). Then to reinforce the premise that forgiveness from God is contingent on one's heart attitude, a solemn admonition is appended to the prayer: "If you do not forgive men their sins, your Father will not forgive your sins" (v. 15).

CARES OF LIFE AND THEIR CURE (MATT. 6:19–34)

Following the prayer, Christ deals with some basic human concerns: money, food, clothing, the future, and how to deal with these matters ethically. Money is not to be hoarded. From a practical perspective, it is difficult to protect assets from the natural laws of disintegration. Real estate deteriorates. The stock market falls. Fraud and incompetence plague the banking system. Waste and careless spending inflate the na-

Part 1

Chapter 3
Transition
from Law to
Grace: The
Sermon on
the Mount

tional debt and devalue government bonds. But an even bigger problem is the twisted perspective that makes material gain a primary goal of life. "Where your treasure is, there your heart will be also" (Matt. 6:21). A minister's most important "treasures" are his time, abilities, and resources invested in the kingdom of God.

Next, the Lord moves into a profound spiritual lesson on "good eyes" versus "bad eyes." Without the vision for eternal things, the human heart is dark, the future uncertain. To value only material gain and its power is to walk in spiritual darkness. And one day the challenge will come to choose between riches and God: One or the other will be the master. Of itself, money is not bad, but serving it and loving it is not only unethical but unholy. "The love of money is a root of all kinds of evil" (1 Tim. 6:10).

Continuing His caution about undue concern over the things of this life, Jesus turns to food and clothing. The lesson is about a reasonable concern for them, not obsessive worry. What a beautiful lesson in relaxing in the arms of a loving Father and trusting Him for the provisions that sustain life! The instruction "'Do not worry about your life'" (Matt. 6:25) is not an admonition to be a poor provider for the family or to waste the resources God has made available. Rather, it is simply wrong—poor ethical conduct—to worry.

We are urged to look around and observe that God provides for the birds both in summer and winter, that He beautifully clothes the flowers in the fields simply because He created them and keeps them for His glory. The child of God must learn this lesson. "We are God's workmanship" (Eph. 2:10). All we do, all we are, is to be to the glory of God.

Then follows the Master's final word on worry. Sound judgment dictates that we not borrow the cares of tomorrow. They will still be there when tomorrow becomes today. Pragmatically speaking, tomorrow is imaginary; it doesn't exist. We live only today. Dread of the future usually paints a darker picture than reality.

Part 1

Chapter 3
Transition
from Law to
Grace: The
Sermon on
the Mount

HONESTY VERSUS HYPOCRISY (MATT. 7:1-20)

In concluding this section of His sermon, Jesus tears off religion's masks of delusion and deception. He attacks the problem of considering oneself better than others. Hypocritical pride motivates one to see a speck of sawdust in others' eyes while permitting a plank of wood to fill one's own. Why is it so easy to ignore our own shortcomings while being disturbed about those of others? In any case, the solution is simple: Mind your own business.

Some years ago, having moved into a new pastorate, my wife and I were greeted by a parishioner who immediately began to enumerate the faults of the previous pastor. This woman was industrious, a good housekeeper, seemed morally upright, and was careful of her appearance. However, she was a vicious gossip, critical of everyone in the church, including her own children, even though counseled about this. Her husband, a forbearing, kind individual, never had really submitted his life to Christ. As their children grew older, they went their way, obviously not interested in maintaining the poor relationship they had known with their mother in growing up. With the death of her husband, she became a lonely, elderly woman who had failed on an important principle: "Do not judge, or you too will be judged" (7:1). To compound the tragedy, she and others like her have yet to face the final judgment and loss of reward for failure to control the most unruly member of all—the tongue (James 1:26; 3:5-8).

In Matthew 7:6-12 Jesus stressed the issue of honest appreciation of eternal values. To disparage spiritual concepts or to minimize matters of eternal consequence in the presence of an unbeliever is to toss what is sacred to the dogs or to throw to the pigs precious jewels along with table scraps. Simply to present a profound spiritual truth to an unconvert-

Part 1

Chapter 3
Transition
from Law to
Grace: The
Sermon on
the Mount

ed person is to face complete rejection of the truth with the possibility that the person may "turn and tear you to pieces" (Matt. 7:6).

When is it quite ethical to pursue a goal so aggressively that one becomes almost rude? When we pray, we are instructed to ask initially, and it will be given us. If greater urgency has gripped us, we are to seek until we find. Finally, emboldened by holy desperation, we will keep knocking until the miracle happens, until the door of God's storehouse of promises swings open. The Son of God explains that if an earthly father is concerned about meeting the needs of his son, "how much more will your Father in heaven give good gifts to those who ask him!" (Matt. 7:11).

When we come to God in true earnestness, our faith is actually trust in the faithfulness and ethics of God as well as in His ability to answer prayer. The love of "our Father in heaven" for us far transcends the love of a father on earth. He will never play a practical joke on a son or daughter; He gives only good gifts. James phrases it nicely: "Every good and perfect gift is from above, coming down from the Father of the heavenly lights, who does not change like shifting shadows" (James 1:17). Test His ethics—He never fails.

As a young Christian, having received the call to the ministry, I realized the necessity of being baptized in the Holy Spirit, according to the pattern of Acts 2. So I began to pray for the gift of the Holy Spirit, but with no results. After months of fruitless asking, I tried to shift into a seeking mode. Still no results. As months stretched into years, I despaired of this heavenly gift. I questioned my worthiness; I doubted my relationship with God; I developed a spiritual inferiority complex around my classmates and friends who had received the baptism in the Holy Spirit. Ultimately, my desperation approached the "knocking" stage. At this point, God sent a minister who through her preaching convinced me that God

Part 1

Chapter 3
Transition
from Law to
Grace: The
Sermon on
the Mount

loved me and that He would not withhold any gift from any of His children. I had actually been questioning God's fairness and ethics. What a glorious occasion it was when I overflowed with the indescribable gift of the Holy Spirit. Beyond the joy and ecstasy, beyond the exhilarating flow of heavenly language, were other marvels of this gift (available to every believer). I discovered a new intimacy with God. His Word seemed more understandable and powerful in my life. I found that my witness for Christ had a greater impact. Today I continue to thank God for bestowing this gift on me.

The essence of ethical behavior is contained in what we know as the Golden Rule, well expressed in the Phillips translation: "'Treat other people exactly as you would like to be treated by them—this is the meaning of the Law and the Prophets'" (Matt. 7:12). In these few words the godly principles drawn from "the Law and the Prophets"—steadfast love, justice, and righteousness—are distilled into a powerful directive for successful Christian living.

In the Golden Rule, Jesus undercut the legalists who had distorted the Law to suit themselves. The role of the legalist as a teacher of the Law is neatly summarized by Norman L. Geisler: "The legalist is one who enters every decision-making situation encumbered with a bundle of predetermined rules and regulations. For him the letter of the Law, not the spirit of the law, prevails."[5] Small wonder that Christ's Spirit-anointed teaching was resented by the teachers of the Law and the Pharisees.

Jesus concluded His discussion of "Honesty versus Hypocrisy" by dealing with the ethics of taking the popular, easy way. Although this road to eternal destiny is wide and well-traveled, it ends in destruction. Its travelers are pleasing themselves in following their own course. They could have selected the narrow

---

[5]Norman L. Geisler, *Ethics: Alternatives and Issues* (Grand Rapids: Zondervan Publishing House, 1971), 61.

Part 1

Chapter 3
Transition
from Law to
Grace: The
Sermon on
the Mount

but fulfilling road to eternal life. This brief analogy rebuked the majority of the people of Christ's day; they
chose to take the popular route of acceptable religious expression rather than the narrow way of His
radical teaching.

As Jesus taught the crowd on the hillside, He un-
masked the hypocritical teacher-prophets who, dis-
guised as sheep, even now circulate among God's
flock, "but inwardly they are ferocious wolves" (Matt.
7:15). Their unethical ministry is destructive and fruitless. Instead of being fruit-producing trees they are
thornbushes and thistles. They may not be identifi-
able when they first appear among those who are sincere, but in time they will be seen as bad trees,
because only bad trees produce bad fruit. Their fate
offers a solemn lesson about engaging in unethical
ministry: They are "cut down and thrown into the
fire" (Matt. 7:19).

Social pressures nudge us all to the wide road. We
reason that everybody else is taking it—why should
we be different? We find ourselves following a set of
rules based on a norm different from the biblical
guidelines we grew up with. While we would never
be guilty of applying situation ethics to our lifestyles,
we may adhere to "generation ethics." Unfortunately,
the ethical standard from generation to generation is
generally a course of decline. David H. C. Read observes: "[T]here is the historical morality which holds
that the standards of our grandparents must be respected, but not necessarily observed."[6] It is especially tragic for ministers to trade biblical morality for
generation ethics, presenting themselves to God's
people as models of His unchanging integrity and morality.

Taking the matter of ministerial integrity even further, Jesus indicated that there are some who have no
hope of eternal life even though they have apparently
been successful in ministry. They may have used His

---

[6]Read, *Christian Ethics*, 56.

Part 1

Chapter 3
Transition
from Law to
Grace: The
Sermon on
the Mount

name to prophesy, cast out demons, and perform miracles, but they will not be allowed to enter heaven, much less to receive any reward for service. The seven sons of Sceva are an example of an unsuccessful attempt to use the name of Jesus to cast out demons (Acts 19:13-16). Others may seem to have success because God, in spite of their falseness, honors His Word and the faith of people who respond. But what a tragic close to years of ministry, never to have really known the Lord or to have been known by Him.

It is heartwrenching to witness the fall of gifted people who have been notable builders of the Kingdom and enjoyed an anointed ministry. How can it be that God will use an unclean instrument to bear His message of hope and healing? What a testimony of the power of the gospel! Out of his own experience Paul described its dynamic and offered his perspective on it, at work during one of his imprisonments: "It is true that some preach Christ out of envy and rivalry, but others out of goodwill. . . . But what does it matter? The important thing is that in every way, whether from false motives or true, Christ is preached" (Phil. 1:15,18). It is not the messenger who brings eternal life, it is the message. Though we may find ourselves embarrassed by some proclaimers of the gospel, we need never be ashamed of the gospel itself. A venerable professor at Wake Forest years ago is quoted as saying, "God has hit many a lick with a crooked stick!" The tragedy is that the instrument of blessing must be cast aside at the Judgment, never to share the joy of eternal life because of a moral failure that was never repented of.

The most shocking part of the judgment of an unethical miracle worker is the statement of the Lord, "'I never knew you'" (Matt. 7:23). Fellow minister, we will do well to humbly acquiesce to the mandate of 2 Corinthians 13:5: "Examine yourselves to see whether you are in the faith; test yourselves. Do you not realize that Christ Jesus is in you—unless, of course, you fail the test?"

Part 1

Chapter 3
Transition
from Law to
Grace: The
Sermon on
the Mount

A Secure Life on a Solid Premise (Matt. 7:24–29)

The illustrated conclusion of the Sermon on the Mount becomes its application. Although this is the greatest sermon ever preached, it has no value unless it is responded to ethically. In this parable of two houses, one is constructed by a wise builder, the other by a fool. There is no apparent reason to believe the houses are not identical in design, structure, and size. The difference? Only the foundations. This is the matter of primary concern. Each house is subjected to the same test, described in exactly the same words in the original Greek text: "The rain came down, the streams rose, and the winds blew and beat against that house" (Matt. 7:25,27).

The difference in the two houses before the storm may not have been apparent, but what a difference after the test! One house stands, a picture of serenity and security; the other falls, a scene of devastation. The point Christ is making is that it is not enough to hear His teaching, agree with it, retain it, or even repeat it to others. None of these involves ethical practice. The key to spiritual success, the ability to be kept safe in the testing time, simply entails being a doer of the Word: "'Everyone who hears these words of mine and *puts them into practice*'" is indeed a wise builder who has staked his eternal destiny on the Rock, the eternal Word of God (Matt. 7:24).

Small wonder that as the Master concluded His explosive, revolutionary sermon, the people gasped in amazement, "because he taught as one who had authority, and not as their teachers of the law" (Matt. 7:29).

Study Questions

1. In what ways did the Pharisees and teachers of the Law fail to observe the principles of Jeremiah 9:24?

2. How should you apply each of the Beatitudes in today's world?

3. In what ways does love fulfill the demands of the Law?

4. In what ways did Jesus go beyond the demands of the Law in the Sermon on the Mount?

5. What is the value of combining fasting with prayer?

6. How does the "Disciples' Prayer" bring out the principles given by God in Jeremiah 9:24?

7. What are some practical ways to apply the words of Jesus about worry and the cares of this life?

8. What are some of the "good gifts" we can expect from our Heavenly Father, and how do we obtain them?

9. What are the keys to spiritual success?

Part 1

**Chapter 3
Transition
from Law to
Grace: The
Sermon on
the Mount**

Part 2

Ethics and Church Doctrine

Part 2: Ethics and Church Doctrine

Chapter 4

Ethical Concepts from Church History

The history of the Church, from John the Baptist to the present, becomes a textbook on ethics with respect to the part it has played in believers' lives and ministries through the ages. The effectiveness and impact of those who have gone before us have been in direct proportion to their practice of Christ-honoring ethics. The contemporary minister will do well to observe the failures and successes of these men and women of God. They remain all-important reflections of Christian conduct and morality.

The mission of John, the man "sent from God," was to introduce Christ and His kingdom. Everything about John—his lifestyle, his message, his philosophy of ministry—declared that he had not come merely to be the friend of the bridegroom but to introduce Jesus as God's lamb (John 1:29,36). He would also help bridge the gap between Law and grace by his radically new ethical concepts. John's audiences had grown weary of rabbinical teaching with its rigid interpretation of an "eye for an eye and a tooth for a tooth" (Exod. 21:24). This concept was meant to bring justice and was modified by mercy even in the Old Testament, something the rabbis overlooked (cf. Matt. 23:23). Now the person who owned two tunics needed to share with the person who had none, and the tax collector could expect to take no more tax than the law required. When the soldiers requested a

83

Part 2

Chapter 4
Ethical
Concepts
from Church
History

new set of orders, John instructed them to neither extort money nor accuse people falsely but be content with their pay (Luke 3:11-15). These concepts took John's Jewish audiences by surprise, causing them to ask if he might possibly be the Christ.

Hardly had the question been framed before John gave a shocking message, a message of how he viewed himself. "'I am not the Christ'" (John 1:20), he insisted, and when He comes, "'He must become greater; I must become less'" (John 3:30). His humble acknowledgment of the limitations of his ministry offered a stunning contrast to his bold declaration of stern principles. In his unique way John the Baptist set the stage for the advent of Jesus, the Savior, and helped prepare a forum for His life-changing teachings on ethical and moral principles.

God's primary design in sending His Son was to make available salvation by grace through faith. We must accept Jesus as Lord and Savior, not just as a good teacher. But this does not diminish the importance of His ethical teachings. They remain essential, enabling every believer to walk and live according to God's will. Even the most casual study of Christ's Sermon on the Mount, His parables, and His example indicates the nature and importance of His proclamation of ethics for His followers. He stressed the obligations imposed by the Law; yet He was able to introduce the remarkable concept that while law keeping was beyond human abilities, it became possible when blended with the love and grace of God. When the law of divine love is applied, we can bless those who curse us, pray for those who mistreat us, and love those who are our enemies (Luke 6:28,35).

Of course, all of Jesus' lessons on the law of love in ethical living are compressed into one great object lesson—Calvary. He died freely forgiving His tormentors (Luke 23:34); He laid down His life for the very people who were bent on killing Him. After His death and resurrection, He encouraged His disciples to believe, and He continued to express the ethic of

Part 2

Chapter 4
Ethical
Concepts
from Church
History

servanthood, even preparing breakfast for them (John 21:12-13). He was also concerned about giving them continuing help after He ascended back to heaven. In the Upper Room He had already told the disciples that He would be sending a "Counselor" ("Comforter," KJV; "Helper," TEV) like himself (John 14:26; 15:26; 16:7,13). Then He promised that the Spirit's power would come upon them, not merely to enhance their witness but to provide power to *be* the successful witnesses He intended them to be (Acts 1:4-5,8).

As the story of Acts unfolds, even before Paul emerged as God's great missionary exponent of ethical principles, the Early Church by word and deed was setting forth the teachings of Christ in a practical way. Even to critics it was apparent that these disciples loved each other: They freely shared what they had, going from house to house breaking bread and expressing their appreciation for each other and for their Christ (Acts 2:44-46). The Holy Spirit stepped sternly into the picture by the death of Ananias and Sapphira, making it clear that God's principles of conduct were to be respectfully and seriously observed (Acts 5:1-10). Even this shocking episode reflected God's love for His family, showing them how He felt about the corruption of fraud and deception.

Against this background of divine intervention in ethical matters, Paul's instructions to deal firmly with doctrinal impurity and immorality express God's attitude toward ethical impropriety. This is not to say that Paul's teaching dealt only with the disciplinary aspects of ethics, but simply reflects the importance of ethics as a guide to a life that pleases God. It is a guide that remains as relevant to us as it was to the Early Church. The central theme of Paul's teaching on Christian ethics is the conflict of the flesh (that is, the sinful nature) with the renewed spirit within the believer. The sinful nature must suffer the death of the Cross so the joy of spiritual victory may characterize the life of God's child.

Part 2

**Chapter 4
Ethical
Concepts
from Church
History**

THE CHURCH FATHERS

Over the centuries, articulated ethical concepts have reflected the spiritual life and vitality of the Church. Following the death of John the beloved, for example, church leadership, during a period known as that of the apostolic fathers, developed ethics based on Scripture and political concepts. They often addressed the same churches that Paul had, though generations removed. Generally, among the best known are Barnabas, Clement, Hermas, Ignatius, and Polycarp. (Of course, other writers whose works remain today also express the influence of the Church on the ethical teaching of the times.)

The *Didache,* or *The Teaching of the Twelve Apostles,* was held in great repute in the Early Church. Of uncertain origin, this handbook of church discipline has been attributed to Barnabas or Hermas. It identified two opposites: the "Way of Life" and the "Way of Death." It dealt with baptism, fasting,[1] and prayer, as well as the discerning of true and false prophets and apostles (not "the Twelve" but those with an itinerant apostolic ministry something like that of missionaries). Among the issues it considered were the responsibility for confession of sins and the respect due bishops and deacons. Reflected in this writing is the decline in authority of the itinerant apostles and prophets who enunciated the ethic and moral code of the Early Church.

Polycarp (A.D. 69–155) was a disciple of the apostle John and served as bishop of Smyrna. He is considered the bridge between the Apostolic Age and the Catholic orthodoxy of the latter part of the second century. Heresy horrified him. In *The Epistle of Polycarp to the Philippians* he warned women, widows,

---

[1]*Didache* 8:1 reads, "Let not your fasts be with the hypocrites [i.e., the Pharisees], for they fast on Mondays and Thursdays, you fast on Wednesdays and Fridays," *Apostolic Fathers*, trans. Kirsopp Lake (Cambridge, Mass.: Harvard University Press, 1975), 1:321.

The Church Fathers **87**

Part 2

Chapter 4
Ethical
Concepts
from Church
History

deacons, young men, virgins, and presbyters alike to beware of heretics, to avoid slander, to be compassionate, and to live blameless lives. He instructed his audience to look to the martyrs as models of faith and well-doing. He himself died as a martyr at age eighty-six.

Clement was bishop of Rome during the last years of the first century. In his two epistles to the Corinthians he expressed concern over strife in the church that had deposed lawful leaders. He reminded the church at Corinth of her glorious past and entreated members to put away envy and jealousy. He pled for humility, obedience, and a forgiving spirit and referred to the evils of dissension in the Old Testament. Opposed to Polycarp's concern about theological problems, Clement viewed the problem as related to relationships within the church.

Hermas wrote *The Shepherd* during the middle of the second century. As a young man Hermas had been sold into slavery and taken to Rome, where he was purchased by a woman named Rhoda. His writings reflect some of his early background, particularly as he expressed the duty of the rich to assist the needy and the duty of the poor to pray for the rich. He presented a Christian version of the Old Testament moral code in one of five "Visions," which constituted part of the twenty-seven tractates making up *The Shepherd.* Grace was warmly embraced in his understanding of the doctrine of repentance and salvation. He taught that although there was only one repentance, it was possible to be cleansed further when necessary. He implied a generous salvation, one that might include those who were not attempting to be serious Christians.

Ignatius, bishop of Antioch and author of seven authenticated letters, was martyred early in the second century. In the fourth of his letters, which was to the church at Rome, he tried to persuade the congregation not to interfere with his death sentence. He was happy to be a martyr and considered the Church a

Part 2

Chapter 4
Ethical
Concepts
from Church
History

place of sacrifice. When he was arrested and taken from Antioch to Rome to be exposed to wild beasts, the procession was greeted along the way by bands of Christians led by bishops. He was able to address them in encouraging tones.

It is noteworthy that in his writings he hardly ever referred to the Old Testament and seemed to express hostility toward Judaistic practices. One of his great concerns was that Antioch did not seem willing to submit to the bishop who was to succeed him. He felt that without the authority of the bishop, baptisms and the Eucharist were invalid. Undoubtedly the dilemma of the church in its inability to submit to authority stemmed from the fact that the Jewish Christians had been accustomed to autonomous synagogues prior to conversion.

Like Ignatius, the writer of the *Epistle of Barnabas* (his identity is uncertain), which appeared in the first half of the second century, took a dim view of the Jewish faith. Its author, not to be confused with the Barnabas of the Book of Acts, expressed extreme hostility toward Judaism; he also contended that the Mosaic law was not literal. Its only purpose was to point to Christendom. The bronze snake (Num. 21:9) foreshadowed the cross, the scapegoat (Lev. 16:10) foreshadowed the Second Coming.

Barnabas's writing took on an even more unusual twist with the declaration that his own salvation and reward were dependent on the health of the churches he had served. "I rejoice all the more for myself, hoping to be saved, because I see in you that the Spirit is poured out upon you from the rich well of the Lord. . . . Reckoning that . . . my service of such spirits as yours will count towards my reward."[2]

A similar letter of this period, *The Epistle to Diognetus,* deals with the superiority of Christianity to the beliefs of both Jews and heathen. The unknown au-

---

[2]Simon Tugwell, *The Apostolic Fathers* (London: Geoffrey Chapman, 1989), 22.

The Church Fathers 89

Part 2

Chapter 4
Ethical
Concepts
from Church
History

thor convincingly contrasts the Christian ethic based on love and good citizenship with the foolish Hellenistic religions and their idol worship. Christianity proceeds directly from God and its intrinsic excellence is proved by its reasonableness and its fruits.

The concepts of *Clement of Alexandria* (ca. A.D. 150-215) are a fitting conclusion to these summaries of the apostolic fathers. He is considered the first Christian thinker to deal specifically with ethics in his writing. In this he is a model to ministers who want to rise above a common morality. Clement became a presbyter and taught in Alexandria for over twenty years. Well read, he quoted freely from both Old and New Testaments. He referred frequently to the writings of Greek poets, dramatists, philosophers, and historians. He studied Homer and Plato. His problem: With educated men coming into the church, were Greek learning and philosophical ideas to be acceptable to the Christian faith? Clement, while open to higher thought, ridiculed the mythology and worship of gods, especially the low standards of morality among the Greeks. He demonstrated that the Christian church was building a society of a higher standard, based as it was on divine character. Especially was this contrast of standards evident at the marketplace, at feasts, at assemblies, and at religious processions. In Clement's view, demarcation between secular and Christian ethics was clear.

The last of the church fathers is *Augustine* (A.D. 354-430), probably one of the most widely read of them. When Alaric the Goth captured Rome in A.D. 410, Augustine had been bishop of Hippo in North Africa for sixteen years. It became his responsibility to answer the charge of the pagans that Rome, the Eternal City, had fallen because of the establishment of the Christian church and the subsequent desertion of the gods.

Augustine's extensive answers to the question, begun in A.D. 412 and continuing for fourteen years, depicted an allegory of two cities, one representing the

Part 2

Chapter 4
Ethical
Concepts
from Church
History

secular world and the other, the spiritual world. He wrote to prove that the neglecting of the gods had nothing to do with the fall of Rome and to worship them could bring no benefit in the present or in the future.

Drawing on the Bible, he taught that there are two ways and that there is a new Jerusalem, the city described in Hebrews 11. However, Augustine insisted on equating the City of God with the kingdom of heaven and the Church. He saw the heavenly city as the present Church worshiping the one true God. The earthly city was condemned to death, the heavenly city blessed with everlasting life. Yet he considered the Roman Empire as not all bad or the Church all good. His concepts, while not acceptable to present-day evangelicals, influenced medieval thought by identifying the City of God with external ecclesiastical organization (that is, with the Roman Catholic Church and its hierarchy). From the fifth century on, the Church played a dominant role in society.

Quotations from Augustine's work, for example, on love, temperance, sin, and war, help show his shaping of ethical thought:

"Who does evil to the man he loves? Love thou: it is impossible to do this without doing good."[3]

"Man, therefore, ought to be taught the due measure of loving, that is, in what measure he may love himself so as to be of service to himself."[4]

"The office of temperance is in restraining and quieting the passions which make us pant for those things which turn us away from the laws of God and from the enjoyment of His goodness, that is, in a word, from the happy life."[5]

---

[3]Norman L. Geisler, ed., *What Augustine Says* (Grand Rapids: Baker Book House, 1982), 201.
[4]Ibid., 202.
[5]Ibid., 205.

The Medieval Era 91

Part 2

Chapter 4
Ethical
Concepts
from Church
History

"Again, there are some sins which would be considered very trifling, if the Scriptures did not show that they are really very serious."[6]

"It is therefore with the desire for peace that wars are waged."[7]

"For it is possible that a wise man may use the daintiest food without any sin of epicurism or gluttony, while a fool will crave for the vilest food with a most disgusting eagerness of appetite."[8]

Generally speaking, these samplings of Augustine's ethical thought might well be held by a conservative Protestant theologian of today. However, when Augustine deals with sex, it is a Roman Catholic attitude that has persisted through the centuries. In *On Marriage and Concupiscence* he contends that bigamy practiced for propagation of the race is better than monogamy practiced for pleasure. Furthermore, he insists that sex for pleasure in marriage is sinful, despite Paul's encouragement to couples to return to their intimate relationship after a time of prayer and fasting (1 Cor. 7:5).

THE MEDIEVAL ERA

With the passing of Augustine and his pronouncements on morals and ethical issues came the somber period of Church and secular history known as the Middle Ages or the Medieval Era. This period, between A.D. 500 and 1500, was characterized by muddled theology and dubious Christian ethics. No interval in Church history illustrates better the fallacies of the monastic life or military force for spreading the Christian faith.

---

[6]Ibid., 206.
[7]Ibid., 209.
[8]Ibid., 213.

Part 2

Chapter 4
Ethical
Concepts
from Church
History

It was a period in Europe's past that has been described as "a thousand years without a bath," particularly referring to peasant life. Thirty to forty percent of the population died during the Black Plague, which began around 1347. The continent was preoccupied with war, famine, the brevity of life, and death. The entire population of Europe was sixty million, only ten percent of which lived in its towns and cities. The majority of the population were vassals to land-owning lords, all part of an agrarian society.

Because of the proliferation of parish churches, monasteries, basilicas, and bishops' cathedrals, the period has been called the Age of Faith. In the words of one historian, "These structures, sometimes splendid, were medieval man's monument to his faith."[9] Nevertheless, they served only to isolate the church's religious and ethical influence from the common people.

Monasticism became symbolic of devotional life in the Roman Catholic Church. The Benedictine Order began in 530. Class was held daily in every parish, including special masses for the souls of the dead—if relatives could afford them. In this setting the system of good works known as "supererogation" (doing more than required) was developed in the Roman Church. This interpretation proposed that an individual could engage in more good works than God required, "meriting" grace that could be imputed to others.

Perhaps the low point in ethical principles during this era was introduced by the Crusades. These expeditions were initiated to protect Christian pilgrims in Muslim lands. The Frankish, English, and German knights, who made the Crusades possible, theoretically observed the code of medieval chivalry: "truth and honor, freedom and courtesy." Ironically, such virtues were scarce.

---

[9]William R. Estep, *Renaissance and Reformation* (Grand Rapids: William B. Eerdmans Publishing Co., 1986), 5.

Early Reformers **93**

Part 2

Chapter 4
Ethical
Concepts
from Church
History

In the first Crusade against Muslim-held Jerusalem, July 15, 1099, an army of forty to fifty thousand (originally more than ten times that number) entered the city and slaughtered Muslims and Jews alike. The unprincipled nature of the Crusades was finally their undoing. The last of the Crusades was financed and led by King Louis IX of France, who upon arriving at the Adriatic port of Ancona, Italy, to embark, found that the ship's crew had deserted. Thus, from start to finish, the Crusades were an ethical and spiritual failure, serving only to antagonize the Muslim world and weaken the Eastern Church.

The latter part of the Medieval Era, known as the Renaissance, covered the period between 1300 and 1517, from Dante to Luther. However, instead of the church wielding a positive influence, the reverse was true. Nonetheless, this was a remarkable period of literary and artistic revival inspired by the classical works of Rome and Greece. Individualism blossomed. A new class of citizens arose, the burghers, who formed communes and city-states as independent republics. With the rise of capitalism came conflict with the church's prohibition of lending money for interest. At the same time, the church fleeced the poor with the sale of indulgences and similar religious artifices. With the rise of capitalism the cry mounted for reform in the church.

EARLY REFORMERS

Among the stronger voices of the reformers was that of John Wycliffe (ca. 1328–1384). Wycliffe, an Oxford scholar and shining example for those who would contend for righteousness in the midst of corruption in the church, earned his doctorate in 1372. He openly questioned the ethics of pardoners selling forged papal bulls and of friars preaching in vulgar language. He condemned clerical celibacy because of its "untoward moral consequences" and "the consecration of physical objects (as akin to necroman-

Part 2

Chapter 4
Ethical
Concepts
from Church
History

cy)."[10] He opposed prayer for the dead, pilgrimages, auricular confession (told privately to a priest), and the preoccupation of the church with arts and crafts.[11]

His solid ethical posture is neatly summarized in a quote from Arthur Dickens in reference to Lollardy, the popular name for Wycliffe's followers and teachings: "It [Lollardy] argued with force that the materialism, the pride, the elaborate ritual and coercive jurisdiction of the Church found no justification in the lives of Christ and his disciples as recorded in the New Testament."[12]

Other early reformers included John Huss, born in Bohemia in 1373, who preached with moral earnestness in his effort to see the decadent church cleansed and reformed. Another not to be ignored was Erasmus, born in Rotterdam in 1467. He had a humanistic view, blended with the persuasion that instruction and righteousness ought to be enough to cope with humankind's sin. He longed to see the church reformed but not destroyed; this rendered ineffective his efforts as a reformer.

MARTIN LUTHER AND LATER REFORMERS

Martin Luther, the most eminent of the reformers, born in Eisleben in 1483, entered an Augustinian monastery in 1505 after having begun studies as a lawyer. Early in his monastic career he became unhappy with the cloistered life, having not found salvation by his works. His struggle at this time is succinctly described in William R. Estep's *Renaissance and Reformation:* "Above all else the inescapable impression is that here was an honest monk seeking God in a medieval maze of misrepresentation

---

[10]Arthur G. Dickens, *The English Reformation* (New York: Schocken Books, 1964), 24.

[11]Ibid.

[12]Ibid., 25.

Part 2

Chapter 4
Ethical
Concepts
from Church
History

with an intensity of purpose born out of the depths of human despair."[13] His trip to Rome in 1510 further disillusioned him as he observed the "Holy City" corrupted by money, luxury, and related evils.

Fittingly, as he turned his back on the city of the Romans, the Book of Romans became to him a portal into the righteousness of God—a door that has remained open to the seeker after His holiness to this day. He wrote:

Then I began to comprehend the "righteousness of God" through which the righteous are saved by God's grace, namely, through faith; that the "righteousness of God" which is revealed through the Gospel was to be understood in a passive sense in which God through mercy justifies man by faith, as it is written, "The just shall live by faith." Now I felt exactly as though I had been born again, and I believed that I had entered Paradise through widely open doors.[14]

Out of Luther's study of Scripture soon emerged some remarkable, often paradoxical, ethical concepts: Christians belonged to two kingdoms, the kingdom of Christ and the kingdom of the world. While those who belonged to the kingdom of Christ had no need for weapons or law, people in the kingdom of the world could not live in peace without the threat of weaponry. While his views were similar to those of Augustine in regard to earthly and heavenly kingdoms, he encouraged Christians to serve as judge, constable, and hangman. He advocated stern measures against rebellious peasants, but at the same time he was critical of the ruling princes in their discharge of duty.

Luther originally taught that in order to be baptized a child must believe and have a faith of his own; to

---

[13]Estep, *Renaissance and Reformation*, 112.

[14]E. G. Schwiebert, *Luther and His Times* (St. Louis: Concordia Publishing House, 1950), 286.

Part 2

Chapter 4
Ethical
Concepts
from Church
History

baptize a child otherwise was to mock and blaspheme God. Later he seemed to reject this position and engage in the practice of infant baptism, supposing that God miraculously imparted faith to the baby. His widely publicized views gave evidence of a troubled conscience that was thrusting him further and further from the sullied positions of the Roman Church. His impassioned plea at the Diet of Worms laid bare the troubled soul of this valiant reformer: "I am mastered by the passages of Scripture which I have quoted, and my conscience is captive to the Word of God. I cannot and will not recant, for it is neither safe nor honest to violate one's conscience. I can do no other. Here I take my stand, God being my helper. Amen."[15]

Other notable reformers who contributed to ethical thought in these turbulent times were men like Zwingli, the Swiss reformer, who in 1522 defended feasting on sausages instead of fish during the Lenten fast preceding Easter. He insisted that people should be free to choose what they eat and that there was no clear scriptural support for fasting at this particular season. John Calvin (1509-1564) contended that Christians must rest entirely on God's pureness and mercy, not on their own merits. Jesus alone is our advocate. It remained for Philip Melanchthon (1497–1560) to produce the first distinct statement of Protestant ethics in his *Epitome of Moral Philosophy*, published in 1538.

It is amusing that the debatable ethics of a bitter opponent of English reformer William Tyndale (1494–1536) turned to the advantage of the Reformation movement. In 1526 Bishop Cuthbert Turnstall arranged to purchase all of the copies of Tyndale's newly translated New Testament in England for burning. Tyndale was delighted inasmuch as he could now improve his next edition, he could get out of debt, many would

---

[15]Estep, *Renaissance and Reformation*, 133.

protest the burning, and Tyndale would be able to produce even more New Testaments. Ultimately, those who could not stop the spread of his New Testaments burned Tyndale at the stake.

It is noteworthy that the sixteenth-century revival of medieval piety and reaction to the Protestant Reformation brought reforms into the Roman Catholic Church as well. Monasticism was reformed, the teaching of the Bible in universities was begun, the education of the clergy was emphasized, and ultimately papal reform came into focus.

Part 2

Chapter 4
Ethical
Concepts
from Church
History

THE WESLEYAN REVIVAL

John Wesley (1703–1791) profoundly influenced eighteenth-century England's ethical thought by his emphasis on holy love. For example, his views on wealth made it incumbent on the rich to give to the poor. He insisted that we owe society all that we accumulate above our needs and those of our dependents, and that the poor have the right to share the wealth of the rich. Although he was not a pacifist in the true sense of the word, Wesley felt that war was irrational; he could not understand why people of reason and piety could not get together and settle the differences that had surfaced in the war with the American colonies.

Wesley approached human suffering from a practical perspective, organizing London into twenty-three sections and appointing two "visitors" to each section to procure medical help, relieve suffering, and render possible service. He believed that the gospel was for the whole world, a concept shared by most evangelical believers to this day. He announced on one occasion, "I am a priest of the Church universal."[16] From this premise he gave impetus to the great missionary

---

[16]W. T. Watkins, *Out of Aldersgate* (Nashville: Board of Missions, 1937), 140.

Part 2

Chapter 4
Ethical
Concepts
from Church
History

movement begun by William Carey's voyage to India in 1793.

Revival was also occurring in America. Deism and rationalism had blighted religious life in America. The strong religious fervor of the Puritans in the New England colonies had faded; their grandchildren had succumbed to spiritual indifference. Then a series of religious revivals sprang up in various parts of the young nation. The Great Awakening had come to America.

THE GREAT AWAKENING

A passing review should suffice to stimulate a desire for a revival that will raise the level of our nation's morality. The Church must promote such a revival to strengthen once again the moral fiber of our country. Here is the story of a few of the dedicated ministers who led in the Great Awakening.

William Tennent in the early eighteenth century started his "Log College" in which he trained his three sons and other ministers as Presbyterians. His eldest son, Gilbert, along with other graduates of the college, preached with such fervency and conviction that revival blazed from Long Island to Virginia.

Jonathan Edwards, the great New England intellectual and Yale graduate, was the associate pastor of a Congregational church in Northhampton in Massachusetts. He preached a series of sermons on justification; the town was profoundly charged with God's presence. By 1740 mass conversions had served to elevate the moral and ethical tone throughout New England. In July 1741 in Enfield, Connecticut, Edwards preached his great sermon "Sinners in the Hands of an Angry God"; its effect was so dynamic that he could not be heard above the cries of distress and weeping as conviction gripped the congregation, forcing him to request silence.

George Whitefield (1714–1770), Wesley's contemporary, came over from England after having

Part 2

Chapter 4
Ethical
Concepts
from Church
History

preached a great nationwide revival with both John and Charles. From 1738 to 1770 he made seven tours of America, adopting the new (and controversial) mode of preaching outdoors—and seeing thousands converted and thousands more quickened by the Spirit. Among the results of the ministry of these and other great spiritual leaders were a strong encouragement of revival and a strengthening of the ethical and moral fiber of the nation. Before the names George Washington and Benjamin Franklin became synonymous with a national cause, the Great Awakening resulted in bringing unity to the colonies through religious leaders like Tennent, Edwards, and Whitefield.[17]

Unfortunately, the Great Awakening in America was followed by a rapid decline in religious fervor and ethical conduct. Between the late eighteenth and early nineteenth centuries, the Church had reached the lowest level of vitality in its history. Western frontiersmen were ignorant and unchurched. Their conduct was marred by quarreling, fighting, hard drinking, and profanity.

Again, a spiritual upsurge swept across the country. It was America's Second Awakening. Revival broke out at Yale College, where one-third of the students were soundly converted. Other New England colleges experienced revival. Camp meetings spread through the West and the South. New denominations sprang into being; home-missionary societies and foreign-missions societies were created. The American Sunday School Union was formed. The American Bible Society and the American Tract Society came into being. The influence of the Church reached into the remotest areas of the country. Small colleges were established by churches in the West that served to maintain the moral and ethical standards that had resulted from the Second Awakening of the nation.

---

[17]B. K. Kuiper, *The Church in History* (Grand Rapids: William B. Eerdmans Publishing Co., 1951), 422.

Part 2

Chapter 4
Ethical
Concepts
from Church
History

RELIGIO-SOCIOLOGICAL INFLUENCES IN AMERICA

During the latter part of the nineteenth century and continuing well into the twentieth, a number of changes took place in the social structure and political life of America. That in turn brought about remarkable changes in the spiritual vitality and understanding of the diverse branches of the Church. The great wave of immigration into America between 1830 and 1870 enabled the Lutheran and Roman Catholic churches to grow immensely. Many Irish-Catholics settled in major eastern cities, which became great centers of Roman Catholicism in America. In these communities the ethics of the average church member were governed by the latitude offered through the confessional and a formal, impersonal worship style. Woven into the spiritual fabric of the communicants was a strong work ethic and an appreciation for the Lord's Day.

German Catholics and Lutherans migrated further inland, to the Midwest. Often their communities, while conscientious about religious ritual, had less regard for Sunday keeping and considered any careful observance of the day as the "Puritan Sabbath."

An even greater influence on the ethical and moral posture of America's people during this period was slavery. Viewed from the twentieth century, the ethical aspects of the issue are shocking to the spiritually sensitive Christian minister. But slaveholding was generally accepted in colonial times (not to mention New Testament times). Jonathan Edwards and other respected ministers were slave owners. However, by the end of the colonial period the principle that "all men are created equal" began to be more clearly and persistently articulated, particularly in segments of the Church. But with the invention of the cotton gin and the blossoming of the textile industry, slavery became even more important to the economy of the South.

Part 2

Chapter 4
Ethical
Concepts
from Church
History

All the while in the North, bitter feelings against slavery emerged, until the Church found itself hopelessly divided on the issue, particularly the Baptists, Methodists, and Presbyterians. Clearly, economics was dictating the moral and ethical posture of the Church and the state. The great tragedy of the Civil War may well have been that although the legal and political aspects of slavery were settled, the nation remained bitterly divided on its ethical and moral aspects.

The expanding industrial revolution of the latter part of the nineteenth century brought to the Church an emphasis on business efficiency as more and more businessmen began to serve on church boards. Church members developed a desire for more education; large gifts were made to schools. During this interval the Church laid a greater emphasis than ever on the social problems of the cities in particular, and the "institutional" church developed.

The goal of the Church was often to help raise the living standard of the people by the promulgation of the "social gospel." There appeared a trend to forget the main purpose of the Church—to preach salvation by grace through faith alone. When the gospel message was diluted, the prospect of changed lives and changed society faded. Christian education was no longer found in the public schools but was now the responsibility of the Church. At the same time, the Church tended to become more formal and liberal in its worship and theology. Foreign missions lost its evangelistic fervor and became simply a spreading of Western culture to backward nations.

LIBERAL THEOLOGY AND ETHICAL THOUGHT

The development of liberal theology is often traced back to Horace Bushnell, a Congregational minister in Connecticut who in 1847 published the book *Views of Christian Nurture*. He criticized the churches who believed in revivalism. There was no need for a con-

Part 2

Chapter 4
Ethical
Concepts
from Church
History

scious conversion experience at salvation; children could be trained and nurtured, becoming Christians without having had a religious experience.

Helping to spread the liberal theology in the 1800s were Henry Ward Beecher and other gifted pulpiteers. Their theology questioned the infallibility of the Bible, ignored the miraculous, and sneered at the concept of Christ's death on the cross providing salvation for a lost world. Out of this liberal background came many of the unique ethical concepts that prevail among liberal theologians and their churches to this day. We will examine some of these concepts from the perspective of both conservative and liberal ethicists.

Between 1910 and 1960, according to Henlee H. Barnette, many American theological seminaries shifted from traditional theological studies to those dealing with the relationship of Christianity to social issues. Barnette sees two divisions, or classes, of Christian ethics: teleological ethics (directed toward an end or shaped by a purpose), which begins with the problem of the end, or goal, of humankind: its perfection; and deontological (moral, obligational) ethics, the ethics of obedience, a radical obedience to the demands of God. The latter has two subgroups: biblical literalists and formal ethicists.

The ethics of liberalism is the "social gospel": the kingdom of God is a social reality on earth. The ethics of fundamentalism is legalism: conformity to a moral code. Ethics and theology, however, cannot be separated. Ethics relates to biblical studies, homiletics, counseling, and missions, as well as to the broad areas of psychology and philosophy.[18]

Norman Geisler presents other models in some detail. With ideal absolutism, norms are sometimes in conflict. The individual is not willing to admit that it is always right to follow the norm imposing the high-

---

[18]Henlee H. Barnette, *Introducing Christian Ethics* (Nashville: Broadman Press, 1961), vii, 5–8.

er obligation. He must then choose the lesser of two evils.[19] With hierarchicalism, whenever norms con-

Part 2

Chapter 4
Ethical
Concepts
from Church
History

Geisler's Ethical Models		
MODEL	**DEFINED**	**ILLUSTRATED**
Ideal Absolutism	Norms sometimes conflict	One chooses lesser of two evils
Hierarchicalism	Lower norms give way to higher norms	Persons more valuable than things
Nonconflicting Absolutism	Universal norms never conflict	Apparent conflicts signal presence of evil
Generalism	No universal norms apparent	Breaking ethical rules leads to evil

flict, it is morally right to break the lower norm to keep the higher one. The individual must be able to determine which is higher.[20] (An example of a higher norm would be that persons are more valuable than things.) As for nonconflicting absolutism, the concept is that ideally the many universal norms never conflict. All conflicts of norms are merely apparent—they don't really exist. When there is a conflict of norms,

---

[19]Norman L. Geisler, *Ethics: Alternatives and Issues* (Grand Rapids: Zondervan Publishing House, 1971), 97.

[20]Ibid., 115.

Part 2

Chapter 4
Ethical
Concepts
from Church
History

evil is inevitable but is excusable or forgivable.[21] Finally, when no universal norms are apparent, the term "generalism" is applied. In this instance the individual keeps the rules, not because it is wrong to perform a forbidden act, but rather because breaking any ethical rules will lead to evil instead of good.[22]

Against this background of various norms stands Joseph F. Fletcher's situation ethics. In attempting to balance his fears of antinomianism (no need to comply with moral laws) and legalism, Fletcher proposed a one-norm absolutism: love over law.[23] Although he himself has been accused of being in the antinomian school, he classified the New Testament libertines, with their lawlessness, and the Moral Rearmament movement, with its "spiritual power," as illustrations of this position. For examples of legalism he pointed to classical Roman Catholicism and Protestantism, as well as to post-Maccabean Pharisees, who believed in the love of duty rather than the duty of love—his situation-based proposal. In Fletcher's view there is only one moral determinant—love. "Only the command to love is categorically good." Other moral rules may be helpful, but they are not unbreakable. The only ethical imperative that remains is to "act responsibly in love." Fletcher contended that "all laws and rules and principles and ideals and norms are . . . only *contingent,* only valid *if they happen* to serve love in any situation."[24] Because his base was a naturalism that denies the reality of divine revelation, he failed to see that we need the guidelines of Scripture if we are really to "act responsibly in love."[25]

---

[21]Ibid., 79, 95.

[22]Ibid., 47.

[23]Joseph F. Fletcher, *Situation Ethics: The New Morality* (Philadelphia: Westminster Press, 1966), 26.

[24]Ibid., 28–30.

[25]Robertson McQuilkin, *An Introduction to Biblical Ethics* (Wheaton, Ill.: Tyndale House Publishers, 1989), 148.

THE RISE OF THE HOLINESS MOVEMENT

Part 2

**Chapter 4
Ethical
Concepts
from Church
History**

From his evangelical perspective, Milton Rudnick points out that evangelicals using the same high view of Scripture sometimes arrive at contrasting standards of ethics. He notes that ideas of right and wrong change over time. People of the same denomination, facing sets of standards in different eras, will have different views. For example, contraception, once deemed wrong, is now generally approved; racial discrimination, once acceptable, is now frowned on. Such changes are brought about in part by social pressure but are always subject to the light of Scripture.

The current ethical revolution in American society is not just the problem of sinning more and obeying less; rather it is a refusal to consider as sin many actions forbidden in the Bible. Virtues are scorned. "The result is a radical ethical relativism bordering on anarchy."[26] Rudnick views the rise or revival of a "holiness movement" as a reaction to the ethical situation of the times. Historically, such a revolt against the moral and ethical decline of the nation is not without precedent.

Even as post-Civil War America was slipping into the dilemma produced by the social gospel and liberalism, God was readying the counterattack. A young man named Dwight L. Moody moved to Chicago at age eighteen and opened a business. Soon his Sunday school endeavors caused him to give up the business and enter the ministry. He conducted revivals across America, with Ira Sankey leading the singing. He preached a gospel of salvation—simple, warm, and sincere. Thousands professed Christ as their Savior, a phenomenon not seen since the days of Wesley and Whitefield.

---

[26]Milton L. Rudnick, *Christian Ethics for Today: An Evangelical Approach* (Grand Rapids: Baker Book House, 1979), 19.

Part 2

Chapter 4
Ethical
Concepts
from Church
History

Moody served as a founder and first president of the YMCA in Chicago, founded the YMCA in Boston, and established Christian boarding schools as well as the religious training school that was to become Moody Bible Institute. Few men have been used more effectively than this converted businessman who helped elevate the ethics and morals of the common people in America.

A further protest against liberal theology was launched in 1910 with a series of twelve pamphlets (the last of which was published in 1915) titled *The Fundamentals: A Testimony to the Truth.* This outline of fundamentalism included (1) the inerrancy of the Scriptures, (2) the Virgin Birth, (3) the substitutionary work of Christ on the cross, (4) the physical Resurrection, and (5) the physical second coming of Christ.

The end of World War I birthed the belief that the end of the world was at hand. Intense Bible study ensued. Out of this revival and renewed devotion came the teaching of premillennialism and the imminent return of Christ. This brought a renewed emphasis on the need to be ready, which profoundly affected the conduct of believers and produced ethical purity.

At about the same time, a new holiness emphasis sprang up in protest against both liberalism and the worldliness that had crept into the Church, where Christian profession was no longer a major concern. Groups began to withdraw from old-line formal churches to form new churches. Between 1880 and 1926 at least twenty-five Holiness and Pentecostal groups emerged.[27] They were most numerous in the Midwest and South. Among them were the Nazarenes, the Christian Missionary Alliance, the Assemblies of God, the Church of God, the Pentecostal Church of Christ, and the Church of God in Christ.

[27]Kuiper, *The Church in History*, 471.

All of them emphasized sanctification as an important work of the Holy Spirit.

Whereas fundamentalism served to identify the need for holy living, the Holiness movement brought the motivation to live a holy life. It remained for the Pentecostals to demonstrate that holy living and high ethical and moral standards are made possible by the energy and power of the Holy Spirit indwelling the believer.

Part 2

Chapter 4
Ethical
Concepts
from Church
History

STUDY QUESTIONS

1. What are some of the ways Jesus expressed His love?

2. In what ways did the apostolic fathers affirm biblical ethics and in what ways did they depart from them?

3. What was good and what was bad about the monasticism that developed in the Middle Ages?

4. What effect did the Crusades have on the Church as a whole?

5. What positive and negative influences helped to produce the Reformation?

6. What lessons can we learn from Luther's ethical concepts?

7. What effects did the Wesleyan revival and Whitefield have on America?

8. How has liberal theology and the social gospel affected the ethics of America?

9. What is the responsibility of Pentecostals with respect to ethics today?

Chapter 5

The Work of the Holy Spirit: The Minister's Response

The Holy Spirit is at work in the Church. But His presence is not always recognized or even welcomed. Yet He is always present, no matter how unethical the response to His overtures may be. The Early Church reveled in His presence. David Read observes: "The 'fellowship of the Holy Spirit' was not a vague theological formula invented by St. Paul to impress first-century mystics and philosophers. It was the Christians' way of referring to the immediate, awe-inspiring, supernatural realization of the presence of God as the living bond of their unity and inward strength of the new community in Christ. The Pentecost experience is decisive for the Christian Church."[1] Without question, Pentecost was essential for the nurturing of the Church. To appreciate the importance of the work of the Holy Spirit in the Early Church, it will be instructive to consider the definitive role He played in great events recorded in the Old Testament.

THE HOLY SPIRIT IN THE OLD TESTAMENT

The Spirit was present at the creation of the world: by His moving, order came out of a formless, empty state. When God fashioned the first human form out of the dust of the earth, it was the breath of the Spir-

---

[1]David Haxton Carswell Read, *Christian Ethics* (Philadelphia: J. B. Lippincott Co., 1968), 36.

Part 2

Chapter 5
The Work of
the Holy
Spirit: The
Minister's
Response

it that gave life to it. No doubt when God spoke to the patriarchs, except when there was an appearance of the angel of the Lord or a manifestation of the Lord himself, it was by the voice of the Spirit (2 Pet. 1:21). It became imperative for Noah, Abraham, Isaac, and Jacob to recognize and heed the words of the Spirit of the Lord.

In the account of the heroic leadership of Joseph and Moses, their submission to the Spirit's guidance illustrates a high level of relational ethics. The Spirit was the giver of the dreams that came to Joseph and even to Pharaoh—dreams that required an obedient response if their world was to be saved. Centuries later, when Moses viewed the burning bush, he was commanded to remove his shoes in response to God's presence. Then after the Exodus, the Spirit that was upon Moses was imparted to seventy elders at his discretion. Throughout Israel's wilderness journey, the Spirit's presence was apparent to God's people in the form of the cloud by day, the fire by night. No doubt the visible presence of the Spirit was a comfort to the Israelites, yet the relationship sometimes seemed remote and impersonal.

When the Spirit began to move upon the judges of the Old Testament, however, the relationship became more personal. This is particularly true of Samson, God's anointed strong man, whose questionable ethics ultimately dissipated the work of the Spirit in his life. The same Holy Spirit came upon David to write the Psalms, those timeless reflections of the nature and ethical demands of God (2 Sam. 23:1-2). When the revelation of the Spirit came to the prophets, they were required to be transparent and straightforward in passing on the message, then fearless before the consequences. Ezekiel's vision of the valley of dry bones highlights God's ability to bring life to a dead army by the breath of the Spirit. What a typology of the ethical change that accompanies spiritual revival!

THE HOLY SPIRIT IN THE NEW TESTAMENT

Part 2

**Chapter 5
The Work of
the Holy
Spirit: The
Minister's
Response**

It is fitting that Christ's ministry provides a transition from the work of the Spirit in the Old Testament to His operation in the New Testament Church. We have noted the Spirit's filling John the Baptist in the womb, participating in the conception of Christ, and affirming the Incarnation by Elizabeth's experience at Mary's greeting. Public affirmation of the anointing of Christ came as the Spirit descended upon Him in the form of a dove after He was baptized by John.

Immediately following this experience, Jesus moved directly into His Spirit-empowered ministry. It is noteworthy that Luke uses the expression "in the power of the Spirit" to describe the nature of Christ's ministry (Luke 4:14). Christ continued to depend on the Spirit's inspiration throughout His earthly life, even giving His final commandments to His disciples "through the Holy Spirit" (Acts 1:2), and finally promising the Spirit for power and witnessing (Acts 1:8).

In speaking of sending the Spirit, Jesus used the Greek term *allos* to identify the Spirit as one like himself (John 14:16). What a powerful illustration this becomes of the perfect unity and harmony of the Godhead, without a trace of jealousy or self-seeking.

Just as Christ's presence was essential to the apostles' ministry as recorded in the Gospels, the Holy Spirit was vital to the Church's work as recorded in Acts and the New Testament books that follow it. Henlee Barnette points out: "So prominent is the Spirit in Acts that this work is frequently called 'The Acts of the Holy Spirit.' In the Epistles, the Spirit becomes the abiding moral guide and sustainer of the Christian life. Only Philemon, 2 and 3 John fail to mention the Spirit. In his writings, Paul shows a close connection between Christ and the Spirit."[2]

---

[2]Henlee H. Barnette, *Introducing Christian Ethics* (Nashville: Broadman Press, 1961), 89.

Part 2

Chapter 5
The Work of
the Holy
Spirit: The
Minister's
Response

Jesus explained to His disciples that when the Spirit came, He would deal directly with the ethical problems of a world that stood in need of correction. He said: "'When he [the Holy Spirit] comes, he will convict the world of guilt in regard to sin and righteousness and judgment: in regard to sin, because men do not believe in me; in regard to righteousness, because I am going to the Father, where you can see me no longer; and in regard to judgment, because the prince of this world now stands condemned'" (John 16:8–11). The Spirit would seek to glorify Christ (John 16:14).

The ethical dimension of the Spirit's work would be not to merely convict but to convert, to bring spiritual rebirth to lost sinners. He would help select and prepare a bride for Christ, imputing holiness and righteousness to the new converts. He would become the fire of evangelism for the Church. That fire would be borne directly to the believer by means of the infilling of the Spirit. This gift of the Spirit's presence would be imparted to all of Christ's followers. Acts 2 makes it clear that when the Holy Spirit descended, He came upon each member of the group, described as "about a hundred and twenty" believers gathered in the Upper Room (Acts 1:15). It is noteworthy that among the disciples named was Mary, the mother of Christ, who like the rest welcomed this dynamic gift.

Given this powerful witness, the Church as a whole naturally became energized to fulfill God's plan for the world. The Pentecostal churches in Jerusalem and Antioch, as well as in cities throughout Asia Minor and the rest of the known world, soon became centers for spreading the gospel. The same spiritual thrust has been available to the Church from the first century forward. With the fresh outpouring of the Spirit at the beginning of the twentieth century, epitomized by the Azusa Street Mission Revival, came an incentive for world evangelism unprecedented in Church history.

Part 2

**Chapter 5
The Work of
the Holy
Spirit: The
Minister's
Response**

The Spirit gave the Church insight into the heart of the gospel: "God so loved the *world"* (John 3:16). The message remains unchanged today. God loves not only America, not only the Jewish people, not only Europe, but the entire world. And the Holy Spirit is being poured out all over the world. The world vision of the Pentecostal church is exemplified by the Assemblies of God, which came into being in 1914 at Hot Springs, Arkansas. Today with an American membership of only 2,324,615, the missionary outreach program of the church has been so effective that the present worldwide total of members and adherents is over 26 million.[3] The success of the Movement is attributable to the Spirit's empowerment, accompanied as it is by miracles of healing and deliverance from the evil one.

Certain aspects of the work of the Spirit in the church are found only through maintenance of the Spirit's anointing on one's ministry. In the preparation of the sermon, as well as in its delivery, the minister must strive to maintain such an anointing. Sermon preparation as a purely intellectual exercise is always laborious and unfruitful. Only when the preacher's mind has been touched by the Spirit do thoughts and studies take on a quality not to be found in the mere compilation of biblical facts and doctrinal precepts. Then, with sermon material immersed in prayer, the minister will be enabled by the Spirit to deliver a God-given message with the impact of the supernatural. Ministers must jealously guard their personal lives as well as their ministries so that the anointing of the Spirit is always present when they speak.

---

[3]According to the Office of the Statistician of the General Council of the Assemblies of God, The Assemblies of God: Current Facts, *Report*, 1995. See also David B. Barrett, "The Twentieth-Century Pentecostal/Charismatic Renewal in the Holy Spirit, with Its Goal of World Evangelization," in *International Bulletin of Missionary Research* 12:3 (July 1988): 119–29.

Part 2

Chapter 5
The Work of
the Holy
Spirit: The
Minister's
Response

Ministers who enjoy the flow of the Spirit in their lives and ministries will covet the same spiritual blessing for their congregations. They will preach frequently on the importance of the Spirit's work, the glorious possibility of receiving the Spirit, and the necessity of a life yielded to the Spirit. The proper emphasis on the significance and availability of the baptism in the Holy Spirit will create spiritual hunger in the church. When believers "hunger and thirst for righteousness," they are sure to be filled (Matt. 5:6). Within moments after the outpouring of the Holy Spirit on the Day of Pentecost, the messenger of the Lord, Simon Peter, made it clear that the promise of the Spirit was for all those in his audience, for all who lived in distant lands, and "for all whom the Lord our God will call" (Acts 2:39). The message remains unchanged. The gift of the Holy Spirit is for all.

THE PROMISE OF THE SPIRIT (ACTS 2:17)

A brief history of the visitation of the Holy Spirit to the Church in the early twentieth century will provide helpful insights into the ethical aspects of spiritual revival. The baptism in the Holy Spirit, as evidenced by speaking with other tongues, is basic to Pentecostalism, having begun as a spontaneous phenomenon in 1900. Of course, there are references to the occurrence of tongues in Church history from the Day of Pentecost forward. Noteworthy among these is the acknowledgment of Edward Irving, prominent minister of the Church of Scotland, who mentioned in a letter to a friend in July 1831, "Two of my flock have received the gift of tongues and prophecy."[4] Although Irving himself was not known to have ever spoken in tongues, interpreted, or prophesied, after having engaged in serious theological reflection on the matter, he felt constrained to allow these super-

---

[4]Vinson Synan, ed., *Aspects of Pentecostal-Charismatic Origins* (Plainfield, N.J.: Logos International, 1975), 19.

natural utterances. As a result he was eventually locked out of his own church by the trustees of the congregation; whereupon he founded another church in Glasgow. Despite his death within two years, he is recognized as a forerunner of the Pentecostal movement because of his reasoned stand on the Spirit's manifestations.

When on January 1, 1901, Agnes Ozman became the first of millions of Pentecostal believers who would experience speaking in tongues in this century, a new aspect of glossolalia came into focus. For the first time in modern Church history, speaking in tongues was considered to be the initial, outward evidence of the baptism in the Holy Spirit.

As the revival spread, the issue of tongues as the evidence of the Baptism became an increasingly divisive matter. Holiness groups felt compelled to take the position that tongues was not scriptural or that it constituted only one of several signs of the infilling of the Spirit. In the course of time even the Assemblies of God, which had come into being as a "tongues movement," was threatened by controversy over the issue; F. F. Bosworth, an influential Pentecostal minister, began to advocate the position that tongues was but one evidence of the baptism in the Holy Spirit. The matter was firmly settled by decisive action at the meeting of the General Council of the Assemblies of God in the summer of 1918: A resolution was adopted declaring speaking in tongues the initial sign of the Baptism. The Council further took the position that it would be unethical, as well as unscriptural, for any of its ministers to attack as error this distinctive testimony of the Movement.

Within a few days after Agnes Ozman's dynamic experience, a number of other students at the Bible school she was attending in Topeka, Kansas, received the experience of the Baptism as she had received it. The revival was on. Although the Topeka school lasted only a year, its founder, Charles F. Parham, continued to propagate the Pentecostal message over the

Part 2

**Chapter 5
The Work of
the Holy
Spirit: The
Minister's
Response**

Part 2

Chapter 5
The Work of
the Holy
Spirit: The
Minister's
Response

next five years throughout Kansas, Missouri, and Texas. The most important result of his ministry was to bring a black Holiness preacher, W. J. Seymour, under the influence of the revival. Within a few months, Seymour, thoroughly convinced of the validity of the Pentecostal experience but not yet a partaker, accepted an invitation to speak in a black Nazarene church in Los Angeles. After his first sermon, which he based on Acts 2:4, he was locked out of the church; he moved his services to the home of some Baptist friends on Bonnie Brae Street.

It was there on April 9, 1906, that seven black believers received a dynamic infilling of the Holy Spirit accompanied by speaking in other tongues. Soon Seymour, too, received the experience. To accommodate the large crowds that wanted to share the excitement, an old Methodist church that had been converted into a livery stable was secured as a meeting place. For three years this humble mission at 312 Azusa Street became the site of constant Pentecostal revival. Ministers, missionaries, and laypersons from across America and from many foreign nations made the pilgrimage to the meeting room where an uneducated black man with a defective eye served powerfully as the leader of largely unstructured prayer services.[5] The place was never closed or empty for the three-year period, during which a multiracial throng came seeking a new dimension in God and went away as human torches, aflame with their new-found spiritual experience.

"Now about Spiritual Gifts" (1 Cor. 12:1)

The Holy Spirit brought to the Pentecostal church not only power for evangelism but also spiritual gifts. By means of spiritual gifts, individual believers enjoy, along with the presence of the Spirit in their life, an

---

[5]William W. Menzies, *Anointed to Serve* (Springfield, Mo.: Gospel Publishing House, 1971), 52.

enhancement of their service. The gifts are not a mark of spiritual superiority; they are all given by grace through faith. Spiritual gifts are needed to bring vitality to the meetings of the church.

The nine gifts mentioned in 1 Corinthians 12:8-10 can be categorized as conceptual gifts, such as the word of wisdom and the word of knowledge; gifts of power, such as healing and the working of miracles; and utterance gifts, including various kinds of tongues and their interpretation. Romans 12:8 adds the gifts of generous giving, leadership, and showing mercy; 1 Corinthians 12:28 lists the gifts of helpfulness and administration.

The necessity for the gifts to function at the highest possible ethical level is highlighted by the fact that following the extensive treatment of this subject in 1 Corinthians 12 comes the great love chapter of the Bible. Here God's perspective on the proper exercise of the gifts is revealed: "Though I speak with the tongues of men and of angels, . . . have the gift of prophecy, . . . understand all mysteries and all knowledge, and . . . have all faith, . . . but have not love, I am nothing" (1 Cor. 13:1-2, NKJV).

Not only does the Spirit bring invisible gifts to the Church, He has gifted its members for the work of the Church: "some to be apostles, some to be prophets, some to be evangelists, and some to be pastors and teachers" (Eph. 4:11). The combination of gifted individuals and the gifts of the Spirit is needed to bring about true maturity in the Church, to equip the saints for service, and to edify the body of Christ (Eph. 4:12-13).

Who is eligible to receive a gift of the Spirit? Scripture makes it clear that God is no respecter of persons; any true believer may be a recipient. The basic requirement is a receptive heart. When Paul met twelve disciples from Ephesus, his question was simply, "'Did you receive the Holy Spirit when [after] you believed?'" (Acts 19:2). When Paul laid his hands on them, they received the Holy Spirit, spoke in

Part 2

Chapter 5
The Work of
the Holy
Spirit: The
Minister's
Response

Part 2

Chapter 5
The Work of
the Holy
Spirit: The
Minister's
Response

tongues just as the disciples did at Pentecost, and received the gift of prophecy.

Once a spiritual gift has been received, it ought to be given expression according to the Spirit's direction. To do otherwise would be unethical. If that gift has been neglected, hear Paul's admonition to Timothy: "Fan into flame the gift of God" (2 Tim. 1:6). Perhaps the gift has been allowed to function only partially, not having been recognized as a gift of God. The result is that one fails to be the instrument of blessing one might otherwise be.

Recognizing one's proper relationship to the Church can alleviate this problem, as Erwin Lutzer points out: "The Body of Christ helps us understand where we fit within the local church framework. The Body enables its members to find their spiritual gifts and is a testing ground for further ministry. Those who are faithful in the least may later be entrusted with greater responsibility."[6]

How important are spiritual gifts to the contemporary Church? In the light of the spiritual and moral decay surrounding the Church, they are needed more than ever. The Church must develop a high ethical standard that influences the world rather than let the low standards of the world influence the Church. The rapid growth of the Church in many nations has created the need for stabilizing, training, and maturing its members. This will come about only as the gifts of the Spirit function freely in the Church.

The return of Christ seems imminent. The gifts of the Spirit help alert the Church to the urgency of the hour. Supernatural signs and wonders, which "accompany those who believe," attract people to Christ (Mark 16:17). To engage in the harvest without all of the equipment furnished by the Spirit handicaps one's work, as well as calling one's judgment into question.

---

[6]Erwin W. Lutzer, *Pastor to Pastor: Tackling Problems of the Pulpit* (Chicago: Moody Press, 1987), 12.

"FITTING AND ORDERLY" (1 COR. 14:40)

Part 2

Chapter 5
The Work of
the Holy
Spirit: The
Minister's
Response

The Bible teaches that the Spirit's gifts should function within the church. It also instructs church leadership about regulation of the gifts. The Bible assumes that the leader of a church service is both ethically and spiritually sensitive, making sure that all that goes on in the church service is "in order." In a service where the Spirit is at work, well-meaning individuals with more zeal than knowledge can overreact to His presence. (All of us react differently to the same stimulus, even in the natural world. Ten people receiving an electric shock simultaneously will react in ten different ways.)

The Bible further assumes that there may well be so many individuals ready to express the gifts of the Spirit in the service that some control is needed. Emotionalism can displace the ministry of the Spirit. It is unethical for leaders not to care what others think. Certainly the admonition not to allow our good to be evil spoken of applies.

Problems sometimes occur in the regulation of spiritual gifts. The leader of the service may have failed to discern the genuineness of a gift. The leader may attempt to regulate the manifestation of the Spirit but may himself be spiritually ignorant. To act in willful ignorance is definitely an ethical problem. As Paul bluntly states it in 1 Corinthians 12:1, "Now about spiritual gifts, brothers, I do not want you to be ignorant."

Some service leaders may be fearful of offending persons who express a gift of the Spirit. If a reprimand upsets them, then it is evident that they are not in the Spirit. On the other hand, should they be in the Spirit and the reprimand is in error, they will be grieved but will, nevertheless, respond lovingly.

Other leaders fear stifling the expression of those who are being used of God. Certainly we do not want to "put out the Spirit's fire" (1 Thess. 5:19). On the other hand, proper regulation of the Spirit brings

Part 2

Chapter 5
The Work of
the Holy
Spirit: The
Minister's
Response

freedom of the Spirit, for participants in the service will know that fanaticism will not be allowed to distort the work of the Spirit.

Then, too, the leader may feel that only the gifts of speaking in tongues, interpretation of tongues, and prophecy need to be directed in the service; this is a mistake. "Everything should be done in a fitting and orderly way" (1 Cor. 14:40).

Unfortunately, some non-Pentecostals are so unskilled in the Scriptures that they grossly misinterpret the teaching on spiritual gifts and their regulation. Having already concluded that speaking in tongues belonged only to the Early Church and that prophecy is in essence merely anointed preaching, these persons lay great emphasis on the teaching of 1 Corinthians 14, that prophecy is superior to speaking in tongues and that anyone who speaks in tongues is not addressing men but God alone. However, they ignore the latter part of verse 5, that the person who prophesies "is greater than one who speaks in tongues, *unless he interprets,* so that the church may be edified." In other words, tongues with interpretation is equal to prophecy.

Even though Paul in concluding the fourteenth chapter of 1 Corinthians instructs the believer to be eager to prophesy, he makes it clear that speaking in tongues is highly desirable, exhorting the Corinthians, "Do not forbid speaking in tongues" (14:39).

Among trained clergy, perhaps the most unethical denigration of speaking in other tongues is the emphasis on the phrase "where there are tongues, they will be stilled" (1 Cor. 13:8). This is followed by an exegesis of verse 10 ("When perfection comes, the imperfect disappears"), twisted to make "perfection" mean the completed canon of Scripture, which supposedly supersedes speaking in tongues. A correct interpretation of verse 8 has to include the fact that along with the cessation of speaking in tongues, prophecies will cease and knowledge will pass away. Are we to believe the gift of knowledge vanished

Part 2

Chapter 5
The Work of
the Holy
Spirit: The
Minister's
Response

with the completion of the New Testament canon? A more rational and ethical approach to this passage would include Paul's statement that "we know in part," verse 9, and his repetition of this clause in verse 12, where he states: "Now I know in part; then I shall know fully, even as I am fully known." The coming of "perfection" and being known "as I am fully known" clearly relate to the return of Christ for His church when the spiritual gifts of prophecy, speaking in tongues, and knowledge will no longer be needed.

The gift of speaking in tongues is relevant to the Church Age for a number of reasons: (1) It is important enough to be the subject of a chapter of the Bible (1 Cor. 14) on the regulation of gifts. (2) It is the initial outward evidence of the baptism in the Holy Spirit, as attested to in Acts 2:4, 10:45–46, and 19:6. (3) In chapter 12 of 1 Corinthians, which deals with the proper function of the gifts and of the members of the body of Christ, speaking in tongues is one of the gifts highlighted in verse 28, and speaking in tongues and interpretation are two of the three gifts listed in verse 30. (4) Speaking in tongues is the only spiritual gift present in the New Testament Church that does not have an antecedent in the Old Testament.

"Do Not Put Out the Spirit's Fire" (1 Thess. 5:19)

The minister must be careful not to overregulate the expression of the gifts of the Holy Spirit in the church service. To attempt to operate the Spirit by pastoral remote control is completely unethical. It is possible to stifle not only the functioning of the gifts of the Spirit but any of the Spirit's expression. We risk ruling out altogether the presence of the Holy Spirit in our services. It is not possible to justify the judgment of the minister who is so biased he is willing to evict the Spirit to still the gifts.

The gifts of the Spirit are absent from many otherwise doctrinally sound, evangelical churches. They

Part 2

Chapter 5
The Work of
the Holy
Spirit: The
Minister's
Response

are non-Pentecostal and happy about it; they have no
interest in spiritual gifts, signs, or miracles. To them,
spiritual manifestations were for a bygone era. It must
be acknowledged that there are also churches bearing
the Pentecostal label that do not welcome the manifestations of the Holy Spirit. This condition often
stems from a fear of emotionalism or extremism. Certainly a balanced approach to spiritual manifestations
is desirable. Yet, it is unethical to exclude the moving
of the Spirit from the service for fear of emotionalism, just as it is unethical to rely on emotionalism to
provide evidence of the Spirit.

The church that is ashamed of its Pentecostal label
has bartered its ethical soundness for a veneer of social acceptability. In other cases, this indicates a lack
of spiritual hunger or desire for spiritual gifts. The
Church needs training in this important area of its life
and ministry. May God place in the Church people
like Paul, who was able to explain the things of the
Spirit to the Ephesian disciples when they confessed,
"'We have not even heard that there is a Holy Spirit'"
(Acts 19:2). Or may there be those among us like Peter, who in response to the Lord could induct Cornelius and his household into salvation as well as into
the baptism in the Holy Spirit. It is important to note
here that God's standard required that a Spirit-filled
man, not an angel, bring this message to the Gentiles.
The angel who visited Cornelius was permitted only
to arrange the evangelistic encounter.

"DO NOT TREAT PROPHECIES WITH CONTEMPT" (1 THESS. 5:20)

In recent years many churches that once took a
strong stand against the Spirit's manifestation in their
services are becoming hungry for His move, both in
the pulpit and in the pew. Many of their members
have received the baptism in the Holy Spirit and His
gifts. As a result of the charismatic movement, an
even more amazing visitation of the Holy Spirit has

Part 2

**Chapter 5
The Work of
the Holy
Spirit: The
Minister's
Response**

come to some of the liturgical denominations of our nation. Remarkable outpourings of the Holy Spirit, replete with gifts and miracles by the power of the Spirit, have occurred among denominations that had resisted dynamic spiritual revival for years. Thus it is important that the Pentecostal church maintain a proper attitude toward those who stand in opposition to its doctrinal persuasion and emphasis on the work of the Holy Spirit. The ethic of steadfast love really works. Proverbs 15:1 remains true, "A gentle answer turns away wrath."

The Pentecostal church is obliged to pray for revival, for the unrestrained moving of the Spirit, not merely in Pentecostal churches but in every denomination where Christ is preached. Since the events of the Book of Acts, Pentecostal phenomena have accompanied revivals, regardless of the church setting where the visitation of the Spirit came.

Our churches must be open to having relationships with those of like precious faith. We need to join the local ministerial alliance and participate in services with other fellowships in our communities. Such relationships are always ethical if they are pursued with the right motivation. When issues related to the work of the Spirit are to be discussed, we ought to be there. However, it is essential that we be informed on the subject and that we maintain a humble attitude in such conversations.

"NOT A GOD OF DISORDER" (1 COR. 14:33)

Many churches and individuals are praying for revival in America like that in many other nations. But we must never succumb to the acceptance of fanaticism or what was labeled in former days as "wildfire." I recall the statement of H. B. Kelchner, an outstanding Pentecostal teacher who had been raised on a farm. He had heard some radical Pentecostals say it is better to have wildfire in the church than no fire at all. Kelchner responded, "No one who has

Part 2

Chapter 5
The Work of
the Holy
Spirit: The
Minister's
Response

ever seen real wildfire could possibly want it in his church." He pointed out the wanton destruction and heartbreak left by an uncontrolled fire.

Although wildfire may not be an imminent danger to the Church, the unregulated, unbalanced reaction to the presence of the Holy Spirit needs to be avoided. The Holy Spirit is gentle. He comes with fire, but it is an inner fire. He comes to destroy personal sin and to empower for service, not to destroy those who may disagree with us. When James and John asked the Lord for permission to call fire from heaven to consume the Samaritans who were not receptive to Him, His response was "'You do not know what manner of spirit you are of. For the Son of Man did not come to destroy men's lives but to save them'" (Luke 9:55–56, NKJV).

The Church must be aware of twisted or false doctrine that results from the mishandling of Pentecostal truth. Those who embrace "Jesus Only" teaching have assumed an erroneous view of the Triune Godhead. Latter Rain adherents exaggerated the imparting of spiritual gifts. The "hyperfaith" group has adopted a position on divine healing that rivals that of Christian Science. Those who practice "positive confession" engage in the questionable ethic of always grasping for things of secondary importance.

Again, Pentecostal ministers need to maintain an ethical attitude toward extremism. They will manifest the steadfast love that has been shown them by a loving Heavenly Father through the power of His Spirit. They will keep communication open with those they can't agree with. They will pray for and promote the revival needed in the land—a revival that not only will thaw the coldness of religiosity devoid of the Spirit's moving, but also will bring a restoration of biblical soundness into the confusion of doctrinal extremism. The Holy Spirit is the greatest teacher of ethics the world has known since Christ ascended to the Father (cf. John 14:26; 16:13).

Part 2

Chapter 5
The Work of
the Holy
Spirit: The
Minister's
Response

STUDY QUESTIONS

1. How was the work of the Holy Spirit in the Old Testament different from His work in the New Testament and today?

2. Why was the use of the Greek word *allos* important with respect to the promise of the Holy Spirit given by Jesus?

3. What was significant about the Azusa Street revival in Los Angeles?

4. How can ministers maintain the anointing of the Spirit on their lives, ministry, and preaching?

5. What part should the preaching of the baptism in the Holy Spirit have in a person's ministry?

6. Why did the General Council of the Assemblies of God declare it is unethical for our ministers to reject speaking in tongues as the initial evidence of the baptism in the Holy Spirit?

7. What is the importance and function of spiritual gifts in the local church today? How can they be encouraged?

8. What are some of the extremes some Pentecostals have adopted, and how can extremes be avoided?

Chapter 6

Belief in the Second Coming: The Minister's Role

Recent national surveys indicate that most Americans, Christian and non-Christian alike, believe that Christ will literally return to the Earth. One survey showed that 60 percent of the total population held this belief and that 74 percent of Protestants did so.

Undoubtedly, one of the more compelling reasons for this widespread expectation of Christ's return is the moral and ethical deterioration of the times. With every revolution of the Earth on its axis, its inhabitants seem to plunge more deeply into immorality, evil, violence, confusion, desperation. The situation cries loudly for a messiah. Those who read the Bible take comfort in the promise of His coming, mentioned over three hundred times in the New Testament alone.

ESTABLISHING THE BIBLICAL BASIS OF THE SECOND COMING

Among this host of eschatological assurances are a number of ethical premises on which this great doctrine of the Church rests.

1. Jesus assured His followers that He would return for them someday (John 14:3). He who is the Way, the *Truth,* and the Life made a commitment that He is ethically bound to fulfill. His integrity must be sustained; as the omnipotent Christ, no force can deter Him.

2. Christ is needed by the Church (2 Thess. 1:10). The completeness of the Church is at stake. He can

Part 2

Chapter 6
Belief in the
Second
Coming: The
Minister's
Role

never "be glorified in his holy people" as the all-glorious Head of the Church if there is no physical union. The Church is incomplete without Him.

3. It is the deep desire of the Lord to be joined with the Church (Rev. 22:12). His statement that He is coming "soon" ("quickly," KJV) indicates His yearning to be united with the Church, His heavenly bride. In Luke 22:15-16 He speaks of His "eager desire" for eternal fellowship with His followers. He longs to have communion, to eat and drink with them in His kingdom.

4. By raising Jesus, the Father has established His Son's rule on Earth (Acts 17:30-31). Paul drives home this truth in concluding his sermon at the Areopagus: insisting that God has "set a day" for this great event and established the highest possible credence of its coming to pass by raising His Son from the dead.

5. The Scriptures repeatedly affirm the establishment of Christ's earthly kingdom (1 Pet. 1:10-11). From the beginning of time, prophecy has provided the key, the proof of the validity of Scripture. Among Old Testament prophets, Isaiah, Ezekiel, and Daniel foretold both the first and second comings of the Lord to Earth. This prophetic word has been reiterated in the New Testament, by the writers of the Gospels, the Epistles, and Revelation.

6. The entire creation longs for the return of Christ (Rom. 8:19-22). We often fail to sense the bondage brought by the curse upon Adam and the rest of creation. Paul sensed in his day "the whole creation . . . groaning as in the pains of childbirth right up to the present time" (v. 22). Thus the Earth unconsciously joins the Church in hoping for the return of the Liberator.

7. Christ alone can bring the world into adjustment morally, socially, and politically (Ps. 72; Isa. 11:3-5). Not until Christ returns to reign on the Earth will the oppressed and the poor be treated fairly; only then will righteousness and peace flourish around the

Part 2

**Chapter 6
Belief in the
Second
Coming: The
Minister's
Role**

world. The moral and ethical criteria for government will at last attain the level of God's design.

RESPONDING RESPONSIBLY TO MESSIANIC PREDICTIONS

The obvious shortcoming of every date-setting prediction of Christ's return is that each has been false. As early as Paul's day, the problem existed. Paul had to reassure the church of Thessalonica that the Day of the Lord had not arrived. And so this false teaching emerged early, to appear again and again from that day even to this. Throughout the history of the Roman Catholic Church and its domination of much of the Western world, any number of popes have been labeled "Antichrist" by those who apparently assumed the last days had arrived. In the nineteenth and twentieth centuries several noteworthy incidents have resulted from false expectations of the Lord's coming. In 1825 Edward Irving, a charismatic, who considered himself both prophet and priest replete with apostolic gifts, predicted the world would end in 1868.[1] He was never called to account for his error, for he died in 1834.

Then in 1843 and again in 1844 William Miller and his followers predicted the coming of the Lord, taking elaborate measures to prepare for it.[2] To Miller's credit, he had the good sense to admit his mistake and remain a devout Christian to his death. Unfortunately, his later followers, notably Ellen G. White, compounded the error by denying the mistake and from her visions developing the doctrines of Seventh-Day Adventism.

A similar travesty was perpetrated by Judge J. F. Rutherford, who assumed the mantle of leadership among the followers of Charles Taze Russell and con-

---

[1]See Stanley M. Burgess and Gary B. McGee, eds., *Dictionary of Pentecostal and Charismatic Movements* (Grand Rapids: Zondervan Publishing House, 1988).

[2]Walter R. Martin, *Kingdom of the Cults* (Minneapolis: Bethany Fellowship, Publishers, 1965), 361.

Part 2

Chapter 6
Belief in the
Second
Coming: The
Minister's
Role

cocted the startling doctrine that Christ had established His reign in 1914 and had come to His temple, Jehovah's Witnesses, in 1918.[3] The fervor and enthusiasm of present-day Witnesses has served only to discredit and confuse the church world regarding this great biblical promise.

As recently as 1988 the evangelical world was stirred by the publishing of a date for the rapture of the Church (considered by many to be the first phase of the return of Christ). True to the unethical nature of all such date setters, when the first date passed, a second date was announced. Without doubt, a few uncommitted Christians and unconverted churchgoers were momentarily motivated to do some serious heart preparation. Yet one wonders what the net result was in these lives, as well as others, when the prediction failed and the inevitable disillusionment followed.

To set a date for the Lord's return in the face of the scriptural declaration that not even the Son knows the day, the hour, or the time (Matt 24:36; 25:13; Mark 13:32–33) is to commit a grave ethical and spiritual error. At the same time, resistance to date setting should not become skepticism about the event itself. Should the date setter's motive be to frighten the lost into the kingdom of God, the tactic may produce a scare. But it will ultimately fail because only godly fear produces the desired result (see 2 Cor. 7:10).

Among my childhood memories is an event that took place during an old-fashioned camp meeting in West Virginia. The aurora borealis began scintillating throughout the northern sky, causing us to gather at the edge of the camp. Witnessing this rare and brilliant display in the heavens, we were certain that the Lord was going to appear at any moment. I clearly recall the soul-searching that went on in my heart as I

---

[3]Ibid., 34, 41, 44, 45, 97.

stood in awe, scanning the sky for His appearing. The experience, rather than producing skepticism, had a wholesome effect on my life.

The Church will die without hope if it allows the promise of His coming to fade. As we approach the turn of the century and enter the next millennium, many believers feel that the Lord's coming cannot be too distant. Many denominations have intensified their evangelistic efforts in this last decade of the twentieth century. The Church is working and praying earnestly for the return of the Lord. It is important that we not allow unethical tactics to discredit this great truth.

Part 2

Chapter 6
Belief in the
Second
Coming: The
Minister's
Role

COPING WITH KINGDOM NOW AND RELATED PHILOSOPHIES

The "kingdom now" doctrine, which has been around since the days of Augustine, takes the radical position that the Church is now in the Kingdom Age. They teach that during this era, which is viewed as quasi-millennial, the Church will become increasingly dominant in the sciences, the arts, and in government. Several widely known church figures have espoused this position, evidently for political or financial reasons. However, it has an unsound basis inasmuch as it justifies aggressive social action and exalts the human above the spiritual. Further, it postulates the Church as a capable Bride empowered to save the world, independently of the Head of the Church. Then the Church, the Bride, will present the fully mature Kingdom to the passive Christ, whereupon she becomes His bride—a mere anticlimax after all that has gone before.

Such an interpretation of Scripture is hopelessly skewed inasmuch as the Scriptures clearly depict Christ as the central figure of the Millennium. He is the Prince of Peace, described in Isaiah 11 as a branch from the roots of Jesse to rule with wisdom and equity on the Earth. His reign of justice will be the perfect fulfillment of God's formula for ethics:

Part 2

Chapter 6
Belief in the
Second
Coming: The
Minister's
Role

steadfast love, justice, and righteousness. His noble governmental leadership will be the perfect antidote to the cruelty, greed, and racial and political hatred that have been increasing as His return nears.

Closely related to the "kingdom now" philosophy is the prosperity teaching based on such Scripture passages as 3 John 2: "Beloved, I pray that you may prosper in all things and be in health, just as your soul prospers" (NKJV). This amazing, unethical twisting of Scripture appeals largely to those charismatics who relish the carnal application of a spiritual truth. The major fallacy of this teaching is that it cannot be universally applied. For example, most third-world Christians would label the entire concept ludicrous or unfathomable at best. Is it not particularly ironic that this teaching has been drawn from the writing of the most spiritually minded of the disciples, who suffered like a pauper, marooned on the desert island of Patmos?

Erwin Lutzer reduces this variation of the materialistic "kingdom now" teaching to its simplest terms: "The new philosophy that 'God wants you to be rich, happy, and healthy' has appealed to a generation that is quick to accept the benefits of Christianity without painful obedience. Like a child standing by a slot machine hoping he can win the jackpot with a single coin, many churchgoers expect maximum return from minimum commitment. When they are not healed or they don't get a promotion, they take their quarter and go elsewhere."[4]

ESPOUSING A DIVERGENT ESCHATOLOGICAL VIEW

Promoting an unbiblical perspective on the second coming of Christ can lead to spiritual destruction. The desire to have a unique point of view on the subject may reflect egotism or simply a desire for notori-

---

[4]Erwin W. Lutzer, *Pastor to Pastor: Tackling Problems of the Pulpit* (Chicago: Moody Press, 1987), 77.

Part 2

Chapter 6
Belief in the
Second
Coming: The
Minister's
Role

ety. Sometimes departure from sound teaching on a given subject is simply a deliberate effort to become a cult figure. "Father Divine," a self-styled messianic figure who held forth in New York's Harlem some years ago, typifies the would-be cult idol who seems to possess almost satanic power over his gullible subjects. Using Jesus' words, "If anyone keeps my word, he will never see death" (John 8:51), Divine insisted that those who followed him would never die. Believing his teaching, many of his people would abandon their deceased members in the apartment where they had died, leaving city authorities to remove the strong-smelling evidence that error ultimately dies. Finally, the death of Divine himself undercut yet another attempt to distort the Word of God.

As has been noted, distortion of the truth relating to the Lord's coming has troubled the Church for centuries. The Church survives, but many innocent souls never escape the snare of an unethical handling of God's Word. On occasion, a group that has espoused incorrect eschatological teaching may manage to remain fairly orthodox in other areas of truth. Yet invariably they manifest an independent, divisive spirit that is detrimental to the cause of Christ. One never ceases to marvel that among fundamentalist ministers are those who persist in trumpeting some pet deviation from the generally held teaching of the literal return of Christ.

INTERPRETING SCRIPTURE FROM A PRE-TRIBULATION PERSPECTIVE

The fellowship I belong to embraces the pre-Tribulation teaching concerning the Rapture but does not consider it a critical point of doctrine. Within the denomination is the latitude needed for its constituents to privately hold to mid-Tribulation and post-Tribulation teaching. However, postmillennialism or amillennialism are considered unacceptable.

The pre-Tribulation catching away, or "rapture," of the Church is supportable from a number of perspec-

Part 2

Chapter 6
Belief in the
Second
Coming: The
Minister's
Role

tives when compared with the alternative views of this truth:

1. To teach the post-Tribulation theory is to essentially set a date for Christ's return when He has said that He will come "at an hour when you do not expect him" (Matt. 24:44). The very emergence of the Antichrist and the events related to his actions, such as his defiling of the temple and breaking the covenant with Israel, will make possible precise date setting for the return of the Lord.

2. The Scriptures teach that the Church is not expected to endure the Great Tribulation. The Church has always suffered persecution, but never anything like the unmitigated suffering and divine wrath of the Great Tribulation.[5]

3. It is not logical that the Church suffer through the Tribulation. The function of this period of history will be to bring the Jewish nation to its senses and to punish a Christ-rejecting world. Would a father subject an obedient, loving child to the same punishment he is meting out to a rebellious child?

4. The Church is not mentioned in any of the events described in the Book of Revelation beyond chapter 4, where John, the writer, is invited to heaven in the Spirit (4:1-2). Christ instructed the Church to pray that it might escape—rather than bear—the things that were to fall on the Earth (Luke 21:36).

5. The kind of experiences that characterize the Tribulation could hardly be classified as suitable preparation for the great marriage of the Bride and her heavenly Bridegroom.

6. The Church would never have been encouraged to look forward to the coming of Christ as a "blessed hope" if it were tainted with the misery of the Great Tribulation (Titus 2:13).

---

[5]See Stanley M. Horton, "The Last Things," in *Systematic Theology*, ed. Stanley M. Horton (Springfield, Mo.: Gospel Publishing House, 1994), 626.

RECOGNIZING THE IMMINENCE OF CHRIST'S RETURN

Part 2

**Chapter 6
Belief in the
Second
Coming: The
Minister's
Role**

How may ministers deal ethically with the expectation of the coming of the Lord, the blessed hope in the hearts of their church members? They will want to encourage those for whom the promise has lost its luster. They will need to reassure those who have become discouraged because of unfulfilled spiritual yearnings. They will need to help rekindle the first love of the lethargic, those who have lost their concern for righteousness. Ministers will need to preach, to live, to act with the same momentary expectation of the coming of the Lord that characterized leaders of the Early Church.

In the light of Christ's return, how should the minister view the ethical implications of the technology and mass of information available today? The ongoing refinement of communication techniques and the computerization of enormous amounts of data—particularly credit and financial information in international banking concerns and military information by NATO and defense commands of leading nations—have already been labeled by some discerning scholars as precursors to the Antichrist. These developments give credence to the possibilities of mind control and authoritarian governments in the not-too-distant future.

Wars, famine, earthquakes, and nations facing political and economic stress seem on the increase. These devastating circumstances may not be more prevalent than in prior years, but the fact that they are more readily reported and more vividly portrayed via the media greatly increases their impact on the Church. In addition, the decline of morals continues. Many of our national leaders have apparently abandoned ethical principles. Murder, rape, drugs, abortion, divorce, homosexuality—a complete catalog of evil—challenge the Church to its very core. Our homes seem to be lacking spiritual vitality. Our schools are without an atmosphere of respect for teaching.

Part 2

Chapter 6
Belief in the
Second
Coming: The
Minister's
Role

Yet along with these doleful signs are exciting, positive indications of a worldwide revival. Souls are being added by the thousands to the Church in nation after nation. Missionary evangelism has never been more effective. For example, the Assemblies of God with a membership of a little over 2 million at home can claim a worldwide constituency of over 26 million.[6] Signs, wonders, and miracles are becoming the order of the day, particularly in Africa and Latin America. Healings are taking place in the local church here in our own nation. Thus, we ministers have the responsibility to invite the presence and power of the Holy Spirit into our lives and into our churches, to encourage expectancy of the return of Christ.

REALIZING ONE'S POTENTIAL AS PROPHET/PRIEST

In the light of the imminent return of Christ, ministers must fulfill the demands of spiritual leadership in the church. They, as servants of God, will find themselves drawn into the dual role of prophet and priest.

As prophets they will preach prophetically and with conviction. They will be led of the Spirit in their ministry. They will warn the indifferent and will help prepare those who are not ready to face the challenges of the hour. They will search the Scriptures to determine their roles in the contemporary situation. Above all, they will be soul winners. When they are engaged in visitation ministry, it will be second nature for them to speak of the second coming of the Lord. They will stand for the truth of this great doctrine, even in dialogues where liberal theology prevails. They will not view the return of Christ as a mere whim of theology but will embrace it as a central reality, driving them to fulfill their call.

---

[6]It has 2,324,615 in the United States and 26,319,015 worldwide as of December 31, 1994, according to the Office of the Statistician of the General Council of the Assemblies of God, The Assemblies of God: Current Facts, *Report*, 1995.

As priests they will lead an exemplary life before their congregations. They will be the priests in their homes. They will recognize the imperative of being the same faithful leader in private as in public.

The most important aspect of the pastor's priestly ministry will be prayer. David H. C. Read highlights its importance in this commentary:

Part 2

Chapter 6
Belief in the
Second
Coming: The
Minister's
Role

> Instead of thinking that we have exhausted the meaning of prayer as it has been practiced in the Church, we might rather consider whether this is not the most neglected area of Christian ethics in our world today. The greatest impact of such ethics, the strongest influence of the Christian spirit on the points of tension with which we are all confronted, will not come from pronouncements of the Church, no matter how ecumenical and unanimous; nor from political action, no matter how considered or how heroic; but from the presence of men and women in whom is revealed the presence of power of their God.[7]

In view of the abundance of Scripture passages that point out the necessity of prayer in the life of God's servants, not only will they want to pray, they will lead their congregations in their prayer life. If a local church is successful, it is because somebody is praying on its behalf. The success that stems from prayer, however, is not always measured by the size of the congregation. A church in Hagerstown, Maryland, with a modest number of constituents, has for years produced scores of outstanding ministers. Another church, in Arlington, Virginia, has not grown to huge proportions, but has poured hundreds of thousands of dollars into world missions over the years. A church in Richmond, Virginia, experienced only moderate growth until the last several years; yet it has been instrumental in starting nine other churches in the area. A church in the suburbs of Baltimore, Mary-

---

[7]David Haxton Carswell Read, *Christian Ethics* (Philadelphia: J. B. Lippincott Co., 1968), 48–49.

Part 2

Chapter 6
Belief in the
Second
Coming: The
Minister's
Role

land, small for many years, exploded into a large church as a result of years of faithful praying.

Priestly leadership in the church calls for prayer to be an important part of the services, a part of the fixed schedule of the church. The ministers will be present at all of the prayer services they possibly can attend and will be the most fervent in prayer. They will preach on prayer. They will promote prayer groups in the church. They will lead special prayer initiatives from time to time.

Ministers will recognize the high premium that God places on prayer. They will be aware that when they pray, they share the company of two Intercessors: According to Romans 8:26, the Holy Spirit intercedes for us, and according to Romans 8:34, Christ, in His exalted position at the right hand of God, does so as well. Jesus dealt with the subject of prayer over and over in the Sermon on the Mount. Then there is that remarkable scene in the midst of the final judgments of humankind in which an angel with a golden censer "was given much incense to offer, with the prayers of all the saints, on the golden altar before the throne. The smoke of the incense, together with the prayers of the saints, went up before God from the angel's hand" (Rev. 8:3-4).

The minister's major concern in praying is that the Lord of the Harvest will send laborers into His field. Such prayer will produce genuine revival in the nation, in the community, in the church, in the home, in the minister's individual life. Genuine revival is an ethical imperative in view of the coming of the Lord. And every major transforming revival has come as the result of prayer.

Prayer not only produces miraculous change in circumstances and in the spiritual and ethical environment in which the servant of God practices ministry, but, more importantly, prayer changes the person of prayer. As ministers pray, they will find the determination and inspiration necessary for successful, ethical living. When ministers fail to pray and to minister under the anointing of the Spirit, ethical practice becomes a laborious, lackluster exercise.

Part 2

Chapter 6
Belief in the
Second
Coming: The
Minister's
Role

In the words of the Lord, directly quoted by His prophet Zechariah, it is "not by might nor by power, but by my Spirit" (4:6). In compliance with this formula, the sincere servant of the Lord succeeds in walking in wholeness in the sight of both God and humankind.

STUDY QUESTIONS

1. What are the chief biblical reasons for believing in the Second Coming?

2. What are the biblical reasons for not setting dates for Christ's return?[8]

3. What have been the results of date setting in the past?

4. What has been the effect of "kingdom now" and related postmillennial philosophies on the hope of the soon return of Jesus?

5. What are the scriptural grounds for the pretribulational view of the Rapture?

6. What signs point to the soon return of Christ?

7. How should the expectation of Christ's return affect our lives and ministry?

8. How can we encourage prayer in the light of Christ's return?

---

[8]See Stanley M. Horton, *Our Destiny* (Springfield, Mo.: Gospel Publishing House, 1996) for more information on this subject.

Chapter 7

Contemporary Moral Issues: The Minister's Stance

The best possible way to approach the major ethical and moral issues of the day is to examine them in the light of God's perspective on sound ethics. We have determined previously that the divine point of view is most clearly and concisely stated in Jeremiah 9:24, "I am the LORD; I act with steadfast love, justice, and righteousness in the earth; for in these things I delight, says the Lord" (NRS).

DIVORCE AND REMARRIAGE

The God who instituted marriage and the family must look with displeasure on the social scene in America today. The alarming rise in the divorce rate in recent years, coupled with the attendant family-relational problems, is cause for deep concern. Waldo Beach observes: "Another important sociological fact is a drastic change in the nature and function of the monogamous family unit in American society. On the surface, it appears sure and secure: 96% of Americans marry. But underneath that surface appearance, the institution itself is insecure. The most startling index of this is the rapid rise in the rate of divorce. In 1870, one of thirty-seven marriages ended in divorce."[1] Currently, "one out of eight marriages will

---

[1]Waldo Beach, *Christian Ethics in the Protestant Tradition* (Atlanta: John Knox Press, 1988), 54-55.

Part 2

Chapter 7
Contemporary
Moral Issues:
The Minister's
Stance

end in divorce."[2] This means that many "children of divorced couples will be brought up in single-parent households. Even when divorced persons marry someone else, as some 75% do, when children are involved, stepparenting brings difficult tensions and adjustments, for instance, in custody rulings. And for the children, the potential split of affections between a natural parent and a stepparent is often traumatic."[3]

The Scriptures are clear and firm on the subject: God hates divorce (Mal. 2:16). Let's consider a few of the problems related to divorce. Almost invariably divorce reflects alienated affections in one or more lives. Divorce flouts the marriage ordinance of God. Divorce destroys a home and the relationships that can make it a haven in a troubled world. Divorce produces bitterness, hatred, broken hearts, loneliness—a whole host of spiritual, social, and psychological problems that never go away. Divorce always warps the lives of the couple and is doubly damaging to any of their children.

Is remarriage the answer? In most cases it is the next step. However, remarriage does not guarantee happiness, no matter how carefully entered into. For example, a major problem can emerge concerning the fair treatment of any children and the respect of their rights as they are brought into the new marriage. Adjustment is also forced on the extended families of both parties.

Certainly some attention should also be given to Scripture on the subject. Jesus bluntly states in Matthew 5 that whoever marries a divorced person commits adultery along with the divorced person. The only exception occurs when one of the partners is involved in fornication.

Henlee H. Barnette supports a conservative position on the issue in this comment:

---

[2]Rayner Pike, "Survey Says True Divorce Rate Is 1 in 8, Not 1 in 2," Associated Press, 28 June 1987.

[3]Beach, *Christian Ethics in the Protestant Tradition*, 54–55.

Contention for remarriage after divorce can only be by an argument from silence and inference. Paul indicates that in the case of separation the parties must remain in that state or be reconciled (1 Cor. 7:10–11). He permits remarriage only in the case of widows, but holds that the new husband must be a Christian (1 Cor. 7:39). The so-called "Pauline privilege" allows for separation when the unbelieving partner chooses it (1 Cor. 7:15). The believer is "not bound." It is argued that this phrase, "is not bound," gives the individual the right to remarry, but this goes against the grain of Paul's total teaching on marriage.[4]

Part 2

**Chapter 7
Contemporary
Moral Issues:
The Minister's
Stance**

Others, however, disagree and find that sound principles of exegesis uphold the right to remarry under these circumstances, and that this does not go against the grain of Paul's total teaching.[5]

The official statement of the Assemblies of God approved by the General Presbytery reads:

The Greek word for "fornication" *(porneia)* may include especially repeated acts of adultery, but usually means habitual sexual immorality of any kind, both before and after marriage. (A *porne* was a prostitute.) . . .

Matthew 5:32 added an exceptive clause. . . . This shows that a husband who divorces a sexually immoral woman does not cause her to commit adultery, since she is already guilty of adultery.

Matthew 19:9 also carried this exceptive clause. . . . It should be emphasized that the exception has in view sexual immorality, not merely a single act. Wherever possible, sexually immoral practices should be dealt with through repentance, confession, forgiveness, and reconciliation, thus saving the marriage. . . .

Jesus did not change the nature of divorce as dissolving marriage. He simply threw out all excuses, reasons, or causes except "fornication" *(porneia,* habitual sexual immorality). However, in no case does He command divorce

---

[4]Henlee H. Barnette, *Introducing Christian Ethics* (Nashville: Broadman Press, 1961), 116.

[5]Assemblies of God, *Where We Stand* (Springfield, Mo.: Gospel Publishing House, 1990), 32.

Part 2

Chapter 7
Contemporary
Moral Issues:
The Minister's
Stance

or remarriage. They are merely permitted under this one
condition. . . .

[First] Corinthians 7:15 also contains an exception. . . .

If a believer is "not enslaved" when an unbelieving
spouse, unwilling to remain in the marriage, divorces him
(or her), he (or she) must be considered set free. Since it is
the unbelieving partner who determines to go and initiates
a divorce, the believer's freedom seems to be more than a
freedom to let him (or her) go, since he (or she) is going
anyway. The plain meaning seems to be that the believer is
set free to remarry if he or she so chooses.[6]

The minister who holds to the foregoing position
faces the problem of offending couples who want to
be married and one (or both) of them has a living ex-
spouse and the biblical exceptions were not present
in their case.

Issues in Christian Ethics raises the question of
whether the pastor can with integrity take his stand
as a faithful interpreter of the ethical standards of his
church or denomination. The following account is offered as one possible response: A couple came to a
pastor asking him to perform their marriage, despite
one of them having a living ex-spouse. The pastor
told them that the regulations of his church, which
he agreed with, would not permit him to. The couple
appreciated his honesty and his standing for what he
believed to be right. They added that they especially
appreciated him because he did not simply brush
them off. He took an hour and a half to converse
with them about their plans and hopes and stayed in
touch with them after their marriage (they went to a
justice of the peace). In the words of the couple, "He
would not perform our wedding ceremony, but he
showed us he cared and he prayed for God's blessing
upon us. He has been concerned about our life ever
since." The husband continued, "I would have lost respect for him if he had said: 'I can't marry you here

[6]Assemblies of God, *Where We Stand*, 29-32.

Part 2

Chapter 7
Contemporary
Moral Issues:
The Minister's
Stance

in the church, but if you will come over to my house I will do so.'"[7] While this little story has a happy ending, often couples are deeply offended by the inability of the minister who for ethical reasons is unable to perform their marriage ceremony. Nonetheless, such a misunderstanding is a small price to pay for an untroubled conscience.

Divorce has become so acceptable today that it has even altered the judgment of the Church. For example, viewpoints of some ministers on this issue have been changed by divorce having touched their immediate families. Such shifts in thinking are understandable, but if the Church and its leaders do not hold the standard of marital relationships high, who is left to do it? There is no other agency, no institution, no force, no class of people who can or will bear the standard of spiritual and ethical resolution on this issue. Troubled families need to know that the Church proclaims an all-powerful God who loves the family and who stands ready and able to reforge the marriage bond.

In *Pastor to Pastor* Erwin W. Lutzer challenges the Church on this subject: "Every Christian couple that divorces causes others to question the power of God. . . . And when we are willing to rationalize sensuality, selfishness, and greed, we are in effect admitting that Christ is unable to free us from sin. As a result, we have nothing to say to this generation."[8]

Of extreme importance at this point is the example set by a church's spiritual leaders. Having been divorced, even the most gifted minister cannot be respected and accepted as the pastoral role model for family relationships in the congregation. This is not to say that there are not many avenues of expression

[7]Paul D. Simmons, ed., *Issues in Christian Ethics* (Nashville: Broadman Press, 1980), 105–6.

[8]Erwin W. Lutzer, *Pastor to Pastor: Tackling Problems of the Pulpit* (Chicago: Moody Press, 1987), 105.

Part 2

Chapter 7
Contemporary
Moral Issues:
The Minister's
Stance

of ministry available to those who have been affected by this problem.

The minister is the one who should lead the church in developing an appropriate attitude toward divorce. First, a mission of the minister and the congregation must be to support the couple in a troubled marriage, making an all-out effort to hold it together. Norman L. Geisler counsels: "The biblical rule is not: 'Divorce is always wrong.' The rule is this: 'A permanent, abiding, and unique relation is always right.' In other words, the Scriptures are concerned with the *permanence* of marriage. The rule is to keep a unique love relation going at all costs as long as it does not mean the perpetuation of an evil or lesser good in favor of a greater good."[9]

Only when both parties in a troubled marriage have given up should divorce be considered, in order to avoid a greater evil.

On occasion a divorced person will turn to the pastor for counsel when the divorce was granted without just cause. Lane A. Scott advises: "In such cases regard for God's call to permanence in marriage makes it appropriate for the pastor to consider with his or her counselee the broken marriage. Is there a possibility of reconciliation even though divorce has occurred? If so, every means ought to be used to effect that end before remarriage takes place."[10]

Scott further insists that whatever course the divorced person chooses to pursue, he or she needs to be faced with the wrong that caused the breakup of the marriage.

Although the minister will lead the church to oppose divorce, its victims are another matter. Divorce can be forgiven, and the church must lead the way in

---

[9]Norman L. Geisler, *Ethics: Alternatives and Issues* (Grand Rapids: Baker Book House, 1989), 207.

[10]Leon O. Hynson, Lane A. Scott, eds., *Christian Ethics: An Inquiry into Christian Ethics from a Biblical Theological Perspective* (Anderson, Ind.: Warner Press, 1983), 197.

expressing that forgiveness. The church will show love and acceptance of those whose lives have been broken by divorce. The pastor by example will teach the congregation to respect the ministries and service offered to the kingdom of God by those gifted individuals who may have had marital difficulties. However, for the sake of the example set before the young people of the church, it will be understood that the office of elder or pastor cannot be filled by a person who is remarried and has a living former spouse (1 Tim. 3:2,5).

Part 2

**Chapter 7
Contemporary
Moral Issues:
The Minister's
Stance**

ABORTION

Abortion presents a serious ethical challenge to ministers; they must be careful that they glorify God as they oppose this practice and express themselves, especially when they encounter believers who do not share their point of view. One reason most ministers reject abortion is suggested by Philip Hughes in *Christian Ethics in Secular Society:* "Throughout the Bible there is no suggestion that abortion is an option for women who are pregnant; indeed, abortion is so foreign to the biblical perspective that it is not even mentioned."[11] Hughes goes on to report the staggering increase in the number of abortions worldwide and the legalizing and approving of this practice by the government of the United States. Then he states the primary reason for the unacceptability of abortion to the Christian: "Even if the question of whether or not an unborn fetus is a viable person should continue to be debated until doomsday, the indisputable fact remains that it is *human* life—not brutish life, but life that is being formed in the image of its Creator."[12]

---

[11]Philip Edgcumbe Hughes, *Christian Ethics in Secular Society* (Grand Rapids: Baker Book House, 1983), 176.
[12]Ibid.

Part 2

Chapter 7
Contemporary
Moral Issues:
The Minister's
Stance

Most Christians, especially evangelical Christians, consider abortion wrong as a means of birth control. The Scriptures make it clear that the taking of life is wrong. That an unborn child, even in the early stages of fetal development, has distinctly human characteristics has been demonstrated by sonograms indicating that the fetus can feel pain.[13] The ethical and moral issues involved in this procedure have been raised again and again by women who have suffered psychological and spiritual trauma from the haunting memory of the experience.

The Scriptures attest that God views the unborn child in the womb as His handiwork and has at times endowed such a child with spiritual blessings before he or she has come into the world. The Psalmist sings these words to his Creator: "You created my inmost being; you knit me together in my mother's womb. . . . My frame was not hidden from you when I was made in the secret place. When I was woven together in the depths of the earth, your eyes saw my unformed body" (Ps. 139:13,15-16). The prophet records God's message to him in these words: "Before I formed you in the womb I knew you, before you were born I set you apart; I appointed you as a prophet to the nations" (Jer. 1:5). Then there is the remarkable scene in Luke 1:41 in which Mary greets Elizabeth, who was in her sixth month of pregnancy: "When Elizabeth heard Mary's greeting, the baby leaped in her womb, and Elizabeth was filled with the Holy Spirit." Of course, it had already been predicted of John the Baptist, the leaping babe, "he will be filled with the Holy Spirit, even from his mother's womb" (Luke 1:15, RSV).

Understandably, attitudes toward abortion vary. While marveling at human birth, many conscientious

---

[13]John T. Noonan, "The Experience of Pain by the Unborn," in *New Perspectives on Human Abortion*, ed. Thomas W. Hilgers, Dennis J. Horen, and David Mull (Frederick, Md.: Aletheia Books, 1981), 205-16.

Christians struggle with pregnancies that may result from rape or incest or may threaten the life of the mother. The parents of an innocent daughter raped by a diseased criminal will feel differently from the couple demonstrating outside an abortion clinic, hoping to discourage a professional woman whose career was interrupted by her pregnancy.

Godly ethics call for compassion and understanding for our fellow Christians when our views differ on this volatile subject. The minister and the church need to take a strong stand on the abortion issue but must be cautious when engaging in proactive politics. Often pro-lifers become so absorbed in their position that they forget to represent the character of Christ. Instead, some have shown hatred, in some cases even leading to murder. Burning clinics or harming those involved in abortion is out of the question for believers. Political leaders have been labeled "murderers" by those who detest any member of a political party that may espouse a contrary view on the subject. The Church's position on pro-life has been sadly weakened as a result of its identifying with or refusing to disassociate itself from radical opponents of abortion.

Mudslinging and dart throwing seldom solve problems, particularly spiritual ones. Godly ethics call for God-approved weapons: "Though we live in the world, we do not wage war as the world does. The weapons we fight with are not the weapons of the world. On the contrary, they have divine power to demolish strongholds" (2 Cor. 10:3–4). "Our struggle is not against flesh and blood, but against the rulers, against the authorities, against the powers of this dark world and against the spiritual forces of evil in the heavenly realms" (Eph. 6:12).

The ethical solution to the problem is for the Church to assume responsibility for the spiritual decline in America that has led to this tragic situation. Erwin W. Lutzer comments: "[W]e [Christians] cannot escape the consequences of killing four thousand unborn babies every day. It's popular to blame the Su-

Part 2

Chapter 7
Contemporary
Moral Issues:
The Minister's
Stance

Part 2

Chapter 7
Contemporary
Moral Issues:
The Minister's
Stance

preme Court, the humanists, and the radical feminists. To be sure they have contributed to the abortion holocaust. But if God is using them to judge us, might not the responsibility more properly be laid at the feet of those who know the living God but who have failed to influence society?"[14]

Along with being armed to do spiritual battle, the Church must manifest the steadfast love integral to God's standard of conduct, regardless of circumstances. The Church must offer practical alternatives for the girls caught in this dilemma and show a loving, forgiving spirit to the families that have been traumatized by it.

EUTHANASIA

The legalization of abortion in the United States created demand for the legalization of active euthanasia (assisted suicide) for the extremely ill or the elderly. As a result of highly publicized cases involving the lingering of comatose patients and the advocacy by laypersons and physicians of what is best described as "mercy killing," the general public is manifesting a remarkable interest in and acceptance of euthanasia. Two important cases were those of Karen Ann Quinlan and Nancy Cruzan. Quinlan lapsed into an irreversible coma in 1975, whereupon her parents asked that she be removed from the respirator. This resulted in the 1976 landmark case in which the New Jersey Supreme Court permitted the Quinlans to disconnect the respirator. Although their daughter breathed on her own and lived another nine years, her case was the first in which a court approved passive euthanasia. In 1983 a car accident left Nancy Cruzan in an irreversible coma. She was placed on a feeding tube that provided hydration and nutrition. A court action in 1990 permitted the family to remove

---

[14]Lutzer, *Pastor to Pastor*, 103.

the feeding tube, after which she died.[15] Both cases could be labeled passive euthanasia with few ethical implications, but they set the stage for crusaders like Derek Humphry, who illegally assisted his wife's death, to come forward with his book, *Final Exit,* advocating assisted suicide. The book sold an astonishing five hundred thousand copies within one year of publication.[16]

Part 2

Chapter 7
Contemporary
Moral Issues:
The Minister's
Stance

Advocacy of euthanasia has been so successful that a 1993 national public opinion poll indicated that 73 percent of Americans support physician-assisted suicide.[17] Jack Kevorkian, a medical doctor, continues to practice and promote active euthanasia despite legal challenges.

Christian physicians, however, have led the opposition to all euthanasia. Dr. C. Everett Koop, former surgeon general of the United States, laid out the battle lines as early as 1976, stating: "In any discussion of euthanasia an understanding of terminology is essential. The deliberate killing of one human being by another, no matter what the motivation might be, is murder."[18] Uncompromising objection to physician-aided suicide continues to be voiced by such dedicated physicians as Ronald Otremba, who states that active euthanasia is never morally justified. "First, there is the principle that life itself is intrinsically valuable. This value is independent of one's physical or mental state of health. It is based on the principle that God is the sole Creator of life and has sovereign authority over life and death."[19]

---

[15]Carol Wekesser, ed. *Euthanasia: Opposing Viewpoints* (San Diego: Greenhaven Press, 1995), 13.

[16]See Derek Humphry, *Dying with Dignity: Understanding Euthanasia* (New York: Carol Publishing Group, 1992), 28.

[17]Wekesser, *Euthanasia,* 14.

[18]Robert N. Baird and Stuart E. Rosenbaum, eds. *Euthanasia: Moral Issues* (Buffalo, N.Y.: Prometheus Books, 1989), 69.

[19]Ronald Otremba, "Euthanasia Is Unethical," in Wekesser, *Euthanasia,* 22.

Part 2

Chapter 7
Contemporary
Moral Issues:
The Minister's
Stance

What considerations should form the basis of the minister's opposition to active euthanasia?

1. Improved pain control by medical science has enhanced the quality of life until there is no excuse for advocating premature death.

2. If the sick or afflicted person is not a Christian, it would be unthinkable to plunge that person into eternity without Christ or hope in the hereafter.

3. God is the giver of life. When it is to cease should be His decision.

4. Christians believe in the supernatural. There have been many miraculous recoveries of terminal cases—involving both believers and unbelievers.

5. Advocacy of euthanasia is primarily a non-Christian stance. Most Protestant denominations as well as Roman Catholicism, Eastern Orthodoxy, and Orthodox Judaism oppose euthanasia.[20]

SEXUAL PROMISCUITY

Another evidence of the downward spiral of our nation's ethics and morality is sexual promiscuity. Unmarried couples cohabiting as husband and wife besmirch the moral standards of the community, defy God's laws, and mock the sacredness of the marriage union.

National surveys reveal an alarming degree of sexual activity among children, in many cases not yet in their teens. The churches and ministers of the land are to be commended for their practice of good ethics when they instruct our children and encourage vows of sexual abstinence until marriage.

Too many national leaders, often elected officials, openly engage in adulterous relationships. In spite of the high degree of publicity these scandalous situa-

---

[20]For the Assemblies of God viewpoint see "The Assemblies of God Perspectives: Contemporary Issues, Social, Medical, Political" (Springfield, Mo.: Assemblies of God Office of Public Relations, 1995), 44–47.

tions receive, the public often seems uncritical and uncaring.

Part 2

Chapter 7
Contemporary
Moral Issues:
The Minister's
Stance

Widely known sports figures boast of their sexual indiscretions and seem to be admired all the more by their followers. There have even been instances where ministers of the gospel have laid biblical ethics aside and have banded together in defense of popular sports personalities, even to declaring their prosecution to be evidence of racial bias.

The Church must hang its head in shame that even high-profile religious figures have succumbed to the trend of the times. Although only a small percentage of ministers experience moral failure, when even one fails, the credibility of the Church as a bulwark of ethics suffers.

On the positive side, we can rejoice that thousands of youths are pure, largely through the teaching and practice of the Church. As Waldo Beach points out, "As a counteroffensive against the exponential rate of teenage sexual activity and teenage pregnancy, one of the most important things a church can do in its educational program . . . is to provide sex education, not just in the physiological facts, but more important in the morality and spirituality of sex, to convey to youth the Christian normative understanding of the relationship of sex and love in responsibility."[21]

Yet running counter to such influence is the sociopolitical approach: the advocacy of "safe sex" instead of abstinence. Such an attitude calls for sounding the note that apart from divine power young people have little hope of preserving their purity.

Caring ministers will teach the beautiful truth of sex within marriage. They will love and protect their young people by prayer, by godly example, by precept. They will reach out to those caught in the snare of immorality as Christ did to the woman taken in adultery. They will not stand ready to condemn but

---

[21]Beach, *Christian Ethics in the Protestant Tradition*, 61.

Part 2

Chapter 7
Contemporary
Moral Issues:
The Minister's
Stance

rather to lead the sinner to forgiveness, wholeness, and acceptance in Christ's church.

PORNOGRAPHY

Pornography is not only closely linked to immorality, but also one of its more diabolical manifestations. The minister must recognize the severity of this problem and the depravity and greed of those responsible for its growth. In *Christian Ethics in Secular Society,* Philip Hughes is struck by the timeless appraisal offered by the apostle Paul:

A more appropriate description of the contemporary purveyors of pornography and perversion would be difficult to come by than that given by the apostle when he writes of persons who are "filled with all manner of wickedness, evil, covetousness, malice," who are "full of envy, murder, strife, deceit, malignancy," and who are "gossips, slanderers, haters of God, insolent, haughty, boastful, inventors of evil, disobedient to parents, foolish, faithless, heartless, ruthless." He adds, in a manner that with incisive accuracy fits those engaged in this multibillion-dollar business, that "though they know God's decree that those who do such things deserve to die, they not only do them but approve those who practice them" (Rom. 1:29-32).[22]

The scriptural description is accurate. The sale of pornographic material is often related to organized crime in the cities. Such material has become one of the more lucrative forms of evil in the nation. There are numerous accounts of men on death row for murder and rape who have acknowledged that their lurid careers began with pornography.

A leading evangelist who fell into immorality later admitted that he had become addicted to pornography as a child. I have known several ministers who have become hooked on pornography and have had to struggle for months to be freed by the power of

---

[22]Hughes, *Christian Ethics in Secular Society,* 175.

Immorality in Films and Television   **155**

Part 2

**Chapter 7
Contemporary
Moral Issues:
The Minister's
Stance**

God. A recent report in a religious periodical high-lighted the immensity of this problem: A government committee had been established to review porno-graphic materials in order to report to a government agency; several members of the committee them-selves got hooked on the material. Despite pornogra-phy's highly addictive quality, our legislatures and courts permit it to survive. Philip Hughes observes: "In the United States one of the most bizarre develop-ments is the now customary appeal to the first amendment of the Constitution as a hallowed charter which guarantees the freedom to publish without control, in print and on film, any and every kind of unseemliness. No less shocking is the measure of ac-ceptance with which this appeal has met. How rest-less must the spirits of the founding fathers be as the freedom of religion they proclaimed is manipulated for the expulsion of Christianity."[23]

The Church and its godly leaders offer the only hope for success in combating this evil. Entire cities, Cincinnati, Ohio, for example, have been freed of this vice through the leadership of ethically minded minis-ters of the gospel.[24] Along with opposition to the evil, ministers must take the ethical stand on the sub-ject before their people. They will recognize the dan-ger. They will warn the youth. They will forewarn the entire church that no child of God needs ever to acquire the type of knowledge that corrupts. They will give the same sound advice to young people that Paul gave to Timothy: "Keep yourself pure" (1 Tim. 5:22).

IMMORALITY IN FILMS AND TELEVISION

Raw pornography is now available in movie the-aters, at video shops, and on television. Particularly

---

[23]Ibid., 170.
[24]Jerry R. Kirk, *The Mind Polluters* (Nashville: Thomas Nelson & Sons, 1985), 187–91.

Part 2

Chapter 7
Contemporary
Moral Issues:
The Minister's
Stance

disturbing is the availability of this material to children and young people.

As the moral sensitivity of our society becomes jaded, for one to object to promiscuous shows—even in Christian circles—is considered narrow and old-fashioned. Such entertainment has no redeeming or artistic value. Even when a wholesome book is being made into a film, sex scenes are introduced merely to obtain an R rating so the film will attract a wider audience.

Here again, spiritual leaders of the church must take a stand. First, by good example, they will not be guilty of attending a theater to view salacious material and will not allow it on their home screens, whether they have children or not. (A recent published report indicated that the TV-watching habits of Christians are the same as non-Christians, if not worse.)

Concerned ministers will promote wholesome programs to their people, especially in view of the decreasing availability of good programs. They will participate in God-honoring protests against the pathetic standards of the film industry. They will promote desirable activities as an alternative to unwholesome entertainment for their young people and the families of the church. They will sponsor religious films and programs with high ethical and moral values.

HOMOSEXUALITY

"Sodom and Gomorrah and the surrounding towns gave themselves up to sexual immorality and perversion. They serve as an example of those who suffer the punishment of eternal fire" (Jude 7). The sin of Sodom has come out of the closet. The perpetrators have been so successful at political and social intimidation that the lawmakers and courts of our land have created an unbelievable situation. Ninety-nine percent of the country is helpless to cope with the flagrant sin and lifestyle of the remaining one per-

Part 2

**Chapter 7
Contemporary
Moral Issues:
The Minister's
Stance**

cent, the actual count of the practicing homosexuals in the country.[25]

If there is any sin that God hates passionately, this is it. The Old Testament and the New Testament are replete with judgment, damnation, and punishment for the sin of homosexuality. Here are some examples: Genesis 19:4-24, the sordid saga of the Sodomites and their destruction is told; Leviticus 18:22, the Law labels homosexuality as an "abomination" (RSV); Deuteronomy 23:17, male prostitutes are excluded from Israel; 1 Kings 15:12, Asa removes the Sodomites from out of the land; Isaiah 3:9, the sin of Sodom is exposed; Romans 1:24-32, men burning with homosexual lust are given over to a depraved mind; 1 Corinthians 6:9, male prostitutes and homosexual offenders will not inherit the kingdom of God. Conclusion: The proper attitude for the minister toward this sin is to hate it as God hates it.

The spread of AIDS demonstrates obviously that the sin of homosexuality has severe consequences; yet its spread goes unchecked by a befuddled government. Instead, the government has shown its compliance by permitting lewd parades and demonstrations, by permitting the election of homosexuals to office, by allowing children to be taught that homosexuality is merely an alternate lifestyle. Our youth are pressured to consider as an option the very practice for which God destroyed the twin cities of the plain centuries ago.

He looks upon it no more lightly today. Despite the clear teaching of the Scriptures on the nature of the sin of Sodom, there are those who profess to be students of the Scripture who have described this sin as inhospitality.

During my research for this book, I stumbled onto this theological illusion. In a conversation in the lunchroom adjacent to the Library of Congress, I was

---

[25]George Grant and Mark H. Horne, *Legislating Immorality* (Chicago: Moody Press, 1993), 113.

Part 2

Chapter 7
Contemporary
Moral Issues:
The Minister's
Stance

witnessing to a young man who had joined me at the table. When the subject of God's judgment on Sodom came up, he insisted that Sodom's sin was merely treating strangers inhospitably and seemed offended by the scriptural definition of the problem. His look of panic, almost horror, when I offered to pray with him still haunts me. Not until later in the afternoon did I learn that it was the day for a homosexual rally in Washington, D.C., and that I had unknowingly been talking to one of the participants. (It is my prayer that he will someday find God and be delivered from his sin.)

Despite years of working with restoration programs for fallen ministers, I know of no cases where a minister who had fallen into this sin was able to recover. Although the fallen minister can be restored, God himself cannot forgive and absolve sin against the will of the sinner.

What should be the attitude of ministers toward this problem? They will love the sinner but hate the sin. They will offer God's redemption and hope, for people bound by this sin have found deliverance and enjoyed complete freedom for the rest of their lives (see 1 Cor. 6:9–11).

The imperative for ministers in dealing with this aberrant lifestyle is to be able to counteract the training in some public school systems and to offset the influence of social groups contaminated by this moral blight. Ministers will insist that no one is born a homosexual; it is a learned aberration. They will work with the parents of children who tend toward an improper relationship with members of their own sex. Ministers will be alert for family relationships of a loving but domineering mother who strongly influences her child, and especially if it includes a father who is extremely passive or perhaps abusive. Often ministers will not be able to modify such circumstances, but with the help of the Lord, they can still offer guidance and assistance.

CHILD ABUSE

Part 2

**Chapter 7
Contemporary
Moral Issues:
The Minister's
Stance**

Child abuse is growing in our society, as is its publicity. Recalling such abuse by means of psychological induction and hypnosis seems almost a fad among adults, casting doubt on the dimensions of the problem. Nevertheless, child abuse is real and it is serious. Furthermore, one of its frequent dimensions is sexual abuse—perpetrated by a parent, a trusted relative, or a friend of the family.

Apart from a miracle of God, pedophilia appears to be untreatable, largely because of the disposition of the heart of the abuser. Pedophiles usually strike again and again and often go undetected for years.

The church has begun to be directly affected as pedophiles volunteer as children's workers. They find the church to be both trusting and eager for volunteer help, for children in the church are always in need of supervision, particularly with the proliferation of single-parent families. Pedophiles have even become trusted leaders in the church and are ultimately responsible for scarring the lives of children over a period of years before being found out.

Ministers will carefully guard the children in their congregations from these wolves in sheep's clothing. They must be doubly careful not to use new, unfamiliar persons as children's workers. They will set up a screening process, using forms available from denominational administrative offices and insurance companies. Before the problem ever surfaces they will be certain to insure the church (including its leaders) against liability. Lawsuits resulting from the incidence of pedophilia are being successfully brought against churches and can easily ruin a church financially, to say nothing of destroying its reputation in the community. It is good economics as well as good ethics to make certain this situation never occurs in the local church.

If ministers become aware of a problem in the church, they must respond ethically. No matter how

Part 2

Chapter 7
Contemporary
Moral Issues:
The Minister's
Stance

painful it may be, they must report the offender. It must be done for the minister's integrity, for the sake of the child and the parents, and for the protection of the church. It has been statistically proven that to show false mercy to a pedophile is to set the stage for his next sinful act.[26]

CRIME AND PUNISHMENT

Our national crime rate rises; prisons fill; more and more of the lives and homes of our parishioners are affected by crime. Not only so, it is astounding to note that crime has crept into the sanctuary. William W. Rankin reports, "Fraudulent and self-serving practices are not unique to those few TV evangelists who recently have been publicly disgraced. Objective evidence suggests, moreover, that 'ecclesiastical crime' is a serious and widespread phenomenon. One cannot say for sure that the perpetrators of ecclesiastical crime are clergy, of course. One *can* reasonably suppose, though, that diligence on the part of clergy could significantly reduce the magnitude of such crime."[27]

Rankin goes on to cite some alarming statistics to support his allegation: skimming, pilfering, or embezzlement amounted to $300,00 worldwide in 1900, rose to $5 million in 1970, climbed to $30 million in 1980, and, unbelievably, topped $650 million by 1988. It is expected that with the aid of computers and clever programming, crime in the church will account for $2 trillion in losses by the year 2000. He then acknowledges that "one does not, of course, encourage clergy or congregational lay leaders to become police investigators," but, he adds, "[w]e have

---

[26]Benjamin Schlesinger, *Sexual Abuse of Children* (Toronto: University of Toronto Press, 1982), 127, 165.

[27]William W. Rankin, *Confidentiality and Clergy: Churches, Ethics, and the Law* (Harrisburg, Pa.: Morehouse Publishing, 1990), 5-6.

Part 2

**Chapter 7
Contemporary
Moral Issues:
The Minister's
Stance**

to be *willing* to operate at the highest levels of institutional and professional stewardship."[28]

Nationally, crime goes unchecked, fueled by drugs and alcohol. Dealing with crime presents a serious ethical problem for the state. Should the state build more prisons? Shorten sentences? Pass tougher laws? Hire more enforcement officers? As the cost of crime soars, so does the cost of punishment.

Should the death penalty be put into practice? The reinstitution of capital punishment is becoming a decided trend in many of our states. Laws are being reenacted to permit the death penalty, and new laws are being drafted to mandate its use.

Should the state empower judges to deal more harshly with violators of the law, to answer the charge of coddling criminals? Should the emphasis be shifted from guarding the criminal's rights to protecting the citizen's rights? Can stronger measures be enacted against drug trafficking before it corrupts the entire nation? The proper responses to these questions will be forthcoming only as Christians pray earnestly for those in authority.

This national crisis raises ethical considerations for ministers and the Church. We must search the Scriptures for God's view of crime and its perpetrators. The Church will love sinners but fight their sin. The Church will recognize that the death penalty was ordained of God and provides the only just way to deal with murder (Rom. 13:4). The Church will engage in jail ministry and rehabilitation programs, at the same time maintaining that only Christ can transform the sinful human heart.

The minister and the church will teach the children and adults alike to love and respect those in authority: schoolteachers and principals, police and judges, military personnel and political leaders. Even when disappointed by the actions of those in authori-

---

[28]Ibid., 6.

Part 2

Chapter 7
Contemporary
Moral Issues:
The Minister's
Stance

ty, we must demonstrate as well as instruct that the office and its related authority are to be honored.

RACIAL PROBLEMS

Since Noah's sons became adults the world has been plagued with racial problems. The very fact of differences in language, customs, and color tends to breed mistrust or fear of one another. For generations in America the racial problems existed primarily between blacks and whites. Periodically, other racial groups have suffered from prejudice, as in the displacement of American Indians and the internment of Japanese-Americans during World War II. However, today, with the influx of large ethnic groups, including Koreans, Latin Americans, Africans, and Middle Easterners, racial unrest crops up between many groups, especially in large cities. Integration into American society is no longer a simple matter for such distinct groups, if it ever has been, and some question whether America remains the "melting pot" of nations.

There is an unfortunate trend back toward the "separate but equal" doctrine that adversely affected school systems and the use of community facilities in the South. The national problems of riots, gang wars, drug wars, armed robbery, and rape are often predicated on racial hatred. Government seems ineffective in curbing racial foment and criminal activity. Only God can remedy some situations.

The minister of sound ethics will practice and preach love for people regardless of their color or creed. He or she will lead the church in opening its doors and arms to persons of all races. It is encouraging to note that currently across the nation, major black Pentecostal denominations and their white counterparts are moving toward a unity and fellowship not known since the Azusa Street revival in Los Angeles.

Though raised in the South and as a youth having

Part 2

**Chapter 7
Contemporary
Moral Issues:
The Minister's
Stance**

found rapport with blacks difficult under some circumstances, I, along with most Spirit-filled believers, have come to love, respect, and appreciate black Christians as well as those of other races. The beautiful bond of the Spirit makes us one.

The need of our great nation, as well as the rest of the world, is revival. No nation or community can achieve lofty ethical or moral goals apart from the transformation that comes at Calvary. At the foot of the cross the vilest of sinners and the noblest of saints are able to subscribe together to God's code of ethics, "steadfast love, justice, and righteousness" (Jer. 9:24, NRS).

STUDY QUESTIONS

1. What can ministers do to help stop the deterioration of the family in America?

2. What are the reasons that God hates divorce?

3. What are the biblical exceptions to Jesus' statement that remarriage after divorce constitutes adultery?

4. How should ministers deal with people who are divorced and remarried when they apply for membership in the church?

5. In what ways should Christians take a stand against abortion?

6. What can the church do to encourage chastity before marriage?

7. What can the church do about the problems of pornography and homosexuality that have become so open today?

8. Why and how should your church be involved in crime prevention and jail/prison ministries?

9. What can ministers do to decrease the racial tensions that still exist today?

Part 3

Ethics in Practical Ministry

Part 3: Ethics in Practical Ministry

Chapter 8

The Minister and the Congregation: Providing Spiritual Leadership

Chapter 9

Ministers and Their Peers: Maintaining Professional Relationships

Chapter 10

The Minister and Money: Filthy Lucre in Clean Hands

Chapter 11

The Minister and Sex: Joy or Jeopardy?

Chapter 12

The Minister and Moral Failure: Finding Restoration through Grace

Chapter 13

The Minister and Influence: Dealing with Power and Authority

Chapter 14

The Minister and Personhood: Being Authentic

Chapter 8

The Minister and the Congregation: Providing Spiritual Leadership

The kind of relationship pastors enjoy with their parishioners is often governed by their reasons for becoming a pastor in the first place. If they accept churches because the salaries are attractive and the benefits appealing, more than likely they will serve the church and relate to the people on the basis of the monetary value they place on their services. Ministerial ethics influenced by the dollar result in the lowest level of integrity. When the time comes for offering correction or the mildest form of discipline, they will shirk such responsibility for economic reasons. The focus of ministry will not be unselfish devotion to godly leadership. The major concern will be, *How will this decision affect my next paycheck or the proposed salary raise for next year?*

A minister I worked with years ago, a highly respected pastor, came to a point in his ministry when he felt he should make a pastoral change. He had successfully pioneered a church and had supplemented his income with a good paying job. When he was interviewed by the board of the church he felt called to, the amount of salary being offered came into question. He exerted pressure on the board, and they conceded that more salary should be offered even though it was a small church with limited income. Before long he began assuming a dictatorial attitude toward the board and the church. There were no strong members on the board or members of the church who felt they could do anything about the

Part 3

Chapter 8
The Minister
and the
Congregation:
Providing
Spiritual
Leadership

problem. Consequently, the pastor maintained his position for years, the church grew progressively unhappy, and spiritual atrophy set in. The pastor finally resigned the church, but not before it had been reduced to a fraction of its former strength. The pastor's unethical motive for assuming the leadership of the church in the first place set the stage for his unsuccessful tenure.

If a minister is invited to pastor a church that does not offer adequate support, generally two choices are available: (1) to accept the church in good faith that the board will permit earning outside income to supplement salary, believing that God will soon bring growth and economic strength to the church to enable it to provide adequate pastoral support, or (2) simply to withdraw as a candidate for the pastorate, which is preferable to driving a hard bargain.

Incidentally, a tidy, ethical means of addressing such a problem is for the resigning pastor, who has earned the respect and love of the church, to insist that the incoming pastor be given a higher salary. Taking just such a course proved to be one of the most fulfilling experiences in my own ministry. I had felt for several years, considering my church's size and income, that it was not providing the proper salary. The Lord had given me an excellent relationship with the board, so I talked to them, heart to heart, just weeks before it was my time to leave and encouraged them to increase the housing allowance and salary for my successor. I pointed out that in failing to do so they would be limiting their candidates to those ministers who could afford to accept the position without having to be financially dependent on its salary. The board, to their credit, offered a substantial increase to the next pastor. As a result, I was able to maintain the love and respect of the church I was leaving, the incoming pastor and his family were blessed financially, and the good relationship between two good friends in the ministry became even better. Best of all, the new pastor could enjoy the respect of his people for not having had to stoop to questionable ethics to be assured of adequate financial provisions for his family.

Part 3

**Chapter 8
The Minister
and the
Congregation:
Providing
Spiritual
Leadership**

LEADER OR FACILITATOR?

Not only does the pastor's attitude toward money determine how he or she will relate to the congregation, but the pastor's philosophy of ministry plays an important part as well. Some pastors prefer that their boards set the church's goals for spiritual advancement as well as for its financial and numerical growth. Such ministers unwittingly become mere facilitators, pleased to allow others to set the boundaries for ministry while they oil the wheels in the fond hope that the operation will run smoothly though it lacks clear direction. Faith shrivels; initiative dies. Lack of innovation destroys the enthusiasm of the people. The pastor is no longer in charge.

But let the pastor come with a true shepherd's heart. The shepherd leads the sheep and discerns the direction the church should take. Without this assurance of a certain course of action, pastors will flounder. You may have seen one of the clever caps on the novelty market. It has two bills pointing at right angles. The message on the cap is "I'm their leader—which way did they go?" Ministers who lose their bearings in leading the church may soon lose their position. Congregations have ways of removing such pastors. Karen Lebacqz writes, "The specifics of removal differ, of course, from denomination to denomination. Ministers are protected better under some forms of polity than under others. Nonetheless, in most denominations, congregations have ways of removing problematic clergy. Far from being in control, therefore, there is a sense in which ministers are at the mercy of their clientele. They are not so much powerful as vulnerable."[1]

---

[1]Karen Lebacqz, *Professional Ethics: Power and Paradox* (Nashville: Abingdon Press, 1985), 141-142.

Part 3

Chapter 8
The Minister
and the
Congregation:
Providing
Spiritual
Leadership

By contrast, true shepherds will confidently pursue the will of God as leaders of the flock and will be the first to experience what they trust their sheep will ultimately experience. They will take spiritual initiatives and pursue directions of ministry from the perspective of high ethical leadership. They will face challenges to the development of the church's spiritual values. They will be aware that their leadership will amount to nothing if they have no followers. They will conduct themselves so ethically and loyally in relating to their flock that members will lovingly choose the path of the pastor's leading. Like any good shepherd, they will be willing to put their lives on the line for the sheep. The sheep will sense the sincerity of the pastor's motivation; they will follow without hesitation; they will be loyal to his direction; they will share the joy of the spiritual momentum that pastoral leadership helps produce.

Should the pastor move into a situation where the board has been dominant in the leadership of the church, establishing godly pastoral leadership will be important. Except in the case of strongly entrenched members who feel their position in the church is being threatened, invariably a good board will respond favorably to strong leadership that is obviously anointed of God. But even in the most difficult cases, ministers must make it clear that they are solidly in place for the long haul. Ethically sound leadership will prevail. The leadership style of the pastor will need to be dictated by the admonition Paul gave to the Corinthian church: "Follow my example, as I follow the example of Christ" (1 Cor. 11:1). With a formula like this in hand, the pastor will be taking the church in a direction not of the pastor's choosing, but that of Christ's, the eternal Head of the Church.

THE POWER OF ETHICAL EXAMPLE

Pastors may sermonize on glowing themes of moral and ethical conduct, righteous living, and integrity, but if they are not setting an ethical example before their people, such preaching will be in vain. Nobody will be impressed. We all know of cases where pastors have undercut their own ministry by unacceptable ethics. For example, pastors may purchase personal items and use the church's tax–exempt status to their advantage. They may encourage parents in the church to designate their own children's tuition as charitable contributions to a religious institution. Pastors may fail to remit to the church treasury those contributions handed to them that would have otherwise been designated to the church's support. In some instances, pastors may receive large amounts of income from the church and label it "a gift" for income tax purposes when they know it is part of their salary. This careless handling and designation of funds becomes a serious ethics problem. When members of the church learn of such tactics, there will be one of two reactions. Either they will completely distrust the pastor or they will follow his unethical example because he is the leader of the church. Either reaction is tragic.

Pastors are in a position to raise the ethical, moral, and spiritual level of the entire congregation simply by the power of their example. By God's grace, they will not succumb to the temptation to make shady business deals, to misrepresent the truth, to engage in shameful conduct (public or private). Blessed is the leader who recognizes that every action sets an example for others. How fulfilling it is when this example brings glory and honor to the God of unchanging ethics.

Should the Holy Spirit in His gentle way remind us that our ethical posture is not glorifying God, let us not resolve halfheartedly to do better; the secret of ethical transformation is complete contrition. As Erwin W. Lutzer states it: "I've found that incomplete repentance often leads to resentment against God The logic is obvious: If He exists for my benefit, w happens when my 'hunger for glory' remains unsat

Part 3

Chapter 8
The Minister
and the
Congregation:
Providing
Spiritual
Leadership

Part 3

Chapter 8
The Minister
and the
Congregation:
Providing
Spiritual
Leadership

fied? Humans are notorious for insisting on their 'rights.' If we don't see ourselves as undeserving sinners, we'll be upset when God doesn't do what we think He ought. . . . Someone has said that the marks of a strong church are wet eyes, bent knees, and a broken heart."[2]

LOVE, RESPECT, OR BOTH?

Everyone wants to be loved, pastors being no exception. What is more rewarding and heartwarming than to be loved by an entire congregation, to be held close to their hearts, next to God and the beloved members of their immediate families? But as important as it may be for the pastor to be loved, it is far more important to be respected. If the pastor must sacrifice one or the other, he or she must at all costs maintain the parishioners' respect. Pastors should never be guilty of selling self-respect for mere affection. When pastors merit the respect of the people, but have not yet received their love, they will ultimately win their hearts by continuing to manifest godly love toward them. On the other hand, if pastors have gotten their love, but their ethics do not merit respect, they will not likely change the situation. True, the people's love for their pastor will cover a "multitude of sins" (James 5:20), but without producing the esteem all ministers of God must have if they are to be effective leaders.

It is only right that pastors be expected to have the highest ethical standard. It is not enough to be respected as a brother or sister in Christ; pastors must be examples, having set their hearts "on things above" (Col. 3:1).

I think of a young pastor who stooped to earn the love of a board member and his family by sharing intimate details of his life, including financial problems

---

[2]Erwin W. Lutzer, *Pastor to Pastor: Tackling Problems of the Pulpit* (Chicago: Moody Press, 1987), 111–113.

he had had prior to coming to the church. Several years later when the church began to face serious financial problems, the board member who had been confided in by the pastor shared those confidences with the board. The result was the young minister's early exodus from the pastorate. His failure to earn and maintain the respect of just one family in the church led to a sad pastoral demise. This case is not unusual. When questions about pastoral integrity cloud the relationship to the parishioners, a storm can be expected to break any day.

Part 3

**Chapter 8
The Minister
and the
Congregation:
Providing
Spiritual
Leadership**

PROBLEMS PECULIAR TO THE PREACHER-COUNSELOR

Counseling ministries are flourishing throughout the church world, nationally (thanks to the media) as well as locally. As a result, many pastors are becoming interested in counseling as an adjunct to their ministry. In some instances the pastor will have had little training in this area, possibly only a few courses taken during ministerial training. William W. Rankin cites some rather harsh criticism of this inadequacy, describing many pastor-counselors "as only 'paraprofessionals' in counseling since, as professionals in ministry, they encounter people with psychological or emotional problems but have not the same level of competence as psychologists to deal effectively with them."[3]

Pastors who counsel will be challenged by the fact that many of their parishioners place a great deal of trust in their counseling. Howard J. Clinebell indicates that 80 percent of those who sought counsel from the clergy reported they were helped, while only 11 percent reported that counseling with clergy had not been helpful. Clinebell concludes: "This study confirms the strategic role clergy persons fulfill

---

[3]William W. Rankin, *Confidentiality and Clergy: Churches, Ethics, and the Law* (Harrisburg, Pa.: Morehouse Publishing, 1990), 12.

Part 3

Chapter 8
The Minister
and the
Congregation:
Providing
Spiritual
Leadership

as counselors in our society. It is obvious that we continue to be on the front lines in the struggle to help burdened people."[4]

Unfortunately, the pastor is not always qualified to provide in-depth counseling for those having serious emotional problems: broken marriages, dysfunctional relationships, depression, suicidal tendencies, severe moral problems, and the like. If this is the case, the pastor will do well to make spiritual counseling a priority. Should supplemental counseling be necessary, the pastor will need to have a good referral list for his or her clients. Pastors should never attempt to step into ministry shoes they cannot fill. They commit a serious breach of ethics to pose as professionals when they are merely amateurs.

David Switzer, in his excellent treatment of the complexities of ministerial counseling, discusses the lack of preparation for this demanding ministry: "There are ministers who are naïve psychologically, ineffective as pastors and counselors, and who hold and communicate attitudes and utilize methods of handling emotions and drives that may be harmful to some persons."[5]

Switzer then concedes that more ministers are being better trained to deal with people and their problems than ever before, and many ministers without formal training are sensitive and competent to help those that come to them within the scope of their vocation as ministers. However, he offers this admonition: "At the same time, since the training of ministers is so varied, when they get into the area of assisting persons in crisis, there is still much to learn from other professionals."[6]

---

[4]Howard J. Clinebell, *Basic Types of Pastoral Care and Counseling: Resources for the Ministry of Healing and Growth* (Nashville: Abingdon Press, 1984), 48–49.

[5]David K. Switzer, *The Minister as Crisis Counselor*, rev. and enl. (Nashville: Abingdon Press, 1986), 253–254.

[6]Ibid.

Part 3

Chapter 8
The Minister
and the
Congregation:
Providing
Spiritual
Leadership

Some of the problems that face the unqualified pastor-counselor include the tendency to become emotionally and intimately involved with the counselee. At the same time, some counselors may actually have more personal problems than the counselee. In other situations, counselors may feel obligated to give complete and authoritative responses to questions, simply because of being cast in the role of a qualified counselor. Often "[a] sympathetic listener may be all the counselee needs. By the very verbalization the person may be able to see the problem more clearly, and to work through to appropriate conclusions."[7]

Even qualified pastor-counselors invite serious problems when providing marital counseling to their church members. To allude publicly to any situation remotely resembling what has been discussed in the counseling session will produce discomfort for both counselor and counselees. In fact, the counselees will probably be uncomfortable no matter what subject the pastor addresses simply because the pastor knows their intimate secrets. The pastor can be fairly certain that under these circumstances such couples will soon be transferring to a new church home.

An even more compelling reason for most pastors not to counsel extensively has to do with its tremendous demand on time and energy. This is the case even though short-term counseling is considered more appropriate to the ministry, according to one professional counselor:

On the whole, the trend has been toward greater personal involvement by the therapist, with fewer sessions.

This is good news for pastors for on the one hand, their essential role calls for a more active involvement with persons, and on the other hand, these overly busy practition-

---

[7]Rex H. Knowles, "The Ethical Decision of Minister as Counselor," in *Ethical Issues in the Practice of Ministry*, ed. Jane A. Boyajian (New Brighton, Minn.: United Theological Seminary, 1984), 55–62.

Part 3

**Chapter 8
The Minister
and the
Congregation:
Providing
Spiritual
Leadership**

ers of the multiple functions that are demanded by the local church very rarely do any of the long-term therapy they might have learned about in seminary. Even if they were quite well trained and emotionally prepared for a depth-counseling relationship of some length, they simply do not often have the time for its regular demands. Personal experience and discussion of counseling practices with many other ministers has led me to conclude that the typical minister sees very few persons for more than six consecutive weekly sessions of one hour.[8]

Unless pastors neglect hospital visitation, spiritual counseling, sermon preparation, administrative responsibilities, and board meetings—to say nothing of time with their families—they will have little, if any, time to counsel. Howard J. Clinebell reports on two regional surveys of hours ministers devoted to counseling. The results indicate a considerable variance in the time allotted by different ministers.

In a study by Richard V. McCann, a group of clergymen was found to spend only 2.2 hours per week in this activity. But a survey of thirty-four suburban Pittsburgh pastors showed that they spent 30 percent of their time in counseling. The fact that the minister is a part-time counselor is, of course, no excuse for incompetence, any more than his being a part-time teacher and preacher excuses slovenly work in those areas. There is no other aspect of a minister's work in which lack of competence can have comparable negative effects. In counseling, the pastor often deals with people at the time of their greatest vulnerability and deepest need. His counseling skill, or lack of it, can have a decisive effect on their future.[9]

Even when ministers are singularly qualified for counseling and are blessed to have staff personnel to free up their schedule, they must be prepared for the severe emotional and physical drain that accompanies

---

[8]Switzer, *The Minister as Crisis Counselor*, 22.
[9]Clinebell, *Basic Types of Pastoral Counseling*, 44.

dealing with persons whom they know and love as members of their congregation. Ethically responsible ministers realize that they have only so many hours, so much energy, so much of themselves, to give to the work of God. In most instances they will do well to leave the major part of the counseling ministry to Christian professionals.

Part 3

**Chapter 8
The Minister
and the
Congregation:
Providing
Spiritual
Leadership**

CONFIDENCE FOR THE KEEPING

There is no surer way for the pastor to destroy the trust of a church member than to break a confidence. Such a pastor will not get a second chance. When approached by a member with a serious problem, the pastor will not want to even hint that another member of the church has ever come with a similar problem. If the parishioner has requested confidentiality, the pastor should share the information with no one—usually not even his or her spouse. The exception would be when the pastor's spouse is spiritually attuned to the ministry and is a source of strength and support in sharing stressful information or circumstances. However, ministers should inform counselees that they would like to share the matter prayerfully with a spouse but will do so only with unqualified approval. Should a counselee insist that absolutely no one share the confidence, the pastor must comply without hesitation, or should practice good ethics by not receiving the confidence in the first place.

The only situations wherein confidence cannot be held by ministers are to prevent a crime from taking place or to avoid becoming an accessory before the fact of a crime. Should the counselor sense that the confidence about to be shared involves criminal intent or action, the counselee should be interrupted and instructed that the counselor cannot keep such confidence. As William Rankin points out,

There are certain kinds of situations clergy encounter in their roles as pastoral counselors that seem to lie close to,

Part 3

Chapter 8
The Minister
and the
Congregation:
Providing
Spiritual
Leadership

and perhaps beyond, the reach of confidentiality. The duty to keep a confidence is limited in cases where a dangerous person intends, or appears to intend, to commit acts of destruction. It is also limited when the pastor is being asked to cover up a crime, especially an ongoing crime. The alleged "privacy right" is not strongly and unambiguously supported in law, so this cannot always be regarded as a strong incentive to keep confidences in complex situations. . . . Not even the initial promise to keep a confidence is an unyielding guarantee against future disclosure if the evidence suggests that innocent others may be made unduly vulnerable thereby—as in the tale of the child molester.[10]

Should the minister-counselor face the challenge of unwittingly receiving confidential information that involves the violation of the laws of the land or the clear teaching of Scripture, the minister must hold to the higher ethic of honoring God. (James 5 and other biblical passages insist that the confessing of our faults is not for the cloaking of our transgressions, but rather to expose them so prayer can be offered, followed by forgiveness and healing.)

When it is evident a confidence will require covering a moral transgression that should be confessed, ministers face a no-win situation. Again, it is better to interrupt the counselee and have him or her take the information to a professional counselor, who may be able to cope with the problem rather than to become unwittingly involved in harboring secret sin. The pastor must make it clear to the would-be counselee that to simply share secret sin with another never solves the problem. At best, it may provide momentary relief.

Of course, sins of the past that have been dealt with or information that would bring harm or shame to others—these are exceptions. In the most complex situations the minister will find divine guidance by

---

[10]Rankin, *Confidentiality and Clergy*, 78.

holding to divine guidelines; in dealing with confidential information, the same untainted premise that was established centuries ago in the writing of the prophet still pertains—"steadfast love, justice, and righteousness" (Jer. 9:24, NRS). Hopefully, ministers will behave so appropriately that parishioners will know they can trust their minister as a keeper of confidences, one who will be faithful to them as well as to God, one they will not burden with compromising information.

Part 3

Chapter 8
The Minister
and the
Congregation:
Providing
Spiritual
Leadership

"NO RESPECTER OF PERSONS"—THE FOLLY OF FAVORITISM

Ministers face one of the stiffest tests of ethical conduct in relating to their admirers, parishioners who love and admire their pastor more than do others. Such members will usually be among the leaders of the church and will offer the pastor company and rapport he sincerely enjoys. No matter how appealing a close relationship with these persons may seem, pastors should maintain a degree of distance. They cannot afford to have the same kind of uninhibited relationship with them that they enjoy with minister friends. To associate too closely with any member of the church will adversely affect the pastor's relationship to the congregation. Pastors cannot help but neglect fellowship with other members of the church if an inordinate amount of time is spent with a few individuals.

The old adage "familiarity breeds contempt" applies. The individual is rare who can maintain a high level of respect for the pastor who has become too close. On the other hand, the people who are not in the pastor's inner circle are going to resent being left out. Many of them will be hurt; some will feel jealousy; others will fail to show the love and respect they would have shown had there been a balanced relationship between pastor and parishioners. These "outsiders" will resent the pastor's close friends, a feeling that will only increase over time.

Part 3

Chapter 8
The Minister
and the
Congregation:
Providing
Spiritual
Leadership

The situation becomes even worse when favorite friends shower the pastor with gifts and other considerations. I recall the sad experience of a young minister who upon moving into his new pastorate was befriended by a prominent couple in the church. They were wealthy and immediately lavished gifts, trips, and affection on the young minister and his family. However, within a few months he had to assert his pastoral authority in a situation that arose with the friendly couple. Immediately, their affection turned to dislike and finally to hatred. They attempted to destroy his ministry and led an effort to have him removed. Although they were not successful, the pastor and his family endured many months of pain and frustration simply because they had used poor judgment in the relationship. They paid an exorbitant price for a few "perks."

Lutzer's ethical study *Pastor to Pastor* makes this observation: "Ironically, sometimes the person who befriends the pastor when he first arrives is the one who later turns against him. The man is attracted to the pastor because he wants to brief him on the way things really are. But if the pastor doesn't agree with him right down the line, he will soon become his adversary. To see the pastor succeed would be his greatest disappointment."[11]

At best, it is in poor taste to accept gifts and favors from those who will naturally expect affection and attention in return. As spiritual leaders, may we never fall into the trap that destroyed the sons of the prophet Samuel: "His sons did not walk in his ways. They turned aside after dishonest gain and accepted bribes and perverted justice" (1 Sam. 8:3).

But what about those members who sincerely appreciate you and your ministry and carry no hidden agenda? It is possible to relate to them without giving preferential treatment, developing a solid, warm rela-

---

[11]Lutzer, *Pastor to Pastor*, 30.

tionship with the understanding that the pastor will not be a respecter of persons. A mature, spiritually motivated parishioner will understand and will help build a healthy, lifelong relationship. Thus, a fresh challenge emerges: How do we handle enduring friendships when pastor or parishioner changes churches?

Part 3

Chapter 8
The Minister
and the
Congregation:
Providing
Spiritual
Leadership

RELATIONSHIPS WITH FORMER PARISHIONERS

Blessed are the ministers who neatly and sweetly break the ties that may bind them to their former congregation. While friendships and fellowship can be maintained with former parishioners to a limited degree, ex-pastors should never exercise an inhibiting influence on a former church as it is building a bond with its new pastor. The relocated pastor will want to follow the highest possible ethical standard by refusing to hold onto the affection of former parishioners. To divide a congregation's loyalties by main-taining ties is absolutely disastrous—to both incoming and outgoing pastors, to individual parishioners, and to the body of Christ in general.

This problem of ongoing relationships becomes especially acute when a pastor has relatives in a former pastorate. However, such situations can be handled smoothly when proper ethics are applied. I especially applaud my own minister father, who pioneered an outstanding church in Pennsylvania a number of years ago. Later, by the time he had been invited to pastor a church in another state, his sister-in-law, my aunt, had married into a large, influential family in the church. She and her husband became pillars in the church, highly respected; however, neither of my parents, despite the relationship, ever attempted to exert any influence over the church or its leadership, even though my father served as a district officer over the church for seven years.

Former pastors do not always handle such relationships in an ethical way. In one instance, a minister

Part 3

Chapter 8
The Minister
and the
Congregation:
Providing
Spiritual
Leadership

actually coached the board of a former church to deal adversely with its new pastor. Admittedly, a minister may be flattered in maintaining a strong influence on a board of a former church; however, it cannot be ethically justified.

When ministers leave a church, they should take with them their influence, their wise counsel, their role as spiritual leaders of the church. To allow parishioners of a former congregation to invite your slightest influence is to be guilty of bringing division into the work of the Lord. Do not the Scriptures warn against such a breech of ethics? "I urge you, brothers, to watch out for those who cause divisions. . . . Keep away from them" (Rom. 16:17).

STUDY QUESTIONS

1. What concerns should be taken into account when a church board is considering a pastor's salary?

2. How does a pastor develop a philosophy of ministry and what should be involved?

3. How can the pastor establish godly leadership even when there are strong personalities on the church board?

4. What are some ways a pastor can show a godly example to the congregation?

5. Why is it more important to have the respect of the congregation than to have their love?

6. To what extent should a pastor give time to counseling?

7. What limits should pastors set to the kind of counsel they give?

8. How can a pastor avoid close and possibly detrimental relationships with members of a church formerly pastored?

Chapter 9

Ministers and Their Peers: Maintaining Professional Relationships

Occasionally a minister who seems to maintain a high standard of ethics may relate inappropriately to fellow ministers. Perhaps professional jealousy or an inflated ego lies at the root of this shortcoming, but whatever the cause, persons who slight their peers should pray for a greater love for the ministry as well as for God. Discerning young ministers soon learn they need the affirmation and respect of fellow ministers. And to earn such responses they must first show them.

Relationship with Your Predecessor in the Pastorate

The success or failure of the minister who preceded you will be a significant factor in the success of your relationships and ministry in your new church. If that person did quite well in filling the pulpit prior to your coming, do not ignore that contribution as you take his or her place. This is particularly true as you begin your ministry in the new pastorate. The most loyal supporters (as well as detractors) of the former pastor are watching you closely to see how you will assume leadership.

Whether you are in a service, in a board meeting, or in mere conversation with associates, and regardless of their agreeing with you, your giving proper credit to this minister of God, one whose work you will have to build on, is important. Everyone will be

Part 3

Chapter 9
Ministers
and Their
Peers:
Maintaining
Professional
Relationships

interested in how you evaluate your predecessor. Fight and pray to resist an unhealthy attitude toward this minister. If you sense jealousy, for example, express it only as a confession to God. And then when He has removed it—confess it only if it is appropriate to a given audience.

Make every reasonable effort to keep in touch with your predecessor as a person with whom you have much in common. Your conversation should never center on the negative aspects of your ministries; rejoice together in the victories you have mutually won. Invite this preacher back to the pulpit from time to time. Those of your congregation who have not been able to accept the transition may well appreciate you more after such a return visit. Those who were not particularly enchanted by the former pastor's person or ministry will admire you for being generous.

What if your predecessor had only a mediocre ministry or one that failed? Never speak of it critically—publicly or privately. If you take an unethical, negative attitude, your ministry will get the same treatment when you have gone.

If your predecessor was eminently successful, you may need to be more direct in your references to him or her in private conversation and in public services. Above all, honor the former pastor as a friend. If you are more successful, you won't need to point out the contrast. Your people are keen analysts. Here again, it will serve you and your ministry well to invite this minister back as an honored guest, probably after some time has elapsed. You will want to continue to be in touch and will probably need to initiate each contact to keep the relationship alive. Your friendship and respect will be a major source of encouragement.

RELATIONSHIP WITH YOUR SUCCESSOR IN THE PASTORATE

You will have no problem in maintaining a proper attitude toward the one who follows you in the pastorate if your heart is right. Ask yourself if you really want the new pastor to succeed. More importantly, do you want the church you left behind to prosper?

During one of my pastorates, I invited a flamboyant minister friend to hold services. Some time before, he had concluded his ministry in a fairly sizable church. The minister who followed him had met serious difficulty in trying to keep the church growing. I was somewhat taken aback when my friend, who had enjoyed success in the pastorate, commented that his successor just didn't have a strong enough ministry to take the church forward. Rather than regretting it, he seemed to be gloating over it.

Outgoing pastors always carry some responsibility for what happens in a church after they leave. If they have not left their predecessor a foundation to build on, they may be more at fault than the one who follows and appears a failure.

Departing pastors face another important question: To what degree should they stay in touch with members of the church they are leaving? The question becomes even more critical when applied to pillars of the church or members of its board. I believe that contact should be minimal. A close relationship with former parishioners benefits neither them nor the minister who maintains the contact—besides being a detriment to the incumbent pastor.

I have known of cases where a minister with a strong personality actually attempted to continue pastoring the church he had left. His refusal to withdraw his influence eventually led to a split in the church, dealing a serious blow to the incumbent pastor, who suffered unbelievable pressures. What could be more unethical and unkind than to make the ministry a misery for your successor.

A problem in ethical relationships can sometimes arise when pastors purchase a home in the town where they minister: When they move to the next town, they may have a problem selling the property, or they may wish to hold it as an investment. Under

Part 3

Chapter 9
Ministers
and Their
Peers:
Maintaining
Professional
Relationships

Part 3

Chapter 9
Ministers
and Their
Peers:
Maintaining
Professional
Relationships

such circumstances, proceed with caution and exercise Christlike courtesy to your original community and the current pastor of the church. If in maintaining such a property you will have to attend to it personally, the local pastor should be made fully aware of your activities in the community on an ongoing basis. In such circumstances, good manners, not to mention good ethical practice, demand consideration of the local pastor.

As a minister, at the top of your prayer list ought to be the name of the one who follows you in a given ministry. Should that person succeed, you share in the victories. Should your successor fail, you fail as well. Keep in mind, after all, it is the kingdom of God that is being built up or dragged down. We have simply been given the honor of being colaborers with Him who in the final reckoning cannot fail. Nevertheless, we will give an accounting of how we ourselves worked with our fellow ministers.

RELATIONSHIP WITH THE TROUBLED NEIGHBORING CHURCH

Nolan B. Harmon makes this point in *Ministerial Ethics and Etiquette:* "Fortunately, interchurch rivalry has died down with the passing years, and the stern denominationalism of an earlier age has all but disappeared. . . . Nevertheless between local churches, especially in small towns, there is considerable head counting, comparing of local efforts, and striving for local prestige."[1]

Consequently, in the smaller community a church in trouble often becomes a microcosm of a community in trouble. Church problems can be horrendous. The facts sometimes lend credence to the observation credited to Reinhold Niebuhr that the Church reminded him of Noah's ark—You couldn't stand the stench within if it weren't for the storm without!

---

[1]Nolan B. Harmon, *Ministerial Ethics and Etiquette*, 2nd rev. ed. (Nashville: Abingdon Press, 1987), p. 77.

Problems in the neighboring church become particularly acute when that church happens to be of your own denomination. Your attitude as pastor, as well as that of your congregation, must be one of true compassion. Never despise a troubled neighboring church. Never take advantage of the situation. Treat that church as you would treat a troubled marriage. Do everything in your power to bring about reconciliation.

When disgruntled or hurt members of the troubled church show up at your church, be prepared with an ethical approach. The first time they attend, it is proper to welcome them but without commentary about why they are present. However, by the second visit you should have a talk with them and then contact their pastor. Your goal is to return these sheep to the proper fold, back to the care of their undershepherd.

During my twelve years at a fine church, I could expect a visit every year or so from a strapping policeman and his wife who lived in the community. They attended a fundamentalist church but would become discouraged from time to time. They would visit our church for a few Sundays and appear to receive a spiritual boost. Then they would quietly slip back to their home church with no negative feelings on anyone's part. We felt that we were performing a service for the Kingdom in providing a temporary haven for them.

Should a family begin attending your church because of difficulty in a neighboring church, they may not prove to be an asset. If they have created some of the difficulty in the church they left, the possibility is great they will create difficulty for you. On the other hand, if they are running from an existing difficulty in the previous church, who is to say they will stand by your church should a problem arise?

To receive a family from a troubled church without attempting to help them to return home or without contacting their pastor is a serious breach of ministe-

Part 3

Chapter 9
Ministers
and Their
Peers:
Maintaining
Professional
Relationships

Part 3

Chapter 9
Ministers
and Their
Peers:
Maintaining
Professional
Relationships

rial ethics. Count the cost of receiving disgruntled members. You will not enhance the reputation of your church in the community nor will you endear yourself to the pastor and congregation of their former church by your actions. Of course, there are times when the circumstances seem to be completely beyond human control. The only hope is to place the situation squarely in the hands of God and leave it to His mercy and grace. Above all, in such awkward situations as this, do your best to stay on good terms with the pastor of the troubled church and encourage him in the Lord.

RELATIONSHIP WITH GUEST MINISTERS

Evangelists are a vanishing breed. Hopefully, genuine hunger for spiritual revival will lead to reactivating the role of these essential men and women of the Word. Since evangelists are difficult to come by, it becomes even more imperative to treat them with respect and appreciation.

First, confirm carefully the dates for an evangelistic crusade with your evangelist. When he or she arrives, be prepared. Treat the evangelist as an honored guest and strive to transfer a degree of the loyalty and love your people have for you as pastor to this coworker in ministry. If you do not show confidence and ethical regard for this person and his or her ministry, your people will tend to feel distrust; the evangelist will not be a source of blessing to the church or lead its members into spiritual renewal. Better not to have an evangelist come to the church than to have one with whom you cannot share the affection and admiration of your church members.

Honor evangelists. Welcome them warmly to your pulpit from service to service. Free them to pursue their ministry. Don't fear the contrasts between your ministry and theirs. If they preach better than you, your people need to hear better preaching. If they are not as gifted in the pulpit as you, your congrega-

Part 3

Chapter 9
Ministers
and Their
Peers:
Maintaining
Professional
Relationships

tion will be happy to hear you again when the evangelist leaves. For better or worse, an evangelist's ministry will provide a needed change for your parishioners, and they will be ready to hear you when the series of services is concluded.

While the evangelist is with your church, be sure to provide good food and accommodations. Take time to have fellowship. Pray with and for your evangelists that God will richly anoint their ministries.

In most cases, lodging the evangelist in the parsonage during the revival series rarely works, either for the evangelist or your family. Although many years have passed since the experience, my wife and I have vivid recollections of serving as the evangelists at a small city church with a very limited budget. The pastor was able to provide a room for us in the parsonage, which, unfortunately, was separated from the adjoining living room by only an arched doorway. The pastor's wife had hung a curtain across the doorway, but we had not reckoned on the all-too-frequent visitor to our quarters: The pastor's hyperactive little son would come flying through the curtain in his pedal car, giving only a three-second warning of "Beep, Beep!"

Once, in a rural setting as evangelists, we were notified by the pastor and his wife that the congregation had not been bringing enough food to stock their spare freezer. The result—we would have only two meals a day. Although a great way to diet, it hardly reflected the appropriate care and courtesy due a guest. This was, of course, an exceptional case, for during those years, when it was often necessary for the host pastor to open his home to the evangelist, we experienced warm, generous treatment time after time.

Pay your evangelists well. They will have lapses in their schedules from time to time. Their budgets must include the expenses of travel as well as of maintaining a home. Because of such accompanying expenses, their weekly salary should in most cases be larger than that of the host pastor. Should your

Part 3

Chapter 9
Ministers
and Their
Peers:
Maintaining
Professional
Relationships

church be unable to generously remunerate guest ministers, you should consider setting up a fund to cover special meetings. The day may well come when your roles will be reversed. As the evangelist, you will want to remember being more than fair to the guest ministers you invited to your church. The Lord himself stated the principle in cogent terms: "'Treat other people exactly as you would like to be treated by them'" (Matt. 7:12, Phillips).

When hosting missionaries or other guests for only one service, plan it carefully: You will want to highlight the unique ministry of your guests. Give them ample time to present their message. Should the speaker be a missionary seeking financial support or a representative of a ministry that deserves funding, as host pastor create an atmosphere of responsiveness and generosity.

The best preparation for a missions appeal is an established missions fund. Even if the church operates on a low budget or a missions service is poorly attended, such a fund keeps the pastor from being embarrassed and the missionary from becoming discouraged. In any event, the honorarium must be generous. The single-service speaker, like the evangelist, has been faced with travel expenses and has had to neglect other responsibilities to be present at your church. When you have a policy of treating your guests well, the word gets around and you and your church come to be appreciated as benefactors of the ministry.

During the actual service with a guest speaker, your remarks need to be carefully chosen. Nolan Harmon suggests that the introduction of the speaker should be simple and clear, avoiding extravagance. At the conclusion of the speaker's sermon, it is best not to comment on it. If it was good, the people will know it. If it was poor, you can't make them believe otherwise.[2]

---

[2]Ibid., 128.

RELATIONSHIP WITH FELLOW MINISTERS IN THE
COMMUNITY

Part 3

Chapter 9
Ministers
and Their
Peers:
Maintaining
Professional
Relationships

Moving into a new community as a pastor can be interesting and sometimes challenging. In some areas of the country you can expect a warm welcome. Neighboring pastors will take the initiative to get acquainted with you. On the other hand, what if you arrive in town and nobody seems to notice? Don't sulk or pity yourself. Seek out your neighboring pastors. Be warm and courteous to everyone, even when you've been coolly received. Participate in the local ministerial alliance. Let the community know you are a coworker in the Kingdom. If you persist in reaching out to your fellow ministers in the community, the dividends will appear in due time.

I was pastoring in a small city where I met some snobbishness and aloofness in a few of the more liberal members of the local ministerial alliance. I determined by the grace of God to respond with Christ-honoring actions and commit the situation to His guidance. Soon a good relationship developed with one of my neighboring pastors, and we were able to arrange an exchange of services, which continued for a number of years.

My second year in the community, a national trans-denominational effort to promote group Bible study, world evangelism, and prayer (Key '73) came along. As a member of the planning committee, I was assigned the task of inviting a well-known liberal pastor from a neighboring community to speak at a special rally. Since part of my assignment was to provide the subject and text for the speaker, I prayerfully chose the passage in Luke 4 that records Jesus' declaration of His mission on earth as He stood in the synagogue at Nazareth. Providentially, this was the exact passage the national committee had selected just prior to the rally. Our guest speaker was so impressed by this "coincidence" that in the course of his message he highlighted the unusual details of the invitation he had

Part 3

Chapter 9
Ministers
and Their
Peers:
Maintaining
Professional
Relationships

received. The Lord graciously used this almost trivial experience to break down some of the relational barriers among the city's religious leaders.

As a result, the ministers of our immediate area, a wide cross section of denominations, formed a bond among themselves. Interdenominational prayer fellowships also formed, and soon weekly Bible studies sprang up in several homes in the community. A highlight of this interfaith activity in our church was a beautiful baptismal service with four other churches. Moving on the hearts of spiritual leaders who previously had been reluctant to join in the Lord's work, the Holy Spirit succeeded in bringing a genuine spiritual awakening.

Pentecostals often find it difficult to enjoy a warm relationship with those of a different theological position or standard of conduct. Yet even the Lord himself did not reject those who did not adhere to His teaching as the disciples understood it. He simply said that "whoever is not against us is for us" (Mark 9:38). We must view ourselves as workers together with those who are bringing others to the foot of the Cross. As we practice Christlike ethics, we will conduct ourselves so that our fellow ministers can trust us and we can trust them. We will mutually work for God's kingdom, confident that none among us are "sheep stealers" or "goldfish-bowl raiders."

It is alarming that at times ministers of the same denomination cannot work in harmony—despite facing common problems. We are all assigned to meet the deep spiritual needs of people. We can and must reinforce each other's ministry. There is no room for rivalry in the family of God, no time for feuding. The hour is short; the harvest is ripe. We must prepare for the return of the great Lord of the Harvest by working together.

RELATIONSHIP WITH YOUR DENOMINATION

The ethics of a wholesome relationship with your denomination calls for loyalty, support, and even a

Part 3

**Chapter 9
Ministers
and Their
Peers:
Maintaining
Professional
Relationships**

sense of pride. That doesn't mean your loyalty must be blind, but you should see your denomination as a fellowship and agree with your brothers and sisters in ministry about doctrine—this is critical to your ethics as a minister.

Upon joining a fellowship, new members affirm the doctrine of the group. As long as their membership continues, they have an obligation to agree with the doctrinal positions of their fellow ministers. Amos 3:3 states it succinctly: "'Do two walk together unless they have agreed to do so?'" To cloak one's theological identity so one might enjoy the advantages of a denominational affiliation shows a lack of integrity. It should be beneath the honor of God's ministers.

Questions or doubts about doctrinal matters are not necessarily wrong. But a person in that state of mind should be pursuing answers. "A double-minded man [is] unstable in all he does" (James 1:8). If a minister cannot resolve the doubts, he ought to do the ethical thing, for himself and his fellowship, by voluntarily withdrawing. Nagging questions and doubts lead only to frustration, bitterness, and spiritual defeat.

How blessed are the ministers who develop a sturdy loyalty to their denomination. Although they may feel there are weaknesses and faults among their fellow ministers, loving them helps overlook those flaws.

Your denomination is your fellowship. The terms "brother" and "sister," unfortunately, are becoming passé, perhaps because Christian love is declining. An examination of our "first love" (Rev. 2:4) may be in order. Sanctified pride in one's fellowship—not in its attainments, its strength, size, or quality—shows appreciation for the bond tying believers together.

A good question to ask yourself: "Is my fellowship stronger because I am a member?" It is an enjoyable experience to be with others of "like precious faith" (2 Peter 1:1, KJV). There is real fun and fulfillment in exchanging stories, enjoying humor, bearing another's burdens, and just being able to vent feelings that

Part 3

Chapter 9
Ministers
and Their
Peers:
Maintaining
Professional
Relationships

develop in the work of the ministry. An extreme, perhaps, but one of my golfing friends admitted that when he teed up a ball, sometimes he was guilty of imagining a troublesome board member on the tee.

Loyal ministers will not begrudge the financial support that is required to maintain good standing with their fellowship. It is better to go beyond the actual requirement, the second mile. Don't begrudge the fiscal demands of a great relationship.

Never forget that you are a part of your denomination by your choice. You were not forced to join. On the other hand, you were chosen by your denomination. Your fellowship was not coerced to select you. We are not members of a body of believers on the basis of our merits, just as we are not a part of the kingdom of God because we deserve our place. He first chose us, then we chose Him. Never allow yourself to become disillusioned and to think of your fellowship as "them" or "they" rather than "us" or "we."

We are all a part of Christ's body and are joined in bonds of love and faith. While it is true that there are no denominational lines drawn in heaven, the same love and respect that bind men and women into earthly fellowships are the same love and respect that bind them into the kingdom of heaven.

STUDY QUESTIONS

1. Why is it important to keep in touch with your predecessor in the pastorate?

2. What should be your relationship with your successor in a pastorate?

3. When church problems arise in a neighboring church, what can you do to help the church?

4. How should you deal with people who come to you from a troubled church?

5. What preparations should you make for guest ministers, evangelists, and missionaries?

6. To what extent and under what circumstances should you participate in a local ministers' alliance?

7. What is involved in loyalty to your denomination?

Part 3

**Chapter 9
Ministers
and Their
Peers:
Maintaining
Professional
Relationships**

Chapter 10

The Minister and Money: Filthy Lucre in Clean Hands

The minister must maintain a right attitude toward money. Money is to be respected but not loved, appreciated but not coveted. A wrong perspective on financial matters has been the undoing of men and women of God on more than one occasion. It has been said jokingly that money isn't everything—it just buys everything! Fortunately, the most important things in life are not for sale at any price. Nonetheless, the proper handling of dollars and cents becomes a critical matter to that person who views money too seriously or too lightly, as the case may be.

In reality, the wise handling of money leads to financial security much more readily than greater earning power. Often when income rises, we unwittingly raise our standard of living to the extent that financial pressure actually destroys the joy of living. Regardless of the level of income, we need to hold a conservative philosophy of spending and saving that will result in a reasonably comfortable lifestyle, both now and in later years.

A few years ago in working with ministers and their spouses in estate planning, I noticed an interesting phenomenon. Older couples who had accumulated relatively sizable estates over time had never been blessed in their lifetimes with good, substantial incomes. Their secret was simply careful money handling, in some cases accompanied by frugal living. By contrast, any number of families within the same de-

Part 3

Chapter 10
The Minister
and Money:
Filthy Lucre
in Clean
Hands

nominational fellowship, having enjoyed considerably higher levels of income for years, were not prepared for the future, which tends to be marred by burdensome medical expenses or reduced family income, perhaps both. For the head of the home to jeopardize the entire family by carelessly using the resources God has provided is a serious matter.

Recognition of the fact that God is the ultimate source of all financial blessing leads us to a serious consideration of the tithing principle as it applies to the church, the minister, and the minister's family. The term "principle" becomes appropriate here with the realization that tithing was instituted in the Book of Genesis as a response to blessing and was reiterated by Christ himself in the New Testament. Abraham, "Father of the Faithful," was the first to return the tithe to God, via Melchizedek, as an act of gratitude for divine assistance when he was rescuing Lot, along with the spoils of war, from his pagan captors (Gen. 14:20). In similar fashion, Jacob made and kept a lifelong vow to the Almighty that he would voluntarily pay tithes of all that God would ever bless him with (Gen. 28:20–22). In neither case did it appear that giving the tithe was a moral obligation but was rather the reflection of gratitude to a gracious God in an era noted for its ingratitude and self-centered actions, even among those called of God.

Jesus made it clear that not only is it ethically sound to practice tithing but it is practical. He admonished the Pharisees to continue to tithe even as He rebuked them for many of their religious practices that had become perfunctory and even hypocritical (Matt. 23:23). He, above all others, was aware that tithing was God's idea. It worked beautifully to provide for the needs of the ministering Levites in the Old Testament (Num. 18:21) and for the spreading of the gospel by the evangelists of the New Testament (1 Cor. 9:13–14).

Tithing is logical. It distributes the burden of caring for the needs of God's program on earth in a remarkably equitable manner. Who but God could have devised a plan whereby all the participants share equally in the blessing of the program although each has given a different amount of support?

The concept of proportionate giving is not always appreciated by would-be tithers. A modern-day parable tells of the young man who approached his pastor with a prayer request for greater income. The pastor prayed and in gratitude the young man promised to tithe faithfully in the future. God heard the petition and in less then a year the man's income soared. He came back to the pastor with a complaint: "Pastor, it was not a problem to pay the tithe when my income was low. But do you have any idea of the size of the check I place in the offering each week at the present?" The pastor's response: "No problem—we will pray again and ask the Lord to reduce your salary to its original amount!"

Even more important than the material benefit the tither enjoys is the spiritual blessing, which always follows obedience to God's injunctions. Malachi 3:8–10 makes it clear that the nontither is considered a God robber whereas the tither can expect the very windows of heaven to be opened in blessing. Even the nation and the surrounding lands will receive the copious showers of the goodness of God without measure. To fail to honor God with the tithe is not only to rob God but also to deprive the minister and the church of the benefits that they are entitled to by merely fulfilling a simple obligation to a benevolent Heavenly Father.

In addition to tithing, the Bible frequently mentions offerings. On one occasion Jesus stood by the treasury box in the temple to observe the donors as they came by. He commended the widow who had given the least offering rather than the rich man who had made a large contribution to the tune of heralding trumpets (Luke 21:2–3). The lesson here from an ethical perspective is this: God rewards faithful giving on

Part 3

Chapter 10
The Minister
and Money:
Filthy Lucre
in Clean
Hands

Part 3

Chapter 10
The Minister
and Money:
Filthy Lucre
in Clean
Hands

the basis of the amount remaining after the gift, not on the total given.

HANDLING FAMILY FUNDS

While failure to meet one's obligations to God is a source of concern to the church family, failure to pay one's personal bills brings reproach on the church and its ministries throughout the entire community. Prompt payment of bills can be achieved by avoiding foolish spending and by having a systematic way of paying the regular and occasional bills that come each month.

For example, it is a good practice to open and check bills as they arrive. On the mailing envelope write the amount and payment date (at least five days before the bill is due). The marked envelopes can be filed or stacked in chronological order to be taken care of on the payment date. The minister who practices paying personal bills promptly will be in an excellent position to insist that the church treasurer keep the credit record of the church in good order.

PROVIDING FOR THE FAMILY

Handling money responsibly includes provision for the family's needs. The Bible teaches that the person who does not provide for his family has denied the faith and is worse than an unbeliever (1 Tim. 5:8). It is better to personally sacrifice some of the comforts and conveniences that are represented as part of the American way of life than to deprive one's dependents of the essentials. When we provide amply for our children, not only do they enjoy the immediate benefit, but we are setting a desirable pattern for their adult lives when they will be practicing what we have "preached" by our example.

When family income is limited through no fault of the income provider, the family in most cases can accept the circumstances and adjust accordingly. However, if the financial problem for the family is the result of irresponsible, selfish spending by the head of the home, resentment is bound to follow. The financial woes that accompany poor money handling will bring not only hardship to the home but ultimately embarrassment and disgrace. Happy is the family where the head of the house makes good decisions in financial matters.

Part 3

**Chapter 10
The Minister
and Money:
Filthy Lucre
in Clean
Hands**

PAYING TAXES WITH PRECISION

When government spending appears excessive, our calculating and paying income tax can produce a strenuous ethical test. This stress is compounded by the fact that taxation in this country is voluntary and self-administered in many respects. Thus even the most responsible citizen can be strongly tempted to pay less than the tax law stipulates from year to year. Who wants to part with hard-earned income to support a wasteful government? The temptation to cheat on one's 1040 form is heightened by the knowledge that only a few tax returns are ever audited, making the risk of being caught minimal. But once again, true to Jesus' promise, the Spirit reminds us of Jesus' teaching (John 14:26): In this instance, "Give to Caesar what is Caesar's" (Mark 12:17). And that is precisely what believers will do. They will calculate and pay their taxes to the dollar—no more, no less.

Ministers enjoy remarkable incentives to comply with the tax laws in light of some of the special provisions they offer. The minister's housing allowance, set in advance each January, is completely excludable from income for tax purposes; it is not to appear on the minister's W-2 form. The total is often a sizable amount, since it includes the cost of furniture, household supplies, utilities, and upkeep. Besides, the amount of tax and mortgage interest paid on the minister's home is to be shown again on the tax form as Schedule A deductions. This "double dip" is available only to ministers and members of the diplomatic service and will probably remain available for some

Part 3

Chapter 10
The Minister
and Money:
Filthy Lucre
in Clean
Hands

time, since it was reinstated several years ago after the IRS's attempt to annul it.

Another current provision for ministers as professionals is the use of an accountable, reimbursed expense plan to enable the minister to pay his or her business expenses from a designated fund established by the church board. The minister simply submits receipts and paid expense records to the church treasurer to substantiate the amounts drawn from the reimbursement fund. Although this particular arrangement for deducting business expenses from income may not be precisely the same from year to year, a good tax manual for ministers will give helpful guidance on a current basis. The total of this accountable fund is excluded from the W-2 report of the minister's income. The minister should not hesitate to take full advantage of these tax breaks. Conserving one's resources will indirectly result in the furthering of the Lord's work. Ministers in most cases will do well to compute and file their own income taxes each year. However, for the first year or two, once they have done their taxes properly, they should have the information reviewed by a CPA or an experienced, well-trained tax preparer. Then they can work from their old 1040 the following year, taking into account the changes (usually minor) in the tax law.

It is to the minister's advantage to fill out the tax forms, for it is in compiling the information that ministers will usually recognize the exceptional provisions available to them; many tax preparers are not aware of these provisions and are not likely to take advantage of anything they do not understand. The minister loses the deduction or special available computation, plus the cost of tax preparation.

In tax filing, as well as other financial involvements, the minister's motto should be "records, records, records." The sure way to survive a tax audit is to be able to substantiate every figure that has been submitted by means of written receipts and records. I learned this lesson rather painfully early in

Spending with Common Sense   203

Part 3

Chapter 10
The Minister
and Money:
Filthy Lucre
in Clean
Hands

my ministerial career. A self-styled expert helped me file my tax form, claiming legitimate deductions—but for which I had no records. Two years later I came away from a tax audit reeling from the impact of an additional tax payment plus penalties. Having learned the value of good record keeping, exactly twenty years later I was able to walk out of an IRS office thoroughly audited but unscathed. How did it happen? I had been able to produce such complete records at the beginning of the audit that as the audit progressed from item to item, the auditor would simply glance at the stack of supporting receipts about to be produced and move on. While accuracy in entering a figure on the form is critical, the auditor can, and often must, reject any entry that has no record to verify it.

Spending with Common Sense

No matter how large the family's income, spending practices determine its financial strength. A good rule of thumb for wise spending: Be conservative in handling the flow of family finance except toward the kingdom of God. For example, driving a car that reflects a higher income than the family actually receives does not make sense. The family budget should not be strained because of pretenses to prosperity with expensive clothing and automobiles. You may have heard of the man who perspired freely during the summer months as he drove around town in an unair-conditioned car with the windows closed tightly! Such foolish hypocrisy can affect one's health, to say nothing of one's wealth.

As to shopping for the family, to look for sales and bargains is a commendable practice. Our budget has been blessed in this regard. My wife, who is the primary shopper of the family, is gifted at finding quality items at sale prices. Shopping at sales has been a way of life for our family for years. Early in our marriage, my wife and I awakened our three-year-old son to an-

Part 3

Chapter 10
The Minister
and Money:
Filthy Lucre
in Clean
Hands

nounce that we had bought a new car. He sleepily responded: "Was it on sale?" How nice to be able to chuckle over the foibles of wise-spending practices— all the way to the bank!

It is unfortunate that the use of credit cards has been labeled not only unethical but practically immoral by many Christian financial advisors. Credit cards, like fire, can become either servant or master. They can be a means of systematically paying bills with a single check, while enjoying the advantage of holding potential payment funds in an interest-bearing account (most cards provide a grace period of twenty-five days for bill paying). Cards also often extend such bonuses as frequent-flyer airline mileage, car-purchasing discounts, or small cash rebates. The key, of course, is to avoid the high monthly interest on the unpaid balance by always paying the full amount of the monthly credit card bill when due. Certainly, if the credit card holder is an undisciplined spender, the card becomes a curse, not a blessing.

Who should be the primary money handler, the husband or the wife? The first response is the one who is best at it. However, the ideal arrangement is for both individuals to learn the art of financial management together and to share the actual paying of bills, making investments, planning the budget, and keeping the budget balanced. Then in the event of an emergency situation, such as illness, accident, or even death, either spouse can continue to handle the family's funds with anxiety-free efficiency. Although joint handling of money matters is ideal, job responsibilities or schedule changes may dictate the shifting of the major share of financial responsibility to husband or wife from time to time.

SOCIAL SECURITY EXEMPTION: CONSCIENTIOUS OBJECTION

Many ministers have been victimized by annuity and investment salespeople who have convinced them that waiving the social security program and investing in a particular retirement program is in their best interest. Too often follow-through on an alternative program is not maintained and a minister can arrive at retirement age without the means to live. Worse, if he becomes unemployed earlier in life because of accident or illness, without social security he has no means of providing for his family. Further, should the minister's life be cut short, there will be no guaranteed income for minor children or the spouse at retirement age.

The mixed blessing of the social security program is that by law the annual tax for the participant is high, and the program has no dropouts. The high cost of social security potentially creates a dilemma for those newly credentialed ministers who can choose to forgo the program. The law states clearly that the only basis for being excluded from participation in social security is conscientious objection to receiving financial benefit payments from the government.[1] In fact, the provision for waiving the program came into being when a sympathetic Congress recognized that the Amish community provided full assistance to their own, whether disabled or retired. The Amish then regularly rejected government-assistance checks although they had been subjected to the FICA tax, which underwrites social security payments.

In light of the true basis for granting exclusion from the program, it is difficult to comprehend how an individual who has been raised as a product of American society can under normal circumstances ethically claim conscientious objection to a program that is completely acceptable to nearly all the country's religious institutions. Despite the high price of involvement, social security provides a sound basis for part of the minister's retirement program. In addi-

Part 3

Chapter 10
The Minister
and Money:
Filthy Lucre
in Clean
Hands

---

[1]See Richard R. Hammar, "Social Security for Ministers," in *Pastor, Church & Law*, 2d ed. (Matthews, N.C.: Christian Ministry Resources, 1991), 199–216.

Part 3

Chapter 10
The Minister
and Money:
Filthy Lucre
in Clean
Hands

tion to its insurance benefits, it offers a cost-of-living adjustment annually to the recipients of retirement checks.

BUILDING A SAVINGS ACCOUNT AND AN
INVESTMENT PORTFOLIO

Savings accounts are best begun in childhood. However, the next best time for the nonsaver to begin putting funds aside is today. A good rule of thumb for most savings-account builders is to put aside 5 percent of one's gross income. Once the habit of saving regularly has been formed, it becomes progressively easier to maintain the practice. The pattern of saving consistently must be introduced into the parsonage early on if financial tranquillity is to prevail in later years.

The ethics of good stewardship calls for the creation of a savings fund by a family for emergencies that will provide on demand the equivalent of at least one to two months' income. This fund needs to be kept at the appropriate level while the long-term savings account is being gradually funded by deposits of 5 percent of the income. After the long-term savings account amounts to the family's income for six months or more, it is time to consider other types of long-range investments. Tax-sheltered funds such as IRAs produce solid growth since the initial tax savings and tax-deferred interest become part of your investment. Another advantage of tax shelters comes from the investor ordinarily being in a more favorable tax bracket at retirement, when he or she begins withdrawing the funds as income.

Once one's basic savings account reflects financial strength and stability, it is time to consider diversifying one's investment. This is simply to reflect the premise that God not only supplies all our needs (Phil. 4:19), He also supplies wisdom to conserve and judgment to invest. An ethical issue does not arise until the investor begins to consider placing funds in high-risk programs, such as a local business venture or the stock market.

Part 3

Chapter 10
The Minister
and Money:
Filthy Lucre
in Clean
Hands

While we must respect the conviction of those Christian businessmen who feel that investing in the stock market is simply gambling in disguise, it should be understood that any investment of funds, even in a federally insured certificate of deposit, is a risk. In other words, common sense rather than an ethical premise will apply to the decision to invest in a volatile fund, using, for example, only those amounts that are not critical to the family's financial well-being. The more conservative investor will choose a low-risk mutual fund, which in some instances carries a guarantee that the principal of the investment will never be violated.

The best possible investment for the minister will be the purchase of a home by means of a housing allowance, which serves as part of the remuneration of the pastorate or other ministry. Making it possible for ministers to purchase a home has become increasingly acceptable to churches of all sizes and in all types of localities over the past twenty years. Church boards are usually happy to be relieved of maintaining a church-owned parsonage, having become aware that the size and location of one parsonage is not going to suit every pastor's family.

Often this realization will prompt a church board, when feasible, to sell the parsonage. The proceeds can provide the housing allowance and even make possible a loan for the pastor's down payment on a home. Such transactions between the church and its pastor must be carried out carefully and ethically inasmuch as the tax laws require that an unencumbered "grant of value" to the minister must be reported as income. If a loan from the church is interest-free or if the interest has been set at an unreasonably low rate, the minister must report the amount of the benefit as personal income. The most acceptable arrangement for a church loan to the pastor is to set

Part 3

Chapter 10
The Minister
and Money:
Filthy Lucre
in Clean
Hands

the interest at the low end of the current interest scale.

When ministers are able to buy their own home, they receive the amazing tax benefit of being able to exclude the full amount of their housing allowance, plus utilities, from their reported income for tax purposes and will list the mortgage interest and real estate taxes for the year as Schedule A deductions on the 1040 form. Furthermore, equity growth provides additional strength for the financial situation of the minister's family.

Another important benefit to ministers and their families in owning their home is realized if the pastor must give up the pastorate on an emergency basis or if he dies suddenly. The pastor and family are not faced with the additional trauma of having to immediately locate a new residence, pack, and move. The trauma becomes an ethical issue when living in a church-owned parsonage and it is not possible to relocate within a reasonable period of time. The church board in turn may be charged with questionable ethics if they put pressure on a bereaved family to move. This unhappy situation is brought about because the church-owned parsonage must be prepared for the next pastor.

As a case in point, the last pastorate my minister father had held for years seemed ideal, with its loving congregation and board and a beautiful, modern parsonage. However, a beautiful situation became chaotic when my father, who was apparently in good health, died in his sleep at age sixty-two. My mother, who had been totally dependent on him in business matters, was faced with the necessity of disposing of rooms of furniture and moving to an apartment in another community almost immediately to make way for the new pastor. The church could not have been more ethical and supportive during the grieving process but was helpless to alleviate the stress brought on by a church-owned parsonage instead of a housing allowance. The church, to its credit, later sold the parsonage and provided a housing allowance for its pastor. On the other hand, subsequent pastors of the same church and others I have known in similar situations have felt more financially secure if the church supplies a parsonage. Nonetheless, the risk factor in buying a home by means of a housing allowance is small and the prospect of such a purchase providing financial and emotional security for the minister's family is great. Both church and pastor should take every reasonable measure to initiate (or maintain) this housing provision.

Part 3

Chapter 10
The Minister
and Money:
Filthy Lucre
in Clean
Hands

PLANNING FOR THE FUTURE

In discussing the handling of money, it is important to look at the major expenditures a family will face over the years. A major outlay will be for a child's college education. In putting aside the necessary funds, the minister should be aware of proper tax-exempt savings programs available to parents of college-bound children. As they face the ever-mounting expense of higher education, parents will recognize the value of instilling a solid work ethic in their children during their early school years. As a result, the children will most likely be eligible for scholarships available to high school graduates who have maintained respectable grades during their academic careers.

In many cases it is desirable for college students to get a job to supplement or even cover the cost of their training. Another possibility for assistance in funding the college training of ministers' children is the discount that is sometimes available in a church-related institution of higher education. Often larger churches will want to help bear the financial burden of the education of their pastor's children as well. Regardless of the avenues of assistance that may be potentially available to ministers in meeting this major financial obligation, they will want to begin preparing for the challenge even before the children arrive.

As the children in the parsonage mature and the excitement of youthful romance lights up the home,

Part 3

Chapter 10
The Minister
and Money:
Filthy Lucre
in Clean
Hands

another financial consideration faces the minister. The most appealing weddings often carry unattractive price tags. Given American custom, the surest way to avoid the financial strain that accompanies the wedding march is for the parents to produce only boys. Since this is not easily arranged, the family blessed with daughters will need to put aside savings well in advance of the date of each wedding.

Some considerations in this regard: First, there ought to be no reason why the bride cannot in some way ease the financial burden of the wedding by being practical in her wedding plans or by sharing some of the expense. Then, too, it would be irresponsible of the family to plunge itself into debt to produce a nuptial extravaganza. Its impression is likely to be fleeting, but its financial burden will remain, likely obscuring many happy aspects of the occasion. How much more desirable to plan a simple but beautiful ceremony at a cost within the family budget. The joy of the hour and the radiance of the bride will remain untarnished in the memories of participants and spectators alike.

As has been noted, the buying of a home is typically a sound investment for ministers and their families. But some important considerations in financial planning should be observed. In making the purchase, the lowest possible interest rate and the longest-term mortgage, offer, of course, the greatest financial advantage. The monthly payments will then be low enough that it will be possible to invest more heavily in savings accounts or retirement programs. In most cases the home purchaser is not likely to live in the same home long enough to complete paying for it. Dollars placed in funds that add compounding interest to the principal will increase net worth much more rapidly than dollars placed in paying off a mortgage carrying a relatively low rate of interest and a slowly diminishing principal balance. Consequently, making extra monthly payments on a mortgage is not a good strategy unless it is to your advantage to increase the amount of your monthly housing allowance. Of course, it is good ethical practice to keep in mind that the housing allowance cannot exceed the fair rental value of the minister's home and its furnishings, plus utilities.

Part 3

**Chapter 10
The Minister
and Money:
Filthy Lucre
in Clean
Hands**

In purchasing a home, its location, of course, safeguards its resale value. If the surrounding homes show evidence of poor upkeep, it is likely that the value of the home being purchased will be adversely affected in due time. The lot the house is on should be properly landscaped for drainage and attractiveness. Above all, the prospective purchaser should have a reliable builder or construction engineer check the house before the purchase contract is signed.

With the possible exception of buying a house, most families, including those of ministers, spend more money for automobiles than all other purchases combined. But cars are poor investments. The purchase of an expensive luxury car seriously calls the average minister's stewardship into question. The sticker price is high, and the rate of depreciation is even higher.

In fact, the minister who drives between fifteen thousand and twenty thousand miles per year for both business and pleasure should consider leasing an automobile. This is particularly the case if one's income puts him in the middle tax bracket or higher. The entire cost of the lease, plus operating expenses, times the percentage of ministry use is chargeable to business expense in computing income tax. An additional advantage of leasing is that only a month's initial payment is invested in the vehicle, leaving funds that would have been invested in the car to accrue interest in a bank account.

Should it be desirable for the minister to purchase a car, it should not be paid for in full, even if funds are available to do so. It is better to make a minimal down payment and procure the best possible financing arrangement to pay for the car. The funds the

Part 3

Chapter 10
The Minister
and Money:
Filthy Lucre
in Clean
Hands

minister has on deposit in the bank or as an investment elsewhere will be compounding favorably while the principal amount of the car loan will be diminishing each month on an accelerating basis. The car purchaser will gain hundreds of dollars over a three-year period with this type of financial arrangement.

Your retirement program should be an essential aspect of financial planning early in your professional career. Many denominations have built ethical soundness into their financial structure by putting a mandatory retirement program in place for all of their credentialed ministers. Almost without exception, all religious bodies have an excellent retirement program available to their ministers. The program may take the form of a tax-sheltered annuity or a tax-deferred compensation arrangement. These programs offer an exceptional advantage to the minister for converting invested funds into a housing allowance at retirement, thus eliminating the tax.

When the denomination's retirement program is voluntary, the individual churches will often fund the minister's retirement account as part of his or her compensation package. In any event, when the retirement provision is voluntary, young ministers should begin serious participation no later than age thirty-five to forty. They will need to carry a considerable amount of inexpensive term insurance in earlier years of ministry to provide for the family's needs should death come prematurely, before the retirement account has built up.

Ministers should be able to lower the amount of term insurance when they leave their forties since the retirement account and other investments will have elevated their net worth. At this interval in their ministerial career the financial responsibility of raising and educating children will have lifted and they will have arrived at the point where their income has peaked. They will then be able to greatly accelerate their retirement and investment programs. They can look forward to that well-earned interval of limited ministry free of financial worries, which is appropriate for the godly minister who has adhered to sound financial and ethical principles in preparing for the future.

Part 3

Chapter 10
The Minister
and Money:
Filthy Lucre
in Clean
Hands

STUDY QUESTIONS

1. What would you consider a conservative style of spending and saving?

2. Is tithing a matter of Law or a response to God's blessing? Explain.

3. Why is it important that ministers pay their bills on time?

4. What must ministers who prepare their own tax reports keep in mind?

5. What rules have you set for yourself to insure commonsense spending?

6. What reasons are there for a minister not to opt out of social security?

7. What plans for the future have you made and what additional plans should you make?

Chapter 11

The Minister and Sex: Joy or Jeopardy?

THE MINISTER AND HIS SEXUALITY

A major ethical dilemma that often faces male pastors stems from their parishioners' notion that he should not have the normal desires and appetites that other men have. They assume that heaven's lofty calling precludes the possibility that a man could retain, much less be subject to, drives that motivate everyone else. The minister must fix in his heart—and in the hearts of those he ministers to—that he is fully acceptable to God and to reasonable people when he enjoys a balanced expression of the interests God has created as part of his makeup.

Several years ago I was enjoying a lively game of volleyball in a city park with a large group from the church I was pastoring. I confess that I was among the more enthusiastic participants in the game that day.

When we stopped for a break, a middle-aged woman who had transferred to our community from a rural area came to me with a concerned look. Her disappointment obvious, she said, "I didn't know preachers played ball." I merely smiled and assured her that some ministers actually did take part in such activities. However, I'm not sure she was ready to accept the sight of her pastor engaging in such an unspiritual performance. But she was merely reflecting the view of many laypeople that a minister simply cannot indulge in enjoyable pastimes and remain true to God's calling.

The fulfillment of sexual desire within marriage is an important aspect of the minister's natural, healthy pursuit of happiness. Having an erotic view of romantic love, marriage, and family relationships courts disaster—morally and spiritually. Acting on such views not only blights the happiness that belongs in the parsonage but can devastate the church as well. Historically, when church leaders hold an unscriptural position in such matters, cultism can result. Blessed are the pastors who realize that they themselves, more than anyone else in their churches, must maintain sound concepts and practice to insure that marital bliss graces the parsonage.

A Biblical View of Sexuality

God created Adam and Eve as sexual beings. However, He gave them the capacity to enjoy sexual relations on an optional basis. Because humankind was instructed to be fruitful, increase in number, and fill the earth (Gen. 1:28), we see that reproduction was not behaviorally automatic, as it was with other living things, depending on an involuntary urge to trigger the reproductive process. Instead, of all the perfect creatures that were spun off the fingers of God, human beings alone were endowed with the awesome capability to engage in the sexual act of their own volition and desire. From creation to the present, humankind has been privileged to enjoy the pleasurable experience of sexual activity as free, moral, ethical beings. With this privilege, however, comes the responsibility of keeping the sex act within marriage. The Creator has given the act a sanctity that remains to this day.

The purity and sanctity of the sexual act are taken for granted in the Genesis account of the men of God who were among the first progenitors of the human race. Enoch, seventh from Adam, walked in such close communion with God that one day He simply allowed Enoch to step from Earth into His presence.

The scriptural record shows that all during Enoch's singular relationship with God, he was enjoying an intimate, upright liaison with his wife. Simply put, he "had . . . sons and daughters" (Gen. 5:22). The lesson here: Even the loftiest spiritual relationship with the Lord does not preclude an intimate, physical relationship in God's scheme of things.

Further evidence of God's approval of physical intimacy within marriage is seen in the problem of plural marriages in Old Testament times. Jesus made it clear that God's plan for marriage from the beginning specified one woman for each man (Matt. 19:4–5,8). However, though plural marriages were never God's will for humankind, the Bible never suggests that the sexual relationship itself within the boundaries of such marriages was improper or unethical. Without question the most polygamous person on record has to be Solomon, king of Israel. Despite the fact that his many wives and concubines proved to be his undoing, Solomon's Song of sensual, romantic love has become the classic expression of spiritual desire and fulfillment for the ages. The Song has been interpreted by Bible scholars over the centuries as a beautiful allegory or typology depicting the pristine love of Christ for the Church and the strength and beauty of the loving response of the Church in the most intimate terms imaginable.

This picture of the holy love of the Lord for the Church elevates the entire concept of a man's sexual relationship with his God-ordained life's companion. Modern authors of sex manuals would do well to draw from biblical sources in dealing with this fascinating subject. Some years ago as a Bible college student in a meeting for "men only," I was introduced to a book on romantic love and marriage entitled *The Torch of Life*.[1] The book (no longer in print) was based on the Song of Solomon, each chapter explicit-

---

[1]Frederick Magee Rosster, *The Torch of Life: A Key to Sex Harmony* (New York: Eugenics Publishers, 1939).

ly amplifying the biblical text. Written by a godly medical doctor, the book was a beautiful treatise on the art of lovemaking in its most exquisite form. A comparable book, easily available and recommended by a widely known Christian psychologist, is *The Gift of Sex: A Christian Guide to Sexual Fulfillment* by Clifford and Joyce Penner.[2] It is especially helpful for both husband- and wife-to-be, enabling them to approach the marriage bed with wholesome anticipation, free of foolish inhibitions. Prescribed by a happily married pastor, the book will serve as an excellent adjunct to both premarital and marriage counseling.

Throughout Christ's life and ministry He never condemned sexuality. He suggested that it was acceptable for a man to be a eunuch, whether by birth, by choice, or by circumstance (Matt. 19:12); yet there was never an indication that this condition reflected spiritual attainment. At the same time, the Lord never hesitated to speak strongly against the evils of fornication and adultery. He considered the marriage bond to be inviolate. To commit mental adultery or to remarry after divorce except under special circumstances was to face God's displeasure. In each instance the sexual act itself is not looked on with disfavor except in the sense that it is in violation of the marriage covenant or the chastity required of the unmarried. Thus when the ethical imperative has been ignored, the natural consequence is moral failure.

Paul the apostle makes a clear statement on the appropriateness and desirability of the marriage bed (1 Cor. 7:3–6). Both husband and wife are encouraged (if not commanded) to render due affection to each other. Abstinence from the sexual relationship is deemed proper only for seasons of prayer and fasting, possibly because of the physical stress that is part of such arduous spiritual engagement. Then the couple

---

[2]Clifford and Joyce Penner, *The Gift of Sex: A Christian Guide to Sexual Fulfillment* (Waco, Tex.: Word Books, 1981).

Marriage, an Extended Romance **219**

Part 3

Chapter 11
The Minister
and Sex: Joy
or Jeopardy?

is instructed to resume their sexual activity "so that Satan will not tempt you because of your lack of self-control." Here the matter of sexual inactivity in marriage leads directly to the moral problem of being tempted to lose self-control.

In the succeeding verses of the same passage (1 Cor. 7:8–9), the apostle again addresses the subject of ethics and morality in sexual matters. He suggests that if the unmarried and widows find it difficult to control themselves in tempting situations, "it is better to marry than to burn with passion." Although recommending the unmarried state as affording more time for service to God, Paul insists that marriage and its accompanying sexual expression are not only acceptable but also commendable. Even in situations wherein a godly woman finds herself married to an unbeliever, Paul's instruction is to remain in the relationship (including its sexual aspect) in the hope of winning the unbelieving spouse to the Lord. Furthermore, he assures his readers that the children of this mixed union will be sanctified by the ethical action of the Christian spouse in remaining in the marriage.

MARRIAGE, AN EXTENDED ROMANCE

God created humankind with sexual drive. With the creation of woman came the injunction that since she was taken from the side of man, the couple would become "one flesh." With this union the man was to leave his father and his mother for the woman's sake and live with her under the smile of God's approval. Centuries later Christ would deal with this very issue in response to the question of the Pharisees as to whether it was lawful for a man to put away his wife for any cause. When Jesus insisted that to put away one's wife was to commit adultery, His disciples were aghast. Their conclusion: "'It is better not to marry'" (Matt. 19:10). It is here that Jesus makes it clear that to live a life of sexual abstinence is not to demonstrate a higher ethical or spiritual standard than that held by married persons. There are eunuchs "born without the ability to marry, and some are disabled by men, and some refuse to marry for the sake of the Kingdom of Heaven" (Matt. 19:11–12, TLB). But the happy, healthy married man will be a loving husband to the wife God has joined him to.

Although God instituted marriage and provided men and women with the capacity to initiate and enjoy lovemaking, it becomes our responsibility to keep the fire of romance burning brightly. Without romance the best marriage will fail. Ministers must strive with enthusiasm to make their marriage happy and exemplary. The marriage relationship in the parsonage, whether by design or coincidence, becomes the model for marriage relationships in the homes of the parishioners as well.

Faced with the responsibility of setting a good example for the church—and the community for that matter—how do ministers and their spouses keep the marriage relationship both interesting and desirable, even exciting at times? This cannot be accomplished unless the marriage itself rests on a bedrock of mutual love and admiration. If the initial attraction that brought the couple together has faded, the first step is to carefully rekindle the flame. Since the Scriptures enjoin the husband to love the wife (while requiring the wife to respect her husband), he must simply fill the God-given role of courting and wooing his mate with genuine affection. He will never stoop to coercion, bribes, or threats to satisfy his sexual urges. To do so is to reduce the act of lovemaking to the unethical practice of using one's spouse.

While the husband recognizes his charge to be the keeper of the flame, the thoughtful wife sees herself as tinder, feeding the flame until it becomes a burning passion and delight. It is her role to be courted. She will be coy, flirtatious, making herself desirable for him to have and to hold. All of this becomes readily possible if care has been exercised in holding fast to the "first love" that initiated the union.

But tragedy lurks behind the bedroom curtains when either husband or wife must seek an artificial stimulus to enable an acceptable performance in bed. I recall with considerable sadness, even to this day, a couple, personal friends, whose marriage and young family were destroyed because they ignored this major danger sign. Their relationship had regressed to the point that the wife found it necessary to read pornographic literature at bedtime before being able to respond to her husband. Within a few months the couple had separated. Divorce soon followed, depriving their two children of the right to a well-ordered upbringing and compromising a ministry that never recovered. Add to the above a troubled congregation to complete yet another of the thousands of similar sad sagas of arrested love affairs.

Here are a few suggestions for maintaining a wholesome marital relationship or possibly even salvaging an unhealthy one:

1. Talk frankly with your spouse about your sexual needs.

2. Work (yes, work!) at maintaining a loving, tender relationship.

3. Don't let an argument turn into a standing feud. (Take the humble part.)

4. Occasionally, go together to a marriage seminar. (Regardless of the benefit, merely going will speak volumes to your mate.)

5. Should the relationship seem to be in trouble, don't let the word "divorce" be uttered before going for counseling.

Make sure you are doing the little things that make for a happy union. For example, remember the special days each year that have romantic overtones for you and your spouse. Choose a romantic spot for dinner or vacation now and then. Affirm your mate with sincere compliments. Dress for your companion, not for others. Take time to make yourself appealing to your mate. Learn to say the words "I love you" without inhibition. Don't make your spouse assume your affection; express your love. Even if at times it seems hypocritical to utter the "three little words," you will never be judged unethical for your efforts. Finally, always honor your spouse, both in public (whether from the pulpit or in conversation) and in private.

COUNSELING IN SEXUAL MATTERS

When is it appropriate for ministers to counsel in marital and sexual concerns? Provided you have had some class instruction on the subject in preparation for pastoral ministry, you should feel competent to conduct a marriage seminar on occasion. However, private counseling on serious marital problems is another thing, requiring special training. Pastors will do well to refer such cases to a competent Christian professional. Even when qualified to help couples with delicate marital problems, pastors face the risk of losing them from the congregation as the result of the counseling experience: Most couples find it difficult to receive the preaching of a minister who is aware of their deepest, and possibly darkest, secrets.

Should the minister feel it essential in ministry to engage in marital or sexual counseling, it is important to get adequate training and be well-read on the subject. Age will often be a factor in the appropriateness of a given counseling situation. If the minister is considerably younger and more immature or significantly older than the counselees, they may be uncomfortable with the arrangement. Above all, the minister must maintain credibility and complete confidentiality with those seeking help. If at all possible, the sessions should be conducted in the church office or at the parsonage with the minister's spouse present. Such an arrangement will not be objectionable to the counselees if they respect the minister's marriage partner and their integrity as a team. If such respect is not present, the counseling session will not be effective anyway.

In short, most ministers will do well to cover the basics of marital counseling from the pulpit in a tasteful, objective way. Since most of the marital difficulties that find their way into the church are primarily spiritual problems, the biblically based sermon is the most effective antidote available to the minister. It is the pastor's responsibility to preach that husbands must love their wives, but just as importantly, wives must show their husbands the deference due them. No home can be happy if the wife constantly seeks to dominate or belittle her husband. The spouse's role is that of a help, remembering that the word "help" in the Bible is usually used of God being a help to His people and therefore does not denote any inferiority. As she elevates the level of her regard and respect for her husband, she elevates her own level of joy in the marriage relationship. Her appreciation of her mate will be the reflection of a warm, fulfilling love affair when he, in keeping with the biblical formula, has set the beautiful standard for their marriage adventure by loving her "just as Christ loved the church and gave himself up for her to make her holy" (Eph. 5:25–26).

SEXUAL PITFALLS TO AVOID

1. Men need to be especially cautious when serving as a source of comfort and renewed self-esteem to a disillusioned woman. She will at this time most likely be yearning deeply for affection from someone she can trust and appreciate. As you offer her support, it can be a natural turn of events for your concern to become an infatuation, particularly if she is a highly desirable woman. But be forewarned: Do not allow your spiritual support for her to become the basis of an improper personal relationship.

2. Never take advantage of the love and trust that the female counselee brings to the session. Since it is not uncommon for a minister to have an ego problem, he may subconsciously welcome the adulation

that results. What began as an innocent mutual appreciation can get out of control unless care is exercised.

3. Do not engage in or encourage the vigorous frontal hugging (and often kissing) that are all too frequently a part of charismatic circles. This activity, in theory at least, is evidence of spiritual bonding between the participants. In practice it easily becomes a snare, as the "bonding" is enjoyed with members of the opposite sex only. What at first is merely deplorable conduct can become a serious morals problem.

A few years ago one of our great churches was rocked by the moral failure of its pastor. He had advocated the exchange of warm affection in public and was on occasion observed by visiting minister friends openly embracing his attractive secretary (incidentally, the wife of another minister) in the halls of the church between services. The ensuing affair brought havoc into the church and destroyed the integrity of the pastor's marriage and that of his secretary.

4. Beware of the unscrupulous woman who makes a play for the minister. What finer prize could she take than a man of the cloth! Blessed is the minister who is alert to this tender trap or whose wife has that God-endowed instinct to spot the problem before it becomes serious. Along with taking every reasonable precaution, the minister must look to the Lord for His help in this area of concern.

In the early years of my pastoral ministry, an attractive young mother came into the church with a letter of good standing from her former pastor. She was talented and appeared modest, but I was disturbed by her practice of wanting to converse with me frequently after services or to arrange private conferences. Of course, I shared the problem with my wife. Within a few months we were shocked to learn that this woman had had an affair five years before with a man claiming to be a minister, even bearing him a child. We thanked God for His faithfulness in providing the warning signal.

5. The minister, as any other man, becomes vulnerable to sexual temptation when he, as well as his wife, is rebounding from a serious misunderstanding or a period of sexual maladjustment. He becomes an easy target for an enterprising woman who can take the role of pursuer before he is fully aware of the problem. How critical it is to "keep the home fires burning"! Any couple enjoying a loving, warm relationship has a primary defense against the temptation, for either spouse, to fall into sexual sin or even to engage in unethical behavior outside the marriage.

CONDUCT WITH MEMBERS OF THE OPPOSITE SEX

Hopefully ministers will be loved and admired by both the women and the men of the church. In response they will want to relate to members of the opposite sex in a wholesome yet fulfilling way. They will find it desirable to establish rapport with all members of the church by drawing prudent lines of personal integrity and adhering to them.

For example, the minister will never publicly embarrass those who may have shown undue affection. In some cases the minister may have misjudged its expression. Even if such people are at fault, they should be dealt with kindly. The wise action of the minister in such awkward circumstances will be far more effective than anything that could possibly be said in correcting a potentially damaging situation. On the other hand, the minister will be careful to avoid situations that may appear to be morally questionable no matter how innocent the individual(s). Nolan B. Harmon observes:

The danger in ministerial service to women is not so much error on the minister's part—though there are doubtless foolish women in churches as well as out; and there are weak brethren—but the causing of comment and gossip that would embarrass the minister's service. The merest nothing will start a scandal, and the sensible minister knows it and acts accordingly.

It has been advised that calls alone on young married women in the absence of the husband should be avoided. It is suggested that some other person accompany the minister, and this is a sensible procedure when calling on a woman in her home. Repeated calls on any one woman should be avoided, since these will give rise to talk. If long-term counseling is necessary it should be conducted in the minister's office. Anything that will cause gossip should be shunned.[3]

What should the minister do when faced with events as intense as those that faced Joseph in the home of his master, Potiphar? Do precisely what Joseph did—run! Regardless of the attraction, regardless of the unlikelihood of discovery, no person of God can afford such a foolish mistake. One needs only to begin to count the cost to be able to resist the temptation. Such moral failure will adversely affect the remainder of one's life and that of one's spouse, children, and other family members. In addition, those affected, both directly and indirectly, will include the other party in the affair, the family, the local church, the minister's denomination, and, above all else, the Lord himself and His kingdom.

A primary consideration for how a man who is a minister relates to members of the opposite sex, and especially to his wife, is the fact that he serves as an important role model for the males in his congregation. If he fails to properly respect his wife or other women in the church, his attitude will be reflected in time by at least some of the men of the church and frequently even by his own sons. Fortunately, in some instances where the minister has been careless and unethical in relating to the opposite sex, his children have been so deeply grieved by their parents'

---

[3]Nolan B. Harmon, *Ministerial Ethics and Etiquette*, 2d rev. ed. (Nashville: Abingdon Press, 1987), 92–93.

unhappiness, they have determined not to make the same mistake.

A pastor's conduct must be such that should there be someone with designs on him in the congregation, that person will know the pastor to be upright and moral. Ethics for the minister in this instance is a reflection of the psychological and mental aspects of proper conduct, whereas the minister's moral standards become the physical expression of what lies within the heart. Jesus stressed the importance of wholesome ethical behavior when He said that for a man to lust after a woman in his heart was tantamount to committing the act (Matt. 5:28). How much wiser for the man to settle the issue in his heart and find forgiveness from his Lord than to ultimately carry out the act of adultery with all its tragic consequences for so many.

Another problem that may face the minister who conducts himself carelessly around women in the church comes from his own home. A jealous minister's spouse is capable of the same reactions to her husband's deplorable conduct as any other woman. Cases are on record in which the spouse of the pastor engaged in her own affair to spite her imprudent husband. The results can be just as devastating as if the minister himself had had a full-blown affair.

When problems of sexual impropriety arise in the lives of prominent ministers, the publicity mushrooms across the country like an atomic detonation. The morsel-hungry media sees to that. However, although the blare of adverse publicity unfailingly points out these cases, thousands of good, clean-living ministers quietly conduct themselves as men of God should. They love and respect their wives and families and are highly esteemed by everyone who knows them and has been blessed by their ministries.

It is encouraging to observe from year to year that in the Pentecostal fellowship I am affiliated with, as well as with many other evangelical Protestant groups around the world, the vast majority of ministers never have a morals problem requiring discipline. This story will never make the headlines of the tabloids, but it is emblazoned in golden characters in the annals of heaven.

STUDY QUESTIONS

1. What is significant about the fact that God created Adam and Eve with the capability of free choice?

2. What Bible passages compare the relationship of God and His people or Christ and the Church to the marriage relationship, and what do these passages teach us about the marriage relationship?

3. What does the Bible have to say about sex acts outside of the marriage relationship?

4. What are some of the ways a marriage can be kept happy and exemplary?

5. Why is it necessary to work at maintaining a healthy, tender, loving relationship between the husband and wife?

6. What precautions should a minister take when counseling someone who has problems in sexual matters?

7. What precautions should ministers take in all their ministry to the opposite sex?

Chapter 12

The Minister and Moral Failure: Finding Restoration through Grace

Any moral failure is tragic. But of all the transgressions a minister may commit, none seems more difficult to recover from than sexual indiscretion. Several years ago a group of evangelical leaders were asked whether a man who had fallen into sexual immorality should be restored to the pastorate. The response was that it was possible but highly unlikely. The same leaders stated that only after a number of years had elapsed would they or their denomination call a pastor back into ministry. Often, the restoration was effective only when the congregation did not know about the minister's past.[1] These responses may be typical among church leaders but the power of God's redeeming grace to restore should never be left out of such considerations.

FACTORS CONTRIBUTING TO MORAL FAILURE

For properly relating to fallen ministers it is helpful to understand the factors contributing to their failure and the process by which they may be restored. Chief among the causes of moral failure is the most obvious one: a spiritual problem. The minister must at all times maintain the attitude that Joseph held toward this kind of failure. He said simply, "'How then could I do such a wicked thing and sin against God?'"

---

[1]Erwin W. Lutzer, *Pastor to Pastor: Tackling Problems of the Pulpit* (Chicago: Moody Press, 1987), 129–30.

Part 3

Chapter 12
The Minister
and Moral
Failure:
Finding
Restoration
through
Grace

(Gen. 39:9). Yet there are many factors that mitigate against the basic attitude of loving God to such an extent that we cannot fail.

Overwork is an enemy of both spiritual growth and moral strength. The tasks of the day produce tremendous emotional strain. Fatigue has a way of warping one's values, crowding out the moments needed to relax and to reflect. It is essential to spend quality time in the presence of God. Far too often the minister becomes guilty of "maintenance prayer," just enough prayer to salve the conscience and maintain spiritual tone for the soul.

Marital discord can contribute in a major way to moral indiscretion. Sometimes an immoral act is merely an act of revenge or spite against one's mate. The act may be the result of jealousy, the archenemy of harmony in the home. If harmony exists in the home and the minister's love affair with his wife is intact, there is little danger from a third party.

The careless pastor may easily be led into a moral trap as a result of his own ego. The minister in his public role may create his own overblown self-image. Even his success in the pulpit can cause him to have a distorted view of himself. He may feel that he is the all-conquering hero, abounding in ability, prepared to engage in the conquest of the most appealing member of the opposite sex who happens to be an admirer.

Then there is the opposite situation. This is the minister with a poor self-image who without warning is overwhelmed when an attractive woman in the congregation appears to be interested in him. He may have failed to win the affection of his congregation, but the affection of this appealing person will make up for it.

Most ministers, thankfully, will never fall into sexual indiscretion. Nonetheless, it is wise to be forewarned of the possibility. "If you think you are standing firm, be careful that you don't fall!" (1 Cor. 10:12). The situation may steal up on the inattentive average minister or the sensitive minister who may have a tendency to identify strongly with those he counsels.

Part 3

**Chapter 12
The Minister
and Moral
Failure:
Finding
Restoration
through
Grace**

NECESSITY OF THE DISCIPLINARY PROCESS

My denomination is among those that view restoration as possible and desirable. Galatians 6:1 calls for restoration: "Brothers, if someone is caught in a sin, you who are spiritual should restore him gently. But watch yourself, or you also may be tempted." Lutzer's commentary on this verse emphasizes the Greek word *katartizō*, "restore to its proper condition," which is also used of setting a broken bone. "Unfortunately, many bones in the Body of Christ have remained out of joint and have never been restored."[2]

Before the healing process can begin, discipline must be administered—for the sake of the fallen minister as well as the other person(s) involved. The minister's feeling of guilt and shame for the sin is appropriate, helping him realize that this kind of failure calls for discipline. Nothing short of firm corrective measures will satisfy the sense of justice among the members of the family of the "other party." The minister's congregation will feel mollified after having been deceived. Discipline will help the offender deal with the personal seriousness of the problem and to be fortified against repeating it.

Discipline is not condemnation. Jesus said, "'Neither do I condemn you. . . . Go now and leave your life of sin'" (John 8:11). Discipline is not primarily punitive; it is restorative. But what is to be restored? Ironically, returning to ministry is usually the highest priority to fallen ministers, but that should be recognized as far less important than other considerations. Although the ministry may have been their livelihood, their return to ministry is not an ethical or spiritual priority. The kingdom of God will survive if they do

---

[2]Ibid., 131.

Part 3

Chapter 12
The Minister
and Moral
Failure:
Finding
Restoration
through
Grace

not return to the pulpit. The critical issue is their return to spiritual wholeness.

First, the minister's relationship with God must be readjusted. If the minister's relationship to God remains in question, it creates an insurmountable problem to beginning the disciplinary and restorative processes. On the other hand, if the minister has made a voluntary confession of sin, there will be a vast difference in the approach to rehabilitation. In most such cases, the restoration process is assured of success.

Next to the relationship with God, it is essential that the minister's relationship with spouse and family be restored. One can never hope to resume a meaningful ministry until the breach in one's closest relationship has been repaired fully. At this point steps may be taken directly toward restoration to the ministry.

For the minister the restoration process involves the return of his self-esteem, his sense of belonging to the community of saints. He must know that he is truly forgiven by God and the people. Then once again he will be able to serve as a fruitful, contributing member of the body of Christ, a trophy of God's redeeming grace.

IMPACT OF A FRIEND'S FAILURE

One closely connected to a fallen minister will likely react in two different ways: First, the individual may feel betrayed and deceived, even hurt, that a close friend has acted so unworthily and inconsiderately of those who love him. The friend can react so intensely that all communication is cut off between them; a bond is forever broken.

An opposite reaction may be that the friend becomes protective and defensive of the erring minister, perhaps even encouraging resentment of and resistance to the restoration process. While it is highly commendable that a friend offer to share the burden of discipline, much of the load must be borne by

Part 3

Chapter 12
The Minister
and Moral
Failure:
Finding
Restoration
through
Grace

the fallen minister alone if it is to accomplish God's purpose. God uses discipline to strengthen His weak children. I read once of a lover of nature who was walking through the woods and spotted a cocoon attached to a tree branch. The cocoon was being violently distorted by a caterpillar struggling to get out. The sympathetic observer broke the cocoon open to assist the creature, but, alas, no butterfly emerged. The creature died.

Regardless of one's reaction, one's relationship to the fallen friend will be changed by that friend's trespass. Only time can heal such hurt. The situation becomes harder to deal with if there has been no previous knowledge of the erring minister's latent weakness. I vividly recall, always with a sinking sensation, a once outstanding minister friend I came to know and appreciate when we were both young and finding our way in the ministry. We were both ordained on the same evening, and each of us had proudly presented a son for dedication on that occasion. We had conducted services together and had enjoyed great times of fellowship, including picnics and outings with our young families. My friend had moved to another state to accept a pastorate when I was shocked by the report of his dismissal on charges of homosexuality. It was as if I had taken a blow to the midsection. My friend requested no help, nor did the district offer any. He moved to another part of the country, and I have not seen him for years. The pain of the separation caused by his sin and his refusal to turn from the past only heightened his ethical dilemma. It became virtually impossible for him to cross the line of separation created by his failure, which was further compounded by a determined resistance to any help that could possibly be offered.

Consequences of the Fall of Nationally Known Figures

It is difficult to feel the emotional and psychological fallout caused by the failure of men who are wide-

Part 3

Chapter 12
The Minister
and Moral
Failure:
Finding
Restoration
through
Grace

ly known and part of one's own denomination other than by going through the experience. Glittering publicity highlights the embarrassment. Media reporters hound every minister who may be able to provide a thread of information on the subject. One's personal friends outside the church are puzzled. Some are inclined to question the integrity of even the most highly regarded ministries. The credibility of the fallen minister's denomination is undermined. The ministry in general is challenged and maligned.

When an internationally known television evangelist failed several years ago, a fellow minister who pastors a good-sized church in the South was faced with a most awkward situation. A wealthy woman who attended the church had made a sizable loan to the church to assist in a building program. When the news of the totally unrelated scandal hit the streets, the woman immediately demanded repayment of the loan, creating a difficult situation for the church and its pastor.

Sad to say, within a short time two other prominent ministers of the same fellowship had moral failures as well. All three were personal acquaintances of mine. Although I had not always agreed with certain aspects of their ministries, I had always appreciated their contributions to the work of the Lord. When their failures became evident, I found myself wondering if they had been sincere at any point in their ministries.

Two of these men have continued with independent ministries, never having accepted the available disciplinary and restorative processes. One of the men not only rejected the rehabilitation program that he had once strongly advocated but also allowed one of his supporters to write a book defending the rejection. His logic was that he really didn't understand the impact of the program until he was experiencing it. Then he felt it was unfair. At that point he claimed that the whole process needed to be changed.

The most damaging fallout of this moral indiscretion is the reinforcement of the human tendency to

Concerns with the Disciplinary Process **235**

Part 3

Chapter 12
The Minister
and Moral
Failure:
Finding
Restoration
through
Grace

generalize, in this instance, to discredit all television ministries. These men, by their base actions, have given credence to the Elmer Gantry stereotype of ministry held by skeptical observers of the religious scene. There remain many sincere, godly men and women who use the media to the glory of God. The tragedy is further heightened by the fact that these fallen ministers profess to be Spirit-filled believers. Were this the case, such disasters could be averted by simply being sure we are among those "who do not live according to the sinful nature but according to the Spirit" (Rom. 8:4).

CONCERNS WITH THE DISCIPLINARY PROCESS

The leadership of the largest international Pentecostal movement in the nation can be justifiably proud of the high standard of its application of the disciplinary process for fallen ministers. In one situation in which the minister was internationally known and had been a heavy contributor to missions causes within the denomination, the leadership refused to back down after dealing with his problem in an even-handed manner. In other situations where the general public has been highly sympathetic with the fallen minister, the denomination has been consistent in meting out the necessary measures to correct each situation.

This denomination has one of the finest restoration programs among the churches of America. It is the policy not to publish the names of those who are being dismissed, provided they will enroll in a two-year rehabilitation program. During the course of the program the minister must attend a church under a mature supervising pastor. The enrollee in the program is then given the privilege of limited ministry, first in the local church, then gradually an expanded ministry until full restoration is achieved. The minister may have his credentials returned at the end of the two-year program.

Part 3

Chapter 12
The Minister
and Moral
Failure:
Finding
Restoration
through
Grace

This program reflects the grace of God in its application but raises a few ethical problems along the way. Since the dismissed ministers' names are not published, it leaves them and their ministry in an ambivalent state. They normally move immediately from their community and are no longer active in ministry. Their close acquaintances and those who know them by reputation must receive the information about their moral problem and proposed rehabilitation by way of the grapevine.

Until recently, the program allowed restored ministers to transfer from district to district without knowledge of their situation being conveyed to those who should be available to encourage and support them in their new environment. It would be far more desirable for leaders of a different district to be fully apprised of the transferee's problem and completion of the rehabilitation program than for them to learn it by chance. The denomination has taken official action recently to correct this problem. Now when ministers transfer to another district, they can expect the prayers and sympathetic concern of the leaders of their new district as well as of their former district.

An even more serious problem related to the withholding of information of moral failure has emerged in the courts. If a pastor has had a morals problem and transfers to another church where he experiences a similar problem, the family members of a subsequent "victim" have a solid legal basis for bringing suit against church leaders who permitted him to transfer and did not share knowledge of the problem.

Along with the legal liability in such situations, the question arises as to whether it is ethically correct to withhold such information from a church about to elect a pastor they assume has an unblemished record of conduct. Just such a situation occurred some years ago when a fellow district officer presented the name of a pastoral candidate to the board of a fine church. The candidate had committed a relatively minor infraction in his former district; it had involved questionable conduct but had not been serious enough to warrant the rehabilitation process. The board, which served as the pulpit committee, approved the candidate and recommended him to the church membership, whereupon he was elected as pastor. A few years later at the new church, the minister was again accused of questionable conduct. At this point, the board of the church learned about the previous problem in his former district and let the leadership of our district know in no uncertain terms that they were upset that the information had been withheld.

This experience highlights the question: Is it proper to withhold information of this nature from a church that will be accepting such a candidate as pastor? It is far better for the church to know the circumstances and to approve the candidate without reservation. In fact, there are cases on record where the congregation expressed even greater appreciation for the candidate after knowing of the problem and his success by the grace of God in overcoming it.

Proper Attitudes toward the Other Party

Often the other party in an affair is in the church pastored by the offender. It is difficult for the other party (as well as family members) to remain in the local church even if everyone involved is fully repentant. When it is feasible for the other party to remain in the church, that person and the family need to be supported and loved by the congregation. Such a person should never be ostracized or forced to carry a burden of shame and guilt. If the congregation is able to forgive all other transgressions among its membership, surely moral indiscretion can be forgiven as well.

The fallen minister has a responsibility to the other person in the affair, including any family. The minister will need to ask forgiveness of the other party and spouse, if married. The minister has sinned against both persons, as well as against his own spouse, and has seriously threatened their marriage. It is impor-

Part 3

Chapter 12
The Minister
and Moral
Failure:
Finding
Restoration
through
Grace

Part 3

Chapter 12
The Minister
and Moral
Failure:
Finding
Restoration
through
Grace

tant that there be a phase of the restoration process that applies to the other party and family members. It is unfortunate that often this part of the restoration process is completely omitted.

MINISTRY TO THE FAMILY OF THE FALLEN MINISTER

The initial phase of the process of restoration will focus on restoring the marital bonds now shattered by the transgression of the minister. Even while the all-important relationship between minister and spouse is being mended, a special effort needs to be made by friends and associates of the family of the minister to encourage them, to show them love, and to boost their spirits. They should be included fully in all the programs of the church they are attending, which will often not be their original church.

The family may need financial support at this time. They have had the expense of moving to a new location, and the head of the household has been without income for a time. The spouse, as well as the minister, needs to go to counseling, which will add a further financial burden to the family, a burden which can easily be shared by the church and the district organization. One of the chief goals of the restorative process is to strengthen the family ties of those involved in this unfortunate situation. The minister's family must be lovingly replanted in the fellowship of believers as well as in the good graces of the local community.

POSITIVE RELATIONSHIP WITH THE DISCIPLINED MINISTER

The fellow ministers of an erring brother or sister must respect the disciplinary process regardless of their personal knowledge and feelings. Despite the difficulty of remaining objective when the focus of the program is a close, personal friend, it is critical that the disciplinary process be fully supported or it will not be effective. Good judgment dictates that all those directly or indirectly involved will be careful

Part 3

Chapter 12
The Minister
and Moral
Failure:
Finding
Restoration
through
Grace

not to bring up suggestions of the unfairness of the program or its lack of objectivity. Such comments do not help the minister friend, the process of restoration, or the denomination.

It is important for fellow ministers to respect the family and to be supportive of them, especially the offended spouse. Where there are children, they are going through a severe traumatic experience. They need tender consideration from all who surround them. The man or woman who is the subject of the rehabilitation process needs the respect and love that others can provide by the power of the Holy Spirit. This is especially the case when the fallen minister has shown a repentant attitude and is firmly committed to come all the way back to a fruitful life and ministry. When the Spirit of Christ prevails among the ministers who make up the fellowship of the erring individual, it is a simple matter to forget and forgive. The Master set a beautiful example for us in this regard after He had been repeatedly betrayed by Simon Peter. Immediately following the Resurrection the angel's instruction to the women inside the empty tomb was "'Go, tell his disciples and Peter'" (Mark 16:7). Completely forgiven by Christ, Peter had been singled out to receive a special invitation.

When the same Spirit that raised Christ from the dead dwells in the Church, we will be enabled to help bring to life again the faith of the fallen minister. We will share in renewing the confidence and assurance of the family. We will rejoice in the restoration of the unity and vitality of the church itself.

STUDY QUESTIONS

1. The text lists contributing factors to moral failure. What are some ways that each of these can be overcome?

2. What lessons can be drawn from Galatians 6:1?

3. What should be involved in the discipline of a

Part 3

Chapter 12
The Minister
and Moral
Failure:
Finding
Restoration
through
Grace

fallen minister?

4. How should friends of a fallen minister help in the restoration process?

5. What effects of the fall of a minister have you observed and what have you done about it?

6. What is involved in the restoration process used by your denomination?

7. What can be done to help the family of a fallen minister?

Chapter 13

The Minister and Influence: Dealing with Power and Authority

By the power of example the pastor wields greater influence than any other person in the church. Often members will unconsciously imitate the pastor's mannerisms, personal tastes, and character. Some members will purchase cars or homes similar to the pastor's. Almost any of the pastor's idiosyncrasies will be reflected by some persons in the church.

Ministers usually attract people to the church who are similar to them in some way. If they happen to be young, young people are attracted. If they are sober or fun loving, they can expect to have either grave or lively people drawn toward their leadership, as the case may be.

Some years ago I attended a clinic conducted by Dr. Clyde Narramore, who discussed this phenomenon of like attracting like. He had known a young minister, a schizophrenic, who over a period of time had apparently pulled in a church full of people with the same malady. Rare though it may be, it illustrates the potential of the minister's influence. Awareness of this should cause conscientious ministers to be doubly careful to model Christlike traits and to use sound judgment before the church and the community.

THE SCOPE OF MINISTERIAL INFLUENCE

Ministers should be the most highly regarded members of the community. They are civic leaders simply

241

Part 3

Chapter 13
The Minister
and
Influence:
Dealing with
Power and
Authority

by virtue of being pastors and will be asked at times to preside over or to participate in important functions in the community. The minister's presence will be expected at sporting events, particularly in smaller towns where it is customary for an all-consuming but wholesome school spirit to prevail. The minister's conduct at such events is important.

A pastor in the community where I also served had been a good athlete when he was younger and had become an umpire for Little League ball games. But his stern, almost belligerent attitude when he was officiating damaged his reputation, limiting the size of his congregation. He had mastered the elements of justice and righteousness but lacked the steadfast love that makes ethics complete. He simply never seemed to show the gentle side of godly ethics.

Ministers are expected to exercise their influence by speaking out for good government and high moral standards in the community. They will often be called upon to lead or support citizens' opposition to pornography shops, bars, and gambling houses in the neighborhood.

Frequently their influence will reach beyond the community, on occasion reaching a statewide or national scope in government or politics. Richard Foster highlights the significance of this use of ministerial authority by observing:

> The state, the arena of politics, needs the life-giving ministry of spiritual power. All believers, but particularly those in democracies, are to call the state to its God-given function of justice for all people alike. We are to commend the state whenever it fulfills its calling and confront it when it fails.
>
> When I speak of the state I am not just referring to national governments, though I certainly mean to include them. By the state I mean all those systems of human organization whereby we empower people to represent and serve the whole. School boards, regulatory agencies, state

legislators, public health organizations, city councils, courts, and many others are all part of the state.[1]

Part 3

Chapter 13
The Minister
and
Influence:
Dealing with
Power and
Authority

At best, the minister's political involvement may be limited, as Otto A. Piper suggests: "Christians will participate in the life of the nation, yet in a detached way. They will consider it their privilege to decide how far they will support a political system or action. Such an attitude entails at times considerable difficulties. . . . We may feel unable, for instance, to support an act of legislation, or a war which our government wages against another country. But we do not give up allegiance to our country." Piper further contends that the Church, in order to maintain its detachment from the non-Christian activities of national life, cannot afford to identify itself directly with the body politic.[2]

I have known several ministers who were mayors or state legislators. They used this broader expression of their ministerial authority to improve local and statewide government, bringing glory to God in the process. To blend a high ethic of ministry with the ethics of political involvement should invariably produce an elevated level of service.

Opportunity for the Church's involvement in politics is at an optimum in our country. According to J. Philip Wogaman: "The Christian church is not dependent upon any particular political order. It has coexisted, in turn, with the Roman Empire, the disintegrated territorial states, the feudal baronies and kingdoms, modern nations and empires, and even totalitarian regimes. But it has been freest to be itself in a democratic environment."[3]

---

[1]Richard J. Foster, *Money, Sex and Power: The Challenge of the Disciplined Life* (San Francisco: Harper & Row Publishers, 1985), 225.

[2]Otto A. Piper, *Christian Ethics* (London: Thomas Nelson & Sons, 1970), 239.

[3]J. Philip Wogaman, *Christian Ethics: A Historical Introduction* (Louisville: Westminster/John Knox Press, 1993), 281.

Part 3

Chapter 13
The Minister
and
Influence:
Dealing with
Power and
Authority

The scope of ministry has been broadened considerably for those ministers engaging in televangelism. Many such ministers, Billy Graham in particular, have used this God-given influence to lead people to Christ or into a closer relationship with Him. Sadly, the unethical principles of a few men engaged in this highly publicized ministry have served to discredit the cause of Christ.

It is important for the men and women of God to realize that, for better or for worse, they will be people of influence. The more ethical and discreet they are, the more impact they will have for the kingdom of God. Their influence will live on in the lives and character of those who have been influenced by their lives and ministry.

BIBLICAL MODELS OF SPIRITUAL AUTHORITY

The Old Testament instructs fathers to be the priests of the home and calls for both fathers and mothers to teach their children the laws and statutes handed down by God through Moses. But even prior to the giving of the Law, Abraham served as a model in his home in leading the family from Ur of the Chaldees and later interceding for Lot and the cities of Sodom and Gomorrah. What a powerful illustration he left us when he chose the highest ethic of obedience to God: offering up Isaac, contrary to his own good judgment! A further tribute to his domestic leadership is found in Sarah's relationship to him, a model for Christian wives: "Sarah . . . obeyed Abraham and called him her master. You are her daughters if you do what is right and do not give way to fear" (1 Pet. 3:6).

Jacob, his character seriously flawed, had his personality and ethics overhauled by a physical encounter with God. Subsequently, he came to be respected by his sons as not only the head of the family, but also as their spiritual leader. His position of authority over his strong-willed sons was highlighted by the family's departure for Egypt; they accepted his decision to be dependents of Joseph and Pharaoh's court.

Part 3

**Chapter 13
The Minister
and
Influence:
Dealing with
Power and
Authority**

In later years the prophets of the Old Testament exercised ethical and spiritual authority to the extent that kings and noblemen often cowed before them. Saul, even in his backslidden state, had high regard for Samuel. Ahab quailed before Elijah. Nathan could point his finger in David's face and say, "'You are the man!'" (2 Sam. 12:7). Elisha's instructions to a proud Syrian general had to be obeyed to the letter in order to produce his healing. At the close of the intertestamental period, John the Baptist, fearless preacher of the doctrine of pure ethics, challenged the adulterous King Herod, who revered and feared him. Even following John's martyrdom, the king lived in dread of his memory.

Perhaps the most striking revelation of Christ's authority came from the lips of the centurion, who reasoned that if he, a man of authority, could order men to do his bidding, it would be a small matter for Christ to bring healing to his servant by a spoken word (Matt. 8:8-10). The centurion's comprehension of spiritual authority was hailed by Christ as the greatest example of faith He had seen in all of Israel. It is worth noting that the entire eighth chapter of Matthew, where the centurion's story is recorded, gives us a number of instances where Christ exercised spiritual authority in accord with the highest ethical standard: He used His authority over space in healing the servant who was a distance away (vv. 6-8,13). He had already taken authority over leprosy, a type of sin (v. 3). He manifested authority over common household illnesses and all types of sickness (vv. 14-16). He amazed His disciples with His control of the stormy winds and seas (vv. 26-27). He shook an entire city by taking command of a host of demons (vv. 28-34).

As the Early Church took form, Peter, whose ethics had been transformed and energized by the power of the indwelling Holy Spirit, became a leader in the Church. Paul had held to an ethical standard that drove him to fight the Church, only to become its

Part 3

Chapter 13
The Minister
and
Influence:
Dealing with
Power and
Authority

representative who would stand before kings, Roman centurions, and the Church itself. He was persecuted, stoned, and beaten, but his spiritual authority was seldom questioned; it was the authority of the Holy Spirit himself.

Along with examples of the proper use of authority, the Bible gives some negative instances as well. Saul, Israel's first king, abused the authority invested in the throne. Later David took unethical advantage of his kingly role in his affair with Bathsheba and the murder of her husband. Balaam is a classic example of the false prophet whose scruples would allow him to make merchandise of God's Word. In the New Testament, Simon's code of ethics, developed through years of practicing sorcery, gave him license to offer money in exchange for spiritual authority.

THE MINISTER'S RESPONSE TO THE LORDSHIP OF CHRIST

To make the proper use of spiritual authority, ministers must bear in mind their relationship to the true Head of the Church. Christ is Lord over the Church and over the minister. The resurrected Christ has given ministries to the Church, among them pastors. Their function is to lead the saints as they "grow up into him who is the Head" of the Church (Eph. 4:11–15). Christ's will must remain paramount in the life of the minister and the church.

Any authority that the minister exercises has been given by Christ. First, Christ modeled the ethical use of spiritual power, then transmitted it by the Spirit to His called ministers. Richard J. Foster in *Money, Sex and Power* points out the sequence:

> Jesus' ministry was marked with authority. Spiritual power and spiritual authority are inseparable. In his Gospel, Mark tells of Jesus' healing of a demon-possessed person, adding that the people "were all amazed, so that they questioned among themselves, saying, 'What is this? A new teaching! With authority he commands even the unclean spirits, and they obey him'" (Mark 1:27). Jesus was not giv-

Part 3

**Chapter 13
The Minister
and
Influence:
Dealing with
Power and
Authority**

ing a new teaching; he was demonstrating a new power. He not only proclaimed the presence of the kingdom of God, He demonstrated its presence with power.

Now if Jesus had been the only one who exercised the ministry of power, we might be able to dismiss it as the privileged domain of the Messiah, but he delegated this same ministry to others.[4]

This delegation of authority stems from the Lord's initial calling to follow Him in dedicated service. With the calling comes moral and ethical empowerment. The power-laden commission, first verbalized to the disciples but transmitted to every called minister through the Scriptures, is clear in its ethical intent: "'I will give you the keys of the kingdom of heaven; whatever you bind on earth will be bound in heaven, and whatever you loose on earth will be loosed in heaven'" (Matt. 16:19). Thus, the minister becomes the ethically authorized instrument through whom the Spirit works "just as he determines" (1 Cor. 12:11).

Empowered by the Spirit, the minister finds a place to function in the body of Christ. The ministry ethics of the members of the Body dictate that there be no hierarchy of power or authority. God has set the members in the Body as has pleased Him. Members that seem less desirable have been given even greater honor than other members. As a result, any glory that comes from the authority and power granted to an individual member of the Body goes directly to God. "'He who glories, let him glory in the LORD'" (2 Cor. 10:17, NKJV). In this connection, Erwin W. Lutzer comments:

The implications for our ministry are obvious. *God's people do not exist for their own benefit but for His benefit.* In our interpersonal relationships, we must remember that we are dealing with God's property, His people redeemed for

---

[4]Foster, *Money, Sex and Power,* 213–14.

Part 3

Chapter 13
The Minister
and
Influence:
Dealing with
Power and
Authority

His own purposes. That's why church leaders are exhorted to humility and not dictatorial leadership: "Therefore, I exhort the elders among you, as your fellow elder, . . . shepherd the flock among you . . . not for sordid gain, but with eagerness; nor yet as lording over those allotted to your charge, but proving to be examples to the flock" (1 Pet. 5:1-3).[5]

No matter what the relationship of one ministry to another, none will function properly without love. First Corinthians 12, dealing with the ethics of the interaction and ministry of the parts of the Body, leads into chapter 13 where the beautiful work ethic of the Bible, love, is revealed. In essence, this passage makes it clear that if I abuse my spiritual authority by applying it without love, I am nothing and all of my efforts are empty, meaningless, and without reward.

Only divine love enables us to relate to Christ and to others in the humble, lowly way Christ related to His Father. Christ is an equal member of the triune Godhead. But He "did not consider equality with God something to be grasped" (Phil. 2:6). He took the form of a servant and became obedient to death on the cross. When He had humbled himself to the fullest possible extent, His Father elevated Him to the highest pinnacle of spiritual power so "that at the name of Jesus every knee should bow, in heaven and on earth and under the earth, and every tongue confess that Jesus Christ is Lord, to the glory of God the Father" (Phil. 2:10-11). In simple, concise form, here is a profound lesson in the ethical application of spiritual authority: the way down is the way up.

The paradoxical nature of the power inherent in true ministry is dealt with extensively in *Professional Ethics: Power and Paradox.* Ministers have power but the structures they work in limit that power.

[Ministers] are both powerful and not powerful. . . .

---

[5]Erwin W. Lutzer, *Pastor to Pastor: Tackling Problems of the Pulpit* (Chicago: Moody Press, 1987), 136.

All professional power is to some extent paradoxical. It is given in order that it be used to serve others. Professional power is meant to be a power *for* rather than a power *over.* It is legitimated only when it is used for the good of another, or of society. . . . Power is necessary to a professional, and yet it threatens to undermine the very thing it is meant to secure—the authority of the trustee.

This is partly why professional codes stress the "servant" aspect of being a professional.[6]

Part 3

Chapter 13
The Minister
and
Influence:
Dealing with
Power and
Authority

MINISTERIAL AUTHORITY AND ETHICAL RELATIONSHIPS

On occasion, ministers who may have learned to handle the authority issue ethically in the local church face a problem of relationship to fellow ministers in the community or in their own denomination. This calls for the tough lesson entitled "Submission." "Do not speak evil of one another, brethren" (James 4:11, NKJV). In Ephesians 5:21 Paul encourages all members of the body of Christ, including ministers, to submit to one another. In 1 Peter 5:5 the apostle recommends that we all "be submissive to one another" (NKJV). Such an attitude becomes more and more difficult to maintain in view of the lofty image the pastor often must assume in the eyes of the board and membership.

William F. May, drawing on the observations of H. Richard Niebuhr, sees the pastor cast in one of three possible leadership roles in the church. The first of these is chief executive officer. Of the three possibilities, this is the most powerful conception of leadership: The CEO leads by command and obedience, directing the church government by fiat. The second posture the pastor may assume in the church is that of executive director, serving as the paid chief of staff for a large voluntary community. Such a pastor's influence is limited because most voluntary organizations do not look to their executive directors for

[6]Karen Lebacqz, *Professional Ethics: Power and Paradox* (Nashville: Abingdon Press, 1985), 146–47.

Part 3

Chapter 13
The Minister
and
Influence:
Dealing with
Power and
Authority

guidance but to their boards of trustees. Consequently, although the CEO possesses too much power, the executive director usually has very little—and can aptly be called the "clerk of the works." The third and most desirable image of the pastor in May's view is the pastor as leader of a republic. In this capacity the pastor handles relations to both professional and nonprofessional staff more effectively since they are collegial rather than hierarchical. The pastor's success in this role lies in the effective use of powers of persuasion.[7]

Because ministers are in a leadership role, they sometimes find it hard to submit to those in authority over them. This appears to be a major problem with many nationally known ministers and ministries who refuse to be accountable to any individual or group. Such an attitude is contrary to the teaching of Hebrews 13:17: "Obey your leaders and submit to their authority. They keep watch over you as men who must give an account." Yet another facet of the problem of submitting to a person in authority appears when that person is obviously wrong in his application of authority or is a weak authority figure. But the Word of God makes no distinction between the types of authority that we are to submit to nor does it give us the right to resist leadership, even if the leadership is of poor quality. Richard J. Foster deals with this problem extensively in his *Celebration of Discipline:*

> What about people who are in "positions of authority" but who do not possess spiritual authority? Since Jesus made it clear that the position does not give the authority, should this person be obeyed? Can we not rather disregard all humanly ordained authority and only look for and submit to spiritual authority? . . .

---

[7]William F. May, "Images That Shape the Public Obligations of the Minister," in *Clergy Ethics in a Changing Society: Mapping the Terrain*, ed. James P. Wind, Russell Burck, Paul F. Camenisch, and Dennis P. McCann (Louisville: Westminster/John Knox Press, 1991), 54–83.

Part 3

**Chapter 13
The Minister
and
Influence:
Dealing with
Power and
Authority**

The answer is not simple, but neither is it impossible. *Revolutionary subordination commands us to live in submission to human authority until it becomes destructive.* Both Peter and Paul called for obedience to the pagan State because they understood the great good that resulted from this human institution. . . .

We should [also] submit to persons in positions of authority who do not know spiritual authority . . . out of common courtesy and out of compassion for the person in that difficult predicament.[8]

Underlying the idea of showing courtesy to the person who does not appear to possess true spiritual authority is simply a recognition that at times we may not correctly discern the presence of spiritual authority. We tend to feel that because the response or directive we received from the person in authority was not what we had expected, the authority is at fault. Many times we have been given words of wisdom but simply did not recognize them under the circumstances.

A young man attempting to plant a church in a promising community in the South attempted to build up his church by emphasizing a supplemental ministry that seemed to fill a need in his community. Despite a strong admonition from an official of his denomination that to be dependent on this particular ministry would be detrimental to the life of the church, the young man persisted with his plan. All of the details fell into place and the community seemed delighted at the turn of events. Later, after having shown poor judgment by ignoring his advisor's wisdom, he committed a second ethical misstep by using the community's affirmation to justify his stubborn persistence. Having failed the test of recognizing and honoring spiritual authority, the young man will find

---

[8]Richard J. Foster, *Celebration of Discipline: The Path to Spiritual Growth*, rev. ed. (San Francisco: Harper & Row Publishers, 1988), 124.

Part 3

Chapter 13
The Minister
and
Influence:
Dealing with
Power and
Authority

himself again enrolled in God's school of ethical training before he will ever succeed in pastoral ministry.

THE EGO PROBLEM

Psychologists have instructed us that one of the
first discoveries we make in our learning as infants is
the ego or "self." Often victims of poor ego development have no true concept of self-discipline or self-
restraint but are concerned only with satisfying their
personal egos, those tiny centers of the small uni-
verse that revolves around them. They go through life
completely out of control, submitting to every dis-
cernible drive of the ego, or sinful, fleshly nature.
This tragic condition is described in *Power Encounter:* "A third area of the works of the flesh is the social—evils committed in the realm of human relations. These include hatred, the attitude, and strife,
the outcome of the attitude. Here also is emulation
(*zeelos,* "zeal or ardor in a bad sense"). By it one feels
jealous of others who hold positions of leadership.
Paul continues to list wrath, rage, and outbursts of
anger as social sins as well as strife, selfish ambition,
or self-seeking of a leadership office by unfair
means."[9]

It takes a special work of grace to bring "self" into
conformity to the will of God. The Scriptures teach
that this work of grace comes in stages: first, one
must rule one's self, then one's home, and finally
God's house. In 1 Timothy 3:2-5, Paul outlines for
the young minister the steps to qualifying to rule in
the church. In verses 2 and 3, the minister exhibits
self-control as an ethical man: "above reproach, the
husband of but one wife, temperate, self-controlled,
. . . not violent but gentle." The next lesson in self-

---

[9]Charles Harris, "Power for Victorious Christian Living," in
Power Encounter: A Pentecostal Perspective, ed. Opal L. Reddin
(Springfield, Mo.: Central Bible College Press Publishers, 1989),
145-72.

Part 3

Chapter 13
The Minister
and
Influence:
Dealing with
Power and
Authority

control takes place at home: "He must manage his own family well and see that his children obey him with proper respect" (v. 4). Then the rhetorical question "How can he take care of God's church?" (v. 5) is without effect. More good advice on managing the personal ego problem in an ethical manner comes to us from 1 Peter 5:3: "Not lording it over those entrusted to you, but being examples to the flock."

To deal with the personal ego problem effectively requires a miracle. That miracle took place at Calvary centuries ago. It is there at the Cross that we find new life, new hope, new control of "self" as never before. The key is found in Galatians 2:20: "'I have been crucified with Christ and I no longer live, but Christ lives in me. The life I live in the body, I live by faith in the Son of God, who loved me and gave himself for me.'" With Christ living in me and through me, His beautiful nature will supersede my egotism and foolish pride.

THE TEMPTATION TO ABUSE POWER

Who among us has not been tempted at times to claim some of the perquisites of spiritual power, to abandon restraint momentarily for personal benefit. This is a temptation we must look at directly, much in the manner described by Richard Foster addressing power and the ministry:

As we go into the desert of the heart, we enter with confidence, knowing that God is with us and will protect us. . . .

There in the desert, alone, we look squarely into the face of the seductive powers of greed and prestige. Satan tempts us with wild fantasies of status and influence. We feel the inner pull of these fantasies, because deep down we really do want to be the most important, the most respected, the most honored. We fancy ourselves before the cameras, in the judge's seat, at the top of the heap. "After all," we muse, "aren't these things nothing more than the desire for excellence?"[10]

Part 3

Chapter 13
The Minister
and
Influence:
Dealing with
Power and
Authority

A peculiar twist often manifests itself in the character of the minister who does not have genuine leadership in his home. He will often succumb, perhaps subconsciously, to the temptation to abuse the power he wields in the church in one way or another. On one occasion in a former pastorate, I had invited a well-known evangelist for a series of consecutive special services in the church. I found it disturbing that he seemed to be overbearing and almost abusive in his relationship with my family and with the musicians who accompanied his singing in the services. I discovered the problem within a few days. This man, who was well proportioned physically and decidedly masculine, confessed that when he was home, he was often afraid to drop off to sleep following a disagreement with his wife, who was an aggressive businesswoman. His story brings to mind the apparently reliable rumors that floated around the town where I once pastored that a particular judge of the circuit court, who traditionally meted out extremely harsh sentences, went home each evening to live as peaceably as possible with a very dominant wife. In this connection one is reminded of King Ahab of the Old Testament, who at times was driven to diabolical extremes by his powerful queen, Jezebel (1 Kings 21:25). Such cases may be the exception, but they do exist.

Another possible explanation for the abuse of power in and out of the pulpit may be that it is simply a reflection of suppression and abuse suffered by the minister during childhood. This could have occurred through abusive parents or a dominating sibling. In other instances, having been completely spoiled as a child could be a factor.

Often the temptation to abuse power is strongest when one moves into a leadership vacuum left by one's predecessor. The incoming pastor may overre-

---

[10]Foster, *Money, Sex and Power*, 222.

Part 3

**Chapter 13
The Minister
and
Influence:
Dealing with
Power and
Authority**

act to this tacit invitation to take control. On occasion ministers may sense that their leadership is being challenged by the board and will react by being abusive with whoever may cross their paths. In relating to staff personnel, power-conscious pastors may unwittingly overload younger or less dynamic associates with unreasonable responsibilities.

The very leadership role we fill as ministers—spiritual father or mother, man or woman in charge, shepherd of the flock, the church's final human authority—is fraught with temptation to exert the power inherent in the office. In *The Minister as Crisis Counselor,* David K. Switzer alerts us to the issue: "The matter of role is a particularly important issue for ministers, for we have a long history, a tradition, which tells us and the larger society something about who the clergy are. Without going into detail here, we need to clarify the difference between certain of our functions as ordained clergy, and ourselves as individual human beings. We need to be able to utilize the symbolic power of our role and the authority it carries, but without hiding behind it or exploiting people with it."[11]

THE MINISTER'S REPUTATION AT HOME AND AWAY

When the minister is a man, how he deals with the authority issue as leader in the home often determines the image he projects in the church. His parishioners come to respect him as their leader when they sense that he is highly ethical in his family relationships. They will accept his teaching, his preaching, and his counsel as proceeding from a true man of God. His reputation will loom larger than life as he fills the God-given role as head of his household. He is viewed from a psychologist's perspective as follows:

---

[11]David K. Switzer, *The Minister as Crisis Counselor,* rev. and enl. (Nashville: Abingdon Press, 1986), 53-54.

Part 3

Chapter 13
The Minister
and
Influence:
Dealing with
Power and
Authority

It is important that the ordained clergy be aware that they are symbols of the reality that underlies the meaningfulness of Christian faith. In other words, quite apart from their own being as persons, clergy are perceived by others as being the physical representation to the community of faith and, at least to some extent, to the larger community of the reality of God. Their very physical presence has the power to stimulate those internal images which, through early learning in a highly emotionally charged relationship of dependence, have become a part of an individual's intrapersonal dynamics. These primitive images are a part of that individual's internal resources and are strong unconscious forces, affecting every aspect of his or her life. . . . Ordained ministers are physical representations of the whole community of faith, of the tradition, of a way of viewing the meaning of life, of the dynamic power of faith, and even of God.[12]

How ministers relate to their church and its leaders in fulfilling the role cast for them becomes known throughout the area where they serve. They and the church will come to be respected, even revered, in the community.

The minister's reputation as a good leader also travels out into his denomination, making way for an expanded ministry and in some cases a leadership role. More important, the enhancement of the minister's ethical reputation serves the minister and the church well. It also gives the world surrounding the church a proper image of the kingdom of God and what the grace of God is all about. When the divine ethic of steadfast love is the basis for the reputation of the minister and the church, God will be glorified. As Jesus expressed it, "'By this all men will know that you are my disciples, if you love one another'" (John 13:35). The church with this kind of reputation will be the church that the neighborhood will look to in time of trouble, in the face of shattering world events.

---

[12]Ibid., 16.

Part 3

**Chapter 13
The Minister
and
Influence:
Dealing with
Power and
Authority**

As a result of the Cuban missile crisis during the Kennedy administration, a young German lady, who had only a passing interest in spiritual things, requested an emergency interview at my office in the church. There she came into a transforming experience with God that has sustained her to this day. She chose our church in her time of fear and distress totally on the basis of the reputation of a congregation known for its love for God and for each other.

Years later, across the street from our church, a retired U.S. Air Force colonel kept watch on the building program of the new sanctuary. As soon as it was completed, motivated entirely by what he had learned about the church from his godly mother-in-law, he made his way to our services and found Christ as Savior. These stories and thousands like them could be repeated by church after church around the world.

It greatly matters that the church and the pastor have earned a reputation for capably carrying on the work of God and that their ministry has reflected the highest ethical standards of leadership and spiritual authority. Without exception, when members of the community face a spiritual problem or begin to search for a church home, they will be drawn irresistibly to such churches and their leaders.

STUDY QUESTIONS

1. Why is it important for a minister to modify personal tastes and lifestyle to be in line with the expectations of the church and community?

2. To what extent and in what ways should ministers deal with community problems that have political overtones?

3. How will a minister's involvement in local or state government affect the growth and spirituality of the local church being pastored?

4. What lessons can we learn from the way Old

Part 3

Chapter 13
The Minister
and
Influence:
Dealing with
Power and
Authority

Testament leaders and prophets exercised spiritual authority?

5. What lessons can we learn from the way Jesus and the apostles exercised spiritual authority?

6. In what ways does the Bible emphasize the importance of loving servant leadership?

7. How can ministers avoid the temptation to build an empire for themselves?

8. What are ways ministers can preserve their reputations as godly leaders?

Chapter 14

The Minister and Personhood: Being Authentic

The tone and quality of the preaching service are often set by the minister and the other participants in the service before the congregation is ever addressed. The leaders of the service will be careful to come out to their positions in an orderly fashion. Too many stage whispers and conversations may take on ethical overtones for the congregation: *Are the leaders unprepared or are they exchanging information that we should know?* Smile—at least give the appearance that this is to be a joyful experience. Be a hearty participant in the singing and worship that precede the message. Make it apparent that you're enjoying the service and the privilege of being with your people.

This evidence of love and appreciation for your people must be present before the service begins and after it ends. The minister must be known as the friend of all the parishioners, both inside and outside the church.

I am always amazed to learn of pastors who leave the church office at five o'clock and want no more contact with any of their members until the next day of business. I find it puzzling when I hear of pastors who do not care to greet any of their parishioners either before or after the service. The attitude seems to be, *These people know who I am and where I am— let them come to me.* With this kind of relationship between pastor and parishioners, they will always be wondering: *Can we really expect help from someone who doesn't seem to care about us?*

Part 3

Chapter 14
The Minister
and
Personhood:
Being
Authentic

THE MINISTER IN THE PULPIT

When ministers stand before the congregation, they will not want to be dressed ostentatiously; neither will they want to appear as though they were preparing to do yard work. They will dress carefully and in good taste to show respect for God, His house, and His people.

On one occasion I was the guest speaker at a pioneer church meeting in a rented hall. Yet even in this humble setting, I could find no excuse for the pastor to stand before his audience with his shirt so disarranged that a portion of his oversized stomach was showing. No matter that his clothes did not reflect high style, he had no excuse for sloppiness. But worse are cases where ministers may wear less than their best clothing to evoke sympathy from the congregation. In the days following the Depression, it was occasionally reported that visiting evangelists would kneel before an audience to reveal a hole in the sole of a shoe to encourage greater generosity at offering time.

The casual look, even in church, seems to be more in vogue than ever. Yet no matter how informal the service, if it is being conducted in God's house, shorts and blue jeans fail to show proper respect for the setting. Ministers and their fellow worshipers surely should have a standard of dress as high as that required to attend a concert or to eat in a nice restaurant. The sense of satisfaction and rapport that comes from being appropriately dressed for an enjoyable social event ought to carry over into the worship of God in His dedicated house.

Just as important as the minister's appearance is his preaching style. Style is often developed early in one's ministry. A younger minister frequently tends to emulate the mannerisms and delivery of some favorite preacher. It is amusing to note how often the devotees of a certain flamboyant preacher use the same

Part 3

Chapter 14
The Minister
and
Personhood:
Being
Authentic

gestures, expressions, and emphasis that they have come to love in their idol.

The minister will need to guard against distracting idiosyncrasies and poor speech habits. Nothing is more annoying to a congregation than dozens of "and-uh's" or sounds like "nnn" to provide time for the next thought to come to mind.

The overuse of a particular gesture may not be unethical but it can become unattractive. Even the style of the gesture is important. Public speaking laboratories should be available to active ministers from time to time. Many irritating speech habits could be corrected when pointed out in a public speaking class. Often the minister's spouse or family members can be of help in correcting such problems.

A minister friend of mine, who has gone to be with the Lord, would laugh as he told of a critique of his song leading. He had formed a habit of using his index finger rather effectively whenever he led songs. However, a friend noticed that when he would come to the last line of *When the Roll is Called up Yonder*, he would conclude with a sweeping gesture, his index finger pointing downward. Fortunately, my songleader friend did not require a change of heart to correct the problem; he needed only to improve his style.

The content of the sermon will be of greater concern to the preacher than the style of delivery. Careful preparation of the message pays big dividends. It has been estimated that on an average, ministers will need approximately ten hours to prepare a sermon that is one-half hour in length.[1] Lack of preparation may well be the reason that many sermons fail to be concise and effective. If the message must extend beyond a half hour, it will have to be excellent. We

---

[1] It is said of Charles Haddon Spurgeon, the great British preacher, that he always had at least a dozen sermons in the process of preparation, but he would never preach one until he felt it was the Lord's specific word for that specific service.

Part 3

Chapter 14
The Minister
and
Personhood:
Being
Authentic

have all suffered through sermons (perhaps our own) where the minister started slowly, seemed to gain inspiration, then reiterated, repeated, reemphasized, restated, until he was back to the starting point—but with a weary and unenthusiastic audience. The minister must learn from the carpenter: Once a nail has been driven in, no more pounding is needed or beneficial.

An anecdote commonly attributed to Mark Twain concerned his experience in a church where the minister was fervently appealing for an offering. Twain got out some money for it but when the minister kept on and on, he put the money away. Finally, when the minister failed to bring his appeal to an end, Twain became so irritated that he was prepared to take money out when the offering plate passed by.

The wise minister stops preaching before the audience stops listening; the brain cannot absorb more than the seat can endure. A pastor tells of an evangelist who spoke for no more than twenty minutes in each of a series of services in his church. The congregation was so appreciative that they brought their friends, and the crowds grew amazingly during the course of the meetings.

The folly of protracted sermons brings to mind the story of the farmer who was used to retiring early but found himself trapped in church past his bedtime as the minister droned on about the minor prophets. When the preacher raised the question in his sermon, "What shall we do with Zephaniah?" the frustrated farmer stood and said, "Let him have my seat, I'm going home."

THE MINISTER IN THE PARSONAGE

As has been observed, the minister who is a man often sets the tone of family relationships in the church by how he functions as father in his own home. He will not need to be stern or formal to command the respect and love of his children and spouse; he will be relaxed and jovial, a pleasure to be around. He will not embarrass his family by immodesty. He will not discuss the problems of the church and his denomination before his family. Many young people have insisted that they were disillusioned with the church as children because unwise parents discussed only the negative side of church relationships in their presence.

Along with making desirable table talk, the minister should have acceptable table manners. He will realize that the example he sets, even at the table, is part of the ethical training of his children. He will not demand prime cuts or the choicest morsels at the table if he loves his family more than himself.

The minister's love will be reflected in his taking part in maintaining the home. He will recognize that as a helpful husband ("houseband") his role is not merely to financially support the family but to assist with raising the children and maintaining the home. He will not have an inflated notion of his role in the home nor will he see his wife as his servant or his children merely as his waiters and waitresses. As Christ loved the Church, so will he love his wife and family. He will recall the example of the Master's washing of the disciple's feet and will want to serve as well as be served. He will gladly and graciously accept his responsibility as a godly model in the home; he will be aware of the powerful example he is setting by what he reads, the TV programs he watches, the games he plays, the kind of conversation he carries on, the nature of the jokes he tells, and the attitudes he portrays.

The minister should be consistent and firm but fair as the co-disciplinarian of the home. As the Scriptures make it clear, the acid test of rulership in the church begins at home: "If anyone does not know how to manage his own family, how can he take care of God's church?" (1 Tim. 3:5). Above all, he will be responsible to lead his children to know the Lord. How

Part 3

Chapter 14
The Minister
and
Personhood:
Being
Authentic

Part 3

Chapter 14
The Minister
and
Personhood:
Being
Authentic

tragic to have been used to bring many to Christ but yet to lose one's own child for all eternity.

The child is more often lost or saved to the kingdom of God because of life in the parsonage rather than life in the church. Children will not respect the preaching they hear in the pulpit if they cannot respect the conversation in the home. We smile at, but perhaps we should be grieved by, the oft-repeated remark of the little girl who said, "Oh no, Daddy wasn't telling the truth—he was only preaching."

The minister should not feel that he is walking on eggs to measure up to his responsibility as husband and father in the home. He will not simply be "acting" to fill his prescribed role; hypocrisy is the worst form of unethical conduct. He will simply be letting the Christ-life shine through. He will realize that it is but a practical evidence of the work of the Spirit within that enables him to be courteous and mannerly, to appreciate simple matters of etiquette, even to know which fork to use, how to properly seat his wife or open doors for her in public places, how to respect elderly persons by rising when it is appropriate. It is in the details of life that we are able to fulfill the command, "If anyone serves, he should do it with the strength God provides, so that in all things God may be praised through Jesus Christ" (1 Pet. 4:11). We all should envy the minister to whom his son said in all sincerity, "Dad, when you walk into the room, I feel as though Jesus just walked in."

THE MINISTER ON PASTORAL BUSINESS

Hospital visitation is high on the pastor's list of responsibilities in ministry. When entering the hospital room, one is dealing with a person who has had time to think about spiritual things and who has time to listen to wise counsel. This patient has been thinking serious thoughts of eternity, of death, of life after death. In case after case God has used illness to bring people to himself.

Part 3

Chapter 14
The Minister
and
Personhood:
Being
Authentic

I have led more people to the Lord in the hospital or the home than in church. In a small community adjacent to a church I pastored, the Lord allowed the head of a highly respected family to become desperately sick and ultimately to die in the hospital. But he found the Lord before his death, and in turn his grown daughter was saved along with other close relatives. Before long a miniature revival had come to the community by the grace of God.

In doing home visitation the minister often faces the problem of having to visit the same sick sheep over and over. It is generally best to concentrate in visitation on young Christians and converts. Of course, the elderly and shut-ins are never to be neglected. The Lord used a shut-in in a former pastorate to shame me into spiritual growth. When I would visit this woman, whose memory was failing her, she would ask me from time to time to assist her in quoting the Scripture passage she was attempting to memorize. After having been embarrassed a few times by my inability to help, I began serious work on my own memorization program, making it a regular part of my devotions. Soon I was able to incorporate Scripture verses into my preaching, which has proved especially effective at funerals and on special occasions.

The key to effective home visitation is to make short calls. Friendly people will tend to monopolize the minister's time. No matter how enjoyable an extended conversation may be, the minister falls victim to poor time management. A kindred temptation is to visit only nicer homes in the parish. James warns of the danger of catering to the rich. Ministers must give of themselves just as gladly to those who cannot repay. This is Christian service of the highest order.

Ministers will want to represent their church well at business establishments. One minister requested a ministerial discount of every business in town until both he and his church were resented. Of course, the day of ministerial discounts is now history, but the temptation lingers to take advantage of any perks

Part 3

Chapter 14
The Minister
and
Personhood:
Being
Authentic

available. On the other hand, ministers' salaries, while not on a par with the incomes of many professionals, are much higher than years ago.

Ministers should dress neatly as they move around town if they expect to have the respect of the community. Sometimes overweight ministers have a problem with an acceptable appearance. If this is the situation, the minister will need to be doubly careful, particularly when wearing casual dress. It should not be difficult to dress without being in any way offensive to our cause and our constituents.

Ministers will be scrupulously honest in business dealings. They will not use undue pressure to get a better deal for the church, much less for themselves. They will be congenial in business contacts and should be the favorite customers of merchants in town.

As a child, it was a highlight of my week to visit the local country store with my minister dad. Here were to be found pickles in barrels, lunch meat by the slice, and candy by the penny's worth. Dad had a great relationship with the merchant, who was not a Christian. It was a pleasure to just stand by and witness the rapport that a man of God could generate in a business relationship.

Ministers will be friendly citizens in the community. They will be as cordial to worldlings as to their own parishioners. They will be friendly to members of the church across town even though it stands on entirely different spiritual principles from their own. They will show Christlike kindness to bartenders in town as well as to persons of unquestionable character. They are God's representatives. More people have been won to Christ by friendliness, simply letting the character of Christ show through, than by any other means. So little investment is required to be the friendliest minister in town, but it pays handsome dividends.

THE MINISTER AT PLAY: PLANNED RECREATION AND RELAXATION

Part 3

Chapter 14
The Minister
and
Personhood:
Being
Authentic

To preserve their mental and physical health, ministers will be sure to observe the Sabbath law. They, like the rest of God's creation, need a day of rest each week: a day off from their church responsibilities, not counting Saturday and Sunday. Their families, along with other staff members and the church board, can help them to maintain the schedule. The keeping of the Sabbath law is an ethical matter. God instituted it. We often tend to confuse the Sabbath with Sunday, which is most likely not a day of rest for the minister.

The value of being able to blend the elements of rest and worship on Sunday, however, is highlighted in Otto Piper's commendable treatment of the subject:

In the Biblical religion, the Sabbath has a twofold function. It is both a day of rest and also a day of worship and sanctification. Hence rest is more than inactivity. . . . We need the hours of rest in order to recover the awareness that there is a God who has made us for His final goal. . . . As a day of recreation and sanctification, the institution of the seventh day serves to remind the Church also of the receptive character of faith. What matters in the celebration of the Sunday is not the strictness in which we refrain from manual work and "worldly pleasures" but rather the rhythm it constitutes. . . . The value of the Sunday does not lie in its institutional character, but in the opportunity it gives us to envisage our daily life in the perspective of God's plan.[2]

I share the personal struggle that many minister friends contend with: how to hold consistently to a day off. I have often used the day for chores around the house, which, although a relaxing experience, is

---

[2]Otto A. Piper, *Christian Ethics* (London: Thomas Nelson & Sons, 1970), 152–53.

Part 3

Chapter 14
The Minister
and
Personhood:
Being
Authentic

still not quite the same as forgetting one's responsibilities for a whole day. I am especially motivated when I recall the sad experience of an elderly minister friend who never had a hobby or any recreational outlet during his ministry. He found all of his fulfillment in a highly successful teaching ministry. Then in his latter years, when he could no longer fill the pulpit, out of sheer frustration and despair he took his own life. His was a classic case of the burned-out minister who refused to heed any warning signs of overwork. Another minister, after a heart attack, said he had learned that those who say they will take their vacation in heaven may take it sooner than they expected.

Ministers need planned recreation, which should usually include the family. How blessed they are if their children enjoy the same type of activity or sport that they enjoy. It is especially desirable if both husband and wife can find a mutual interest in some recreational outlet. To do so may require flexibility and the highest possible ethic—love.

Vacations are a must. Some ministers prefer shorter vacations, more than one per year. Even so, ministers should probably vary their schedules and take a longer vacation every other year with the shorter vacations on the alternate years. Often ministers can enjoy some vacation time along with attending conventions or conferences, perhaps adding a couple of days to the trip at their own expense. They will often be able to save the church money on travel costs by staying overnight on Saturday or another day as specified by the airline or travel agency.

If the minister and his family are enjoying vacation over a weekend, they will want to be certain to attend church on Sunday. The man and woman of God will recognize what a powerful example this will be to their family and their parishioners. They will not want to abandon their devotional life during vacation. After all, the Lord is taking the trip with His ministers as well.

Keeping up with sports news and reports has become important in many ministers' homes as a means of relaxation. This form of entertainment usually provides a wholesome part of the day's news via TV or newspaper. Particularly when the interest in sports involves physical participation, this outlet can be healthful as well as interesting. However, interest and involvement in sports can become dominant, even detrimental. If sports is your recreational release, monitor your involvement so it doesn't take over your weekly schedule.

Over a period of several years, three neighboring pastors and I enjoyed a weekly round of golf. We formed a well-matched foursome and enjoyed good fellowship during our matches. However, it grew to be a sunrise-till-sunset experience: driving to a distant course, playing eighteen holes, and enjoying a lunch break. Furthermore, one of us would return home invariably frustrated from a bad round of golf. And I began to experience a twinge of conscience because I had spent no time with my family. Consequently I changed to tennis, a more concentrated exercise with a more acceptable schedule.

Other sports that produce a good workout in a reasonable amount of time are basketball, bicycle riding, racquetball, and jogging. Of course, besides being something you thoroughly enjoy, the activity should be something you can physically do without abusing yourself.

A minister need not be the best-dressed sportsman in town, but he will dress as befits a Christian gentleman. He will not be immodest in his appearance or wear ragged, dirty attire, becoming an embarrassment to family and parishioners. Neither will he stretch the family budget to buy inordinately expensive clothing and equipment.

Maintain a sensible balance in the family's time at work and play. Keep in mind the expense, the time, and the kind of leisure—but recreation and play must be built into your family's lifestyle, especially in view

Part 3

Chapter 14
The Minister
and
Personhood:
Being
Authentic

Part 3

Chapter 14
The Minister
and
Personhood:
Being
Authentic

of growing pressures on the ministry and the family. A sensible recreational program will help assure longevity in the ministry and in the family. Recreational activity is always much less expensive than an occasional hospital stay or even a moderately priced funeral. In other words, time, money, fellowship, and family will be a consideration in choosing a recreational pastime. When all of these factors have been balanced, you are ready to make a decision.

Finally, a highly important aspect of the life and ministry of the man and woman of God is the recognition that they are physical temples of the Holy Spirit. To neglect care for one's temple is to court ethical failure and to be physicaly unable to fulfill one's calling. On the other hand, taking the time to enjoy recreational activity is a great way to strengthen and restore the temple.

STUDY QUESTIONS

1. Why should ministers be careful about their physical appearance and dress at all times?

2. What should be involved in the preparation of sermons?

3. On what occasions might a sermon be longer than twenty to thirty minutes?

4. What responsibilities should the minister accept and carry out in the home?

5. What should ministers keep in mind when visiting in homes and in hospitals?

6. What is the importance of rest, recreation, and vacations, and what types should the minister enjoy; and what types should be avoided?

Selected Bibliography

The Apostolic Fathers. Trans. Kirsopp Lake. 2 vols. Cambridge, Mass.: Harvard University Press, 1975.

Bailey, Derrick Sherwin. *Common Sense about Sexual Ethics: A Christian View.* London: V. Gollancz, 1962.

Barclay, William. *Ethics in a Permissive Society.* New York: Harper & Row, Publishers, 1971.

Barker, Charles Joseph. *The Way of Life: A Study in Christian Ethics.* London: Lutterworth Press, 1946.

Barnette, Henlee H. *Introducing Christian Ethics.* Nashville: Broadman Press, 1961.

Beach, Waldo. *Christian Ethics in the Protestant Tradition.* Atlanta: John Knox Press, 1988.

Birch, Bruce C., and Larry L. Rasmussen. *Bible and Ethics in the Christian Life.* Minneapolis: Augsburg Publishing House, 1989.

Böckle, Franz. *Fundamental Moral Theology.* Trans. N. D. Smith. New York: Pueblo Publishing Co., 1980.

Bonhoeffer, Dietrich. *Ethics.* Ed. Eberhard Bethge. New York: Macmillan Publishing Co., 1955.

Booth, Edwin P. *Martin Luther: Oak of Saxony.* Nashville: Abingdon Press, 1966.

Boyajian, Jane A., ed. *Ethical Issues in the Practice of Ministry.* New Brighton, Minn.: United Theological Seminary, 1984.

Brown, David. *Choices: Ethics and the Christian.* Oxford: B. Blackwell, 1983.

Browning, Don S., ed. *Religious Ethics and Pastoral Care.* Philadelphia: Fortress Press, 1983.

Brunner, Emil. *The Divine Imperative: A Study in Christian Ethics.* Trans. Olive Wyon. Philadelphia: Westminster Press, 1947.

Butterworth, G. W., trans. *Clement of Alexandria.* Cambridge, Mass.: Harvard University Press, 1939.

Cahill, Lisa Sowle. *Between the Sexes: Foundations for a Christian Ethics of Sexuality.* Philadelphia: Fortress Press, 1985.

Campbell, Dennis M. *Doctors, Lawyers, Ministers: Christian Ethics in Professional Practice.* Nashville: Abingdon Press, 1982.

Childs, James M. *Faith, Formation, and Decision: Ethics in the Community of Promise.* Minneapolis: Fortress Press, 1992.

Clinebell, Howard J. *Basic Types of Pastoral Counseling.* Nashville: Abingdon Press, 1966.

Cook, David. *The Moral Maze: A Way of Exploring Christian Ethics.* London: Society for Promoting Christian Knowledge, 1983.

Cronin, Kieran. *Rights and Christian Ethics.* Cambridge, England: Cambridge University Press, 1992.

Cross, F. L. *The Early Christian Fathers.* London: Gerald Duckworth & Co., 1960.

Cupitt, Don. *The New Christian Ethics.* London: SCM Press, 1988.

Dewar, Lindsay. *A Short Introduction to Moral Theology.* London: A. R. Mowbray, 1956.

Dickens, Arthur G. *The English Reformation.* New York: Schocken Books, 1964.

Donagan, Alan. *The Theory of Morality.* Chicago: University of Chicago Press, 1977.

Driver, Tom Faw. *Christ in a Changing World: Toward an Ethical Christology.* New York: Crossroad Publishing Co., 1981.

Duffy, Martin. *Issues in Sexual Ethics.* Souderton, Pa.: UCP-BW, 1979.

Estep, William R. *Renaissance and Reformation.* Grand Rapids: William B. Eerdmans Publishing Co., 1986.

Fairweather, Ian C. M. *The Quest for Christian Ethics: An Inquiry into Ethics and Christian Ethics.* Edinburgh, Scotland: Handsel Press, 1984.

Finnis, John. *Fundamentals of Ethics.* Washington, D.C.: Georgetown University Press, 1983.

Fitti, Charles J. *Between God and Man.* New York: Philosophical Library, 1978.

Fletcher, Joseph F. *Situation Ethics: The New Morality.* Philadelphia: Westminster Press, 1966.

_____. *Situation Ethics: True or False? A Dialogue between Joseph Fletcher and John Warwick Montgomery.* Minneapolis: Bethany Fellowship, 1972.

Forsyth, Peter Taylor. *The Church, the Gospel, and Society.* London: Independent Press, 1962.

Foster, Richard J. *Celebration of Discipline: The Path to Spiritual Growth.* San Francisco: Harper & Row, Publishers, 1988.

_____. *Money, Sex and Power: The Challenge of the Disciplined Life.* San Francisco: Harper & Row, Publishers, 1985.

Geisler, Norman L. *Christian Ethics.* Grand Rapids: Baker Book House, 1989.

_____. *Ethics: Alternatives and Issues.* Grand Rapids: Zondervan Publishing House, 1971.

_____, ed. *What Augustine Says.* Grand Rapids: Baker Book House, 1982.

Goldman, Alan H. *The Moral Foundations of Professional Ethics.* Totowa, N.J.: Rowman & Littlefield, Publishers, 1980.

Gustafson, James M. *Theology and Christian Ethics.* Philadelphia: United Church Press, 1974.

Hammar, Richard R. *Pastor, Church & Law.* 2d ed. Matthews, N.C.: Christian Ministry Resources, 1991.

Harkness, Georgia Elma. *Christian Ethics.* New York: Abingdon Press, 1957.

Harmon, Nolan B. *Ministerial Ethics and Etiquette.* 2d rev. ed. Nashville: Abingdon Press, 1987.

Harned, David Baily. *Faith and Virtue.* Edinburgh, Scotland: St. Andrew Press, 1973.

Hebblethwaite, Brian. *The Adequacy of Christian Ethics.* London: Marshall, Morgan, & Scott, 1981.

_____. *Christian Ethics in the Modern Age.* Philadelphia: Westminster Press, 1982.

Selected Bibliography

Higginson, Richard. *Dilemmas: A Christian Approach to Moral Decision Making.* London: Hodder & Stoughton, 1988.

Holmes, Arthur Frank. *Ethics: Approaching Moral Decisions.* Downers Grove, Ill.: InterVarsity Press, 1984.

Hopkins, Mark. *The Law of Love and Love as a Law; or, Christian Ethics.* New York: Charles Scribner & Co., 1871.

Horton, Stanley M., ed. *Systematic Theology.* Springfield, Mo.: Gospel Publishing House, 1994.

Hughes, Philip Edgcumbe. *Christian Ethics in Secular Society.* Grand Rapids: Baker Book House, 1983.

Hynson, Leon O., and Lane A. Scott, eds. *Christian Ethics: An Inquiry into Christian Ethics from a Biblical Theological Perspective.* Anderson, Ind.: Warner Press, 1983.

Jersild, Paul T. *Making Moral Decisions: A Christian Approach to Personal and Social Ethics.* Minneapolis: Fortress Press, 1990.

Jessop, T. E. *Law and Love: A Study of the Christian Ethic.* London: Epworth Press, 1948.

Keeling, Michael. *The Foundations of Christian Ethics.* Edinburgh, Scotland: T. & T. Clark, 1990.

Kirby, Gilbert Walter. *The Way We Care.* London: Scripture Union, 1973.

Kuiper, B. K. *The Church in History.* Grand Rapids: William B. Eerdmans Publishing Co., 1951.

Lebacqz, Karen. *Professional Ethics: Power and Paradox.* Nashville: Abingdon Press, 1985.

Lewis, C. S. *Christian Behaviour.* New York: MacMillan Co., 1943.

Long, Edward Le Roy. *A Survey of Christian Ethics.* New York: Oxford University Press, 1967.

Lutzer, Erwin W. *The Morality Gap: An Evangelical Response to Situation Ethics.* Chicago: Moody Press, 1972.

_____. *Pastor to Pastor: Tackling Problems of the Pulpit.* Chicago: Moody Press, 1987.

_____. *The Necessity of Ethical Absolutes.* Grand Rapids: Zondervan Publishing House, 1981.

Maguire, Daniel C. *The Moral Choice.* Minneapolis: Winston Press, 1978.

Manson, Thomas Walter. *Ethics and the Gospel.* London: SCM Press, 1960.

McQuilkin, Robertson. *An Introduction to Biblical Ethics.* Wheaton, Ill.: Tyndale House Publishers, 1989.

Menzies, William W. *Anointed to Serve.* Springfield, Mo.: Gospel Publishing House, 1971.

Mortimer, Robert Cecil. *Christian Ethics.* London: Hutchinson's University Library, 1950.

Nowell-Smith, Patrick H. *Ethics.* Baltimore, Md.: Penguin Books, 1954.

Noyce, Gaylord B. *Pastoral Ethics: Professional Responsibilities of the Clergy.* Nashville: Abingdon Press, 1988.

Outka, Gene H., and Paul Ramsey, eds. *Norm and Context in Christian Ethics.* New York: Charles Scribner's Sons, 1968.

Pannenberg, Wolfhart. *Ethics.* Trans. Keith Crim. Philadelphia: Westminster Press, 1981.

Penner, Clifford, and Joyce Penner. *The Gift of Sex: A Christian Guide to Sexual Fulfillment.* Waco, Tex.: Word Books, 1981.

Piper, Otto A. *Christian Ethics.* London: Thomas Nelson & Sons, 1970.

Prior, Kenneth F. W. *God and Mammon: The Christian Mastery of Money.* Philadelphia: Westminster Press, 1965.

Quinn, Philip L. *Divine Commands and Moral Requirements.* Oxford: Clarendon Press, 1978.

Ramsey, Paul. *Deeds and Rules in Christian Ethics.* Lanham, Md.: University Press of America, 1983.

Rand, Ayn. *For the New Intellectual: The Philosophy of Ayn Rand.* New York: Random House Publishers, 1961.

Rankin, William W. *Confidentiality and Clergy: Churches, Ethics, and the Law.* Harrisburg, Pa.: Morehouse Publishing Co., 1990.

Read, David Haxton Carswell. *Christian Ethics.* Philadelphia: J. B. Lippincott Co., 1968.

Reddin, Opal L., ed. *Power Encounter: A Pentecostal Perspective.* Springfield, Mo.: Central Bible College Press Publishers, 1989.

**Selected
Bibliography**

Reeck, Darrell. *Ethics for the Professions: A Christian Perspective.* Minneapolis: Augsburg Publishing House, 1982.

Robinson, Norman H. G. *The Groundwork of Christian Ethics.* London: William Collins' Sons & Co., 1971.

Rogers, Isabel Wood. *In Response to God: How Christians Make Ethical Decisions.* Richmond, Va.: CLC Press, 1969.

Roper, Lyndal. *The Holy Household: Women and Morals, in Reformation Augsburg.* Oxford: Clarendon Press, 1989.

Ross, John Elliot. *Christian Ethics: The Book of Right Living.* New York: Devin-Adair Company, 1924.

Rudnick, Milton L. *Christian Ethics for Today: An Evangelical Approach.* Grand Rapids: Baker Book House, 1979.

Saint Augustine. *Confessions.* Trans. Henry Chadwick. Oxford: Oxford University Press, 1991.

Schlesinger, George N. *New Perspectives on Old-Time Religion.* Oxford: Clarendon Press, 1988.

Schwiebert, E. G. *Luther and His Times.* St. Louis: Concordia Publishing House, 1950.

Seifert, Harvey. *Power Where the Action Is.* Philadelphia: Westminster Press, 1968.

Simmons, Paul D., ed. *Issues in Christian Ethics.* Nashville: Broadman Press, 1980.

Smart, J. J. C. *Ethics, Persuasion, and Truth.* Boston: Routledge & Kegan Paul, 1984.

Smedes, Lewis B. *Sex for Christians: The Limits and Liberties of Sexual Living.* Grand Rapids: William B. Eerdmans Publishing Co., 1976.

Smyth, Newman. *Christian Ethics.* New York: Charles Scribner's Sons, 1901.

Solle, Dorothee. *Beyond Mere Obedience: Reflections on a Christian Ethic for the Future.* Minneapolis: Augsburg Publishing House, 1970.

Switzer, David K. *The Minister as Crisis Counselor.* Rev. and enl. Nashville: Abingdon Press, 1986.

Synan, Vinson, ed. *Aspects of Pentecostal-Charismatic Origins.* Plainfield, N.J.: Logos International, 1975.

Tillman, William M. *Christian Ethics: A Primer.* Nashville: Broadman Press, 1986.

Tugwell, Simon. *The Apostolic Fathers.* London: Geoffrey Chapman, 1989.

Von Hildebrand, Dietrich. *Ethics.* Chicago: Franciscan Herald Press, 1972.

Wand, J. W. C., trans. *St. Augustine's City of God.* London: Oxford University Press, 1963.

Watkins, W. T. *Out of Aldersgate.* Nashville: Board of Missions, 1937.

Wellman, Carl. *The Language of Ethics.* Cambridge, Mass.: Harvard University Press, 1961.

Wesberry, James P. *The Lord's Day.* Nashville: Broadman Press, 1986.

Westermarck, Edward. *Christianity and Morals.* Freeport, N.Y.: Books for Libraries Press, 1969.

White, Reginald E. O. *Christian Ethics: The Historical Development.* Atlanta: John Knox Press, 1981.

Wiest, Walter E., and Elwyn A. Smith. *Ethics in Ministry: A Guide for the Professional.* Minneapolis: Fortress Press, 1990.

Wind, James P., et al. *Clergy Ethics in a Changing Society: Mapping the Terrain.* Louisville: Westminster/John Knox Press, 1991.

Wogaman, J. Philip. *Christian Ethics: A Historical Introduction.* Louisville: Westminster/John Knox Press, 1993.

_____. *Christian Moral Judgment.* Louisville: Westminster/John Knox Press, 1989.

Wood, Frederic C. *Sex and the New Morality.* New York: Association Press, 1968.

Woolf, Bertram Lee, ed. *Reformation Writings of Martin Luther.* 2 vols. New York: Philosophical Library, 1953.

Wynn, John Charles. *Sex, Family, and Society in Theological Focus.* New York: Association Press, 1966.

Zink, Sidney. *The Concepts of Ethics.* London: Macmillan & Co., 1962.

Scripture Index

OLD TESTAMENT

New Testament

Subject Index